# TRAFFICKING CULTURE

*Trafficking Culture* outlines current research and thinking on the illicit market in antiquities. It moves along the global trafficking chain from 'source' to 'market', identifying the main roles and routines involved. Using original research, the authors explore the dynamics of this 'grey' market, where legal and illegal goods are mixed and conflated. It compares and contrasts this illicit trade with other 'transnational criminal markets', such as the illegal trades in wildlife and conflict diamonds.

The analytical frames of organized crime and white-collar crime, drawn from criminology, provide a fresh perspective on a problem that has tended to be seen as archaeological, rather than criminological. Bringing insights from both disciplines together, this book represents a productive discourse between experts in these two fields, working together for several years to produce the evidence base that is reported here.

Innovative forms of regulation are the most productive way to explore crime control in this field, and this book provides a series of propositions about practical crime reduction measures for the future. It will be of interest to academics working in the fields of archaeology, criminology, art history, museum studies and heritage. The book will also be a vital resource for professionals in the field of cultural property protection and preservation.

**Simon Mackenzie** is Professor of Criminology at Victoria University of Wellington and Professor of Criminology, Law and Society in the Scottish Centre for Crime and Justice Research at the University of Glasgow, in the College of Social Sciences. He is author of *Going, Going, Gone: Regulating the Market in Illicit Antiquities* (2005) and co-editor of *Criminology and Archaeology: Studies in Looted Antiquities* (2009).

**Neil Brodie** is a Senior Research Fellow on the Endangered Archaeology of the Middle East and North Africa (EAMENA) project at the University of Oxford. He co-edited *Archaeology, Cultural Heritage, and the Antiquities Trade* (2006), *Illicit Antiquities: The Theft of Culture and the Extinction of Archaeology* (2002), and *Trade in Illicit Antiquities: The Destruction of the World's Archaeological Heritage* (2001).

**Donna Yates** is a Senior Lecturer in Antiquities Trafficking and Art Crime at the Scottish Centre for Crime and Justice Research at the University of Glasgow. She completed her PhD in Archaeology at the University of Cambridge, and is the lead educator for the University of Glasgow's Postgraduate Certification in Antiquities Trafficking and Art Crime.

**Christos Tsirogiannis** is Associate Professor in the Faculty of Arts at the Museum of Ancient Art, University of Aarhus. He conducts multi-disciplinary research on international networks trafficking in illicit antiquities. Recent article topics have included museum ethics, market 'due diligence' and the evidential basis for repatriations, to which his identifications of illicit objects frequently lead.

# TRAFFICKING CULTURE

New Directions in Researching the
Global Market in Illicit Antiquities

*Simon Mackenzie, Neil Brodie, and Donna Yates,
with Christos Tsirogiannis*

Routledge
Taylor & Francis Group

LONDON AND NEW YORK

First published 2020
by Routledge
2 Park Square, Milton Park, Abingdon, Oxon OX14 4RN

and by Routledge
52 Vanderbilt Avenue, New York, NY 10017

*Routledge is an imprint of the Taylor & Francis Group, an informa business*

*British Library Cataloguing-in-Publication Data*
A catalogue record for this book is available from the British Library

*Library of Congress Cataloging-in-Publication Data*
A catalog record has been requested for this book

ISBN: 978-1-138-69250-3 (hbk)
ISBN: 978-1-138-69249-7 (pbk)
ISBN: 978-1-315-53221-9 (ebk)

Typeset in Bembo
by Taylor & Francis Books

MIX
Paper from
responsible sources
FSC
www.fsc.org   FSC™ C013985

Printed in the United Kingdom
by Henry Ling Limited

# CONTENTS

# ILLUSTRATIONS

## Figures

**Tables**

# PREFACE

This book is an outline of current research and thinking on the illicit market in cultural objects, in particular a subset of cultural objects known as antiquities, which are older, often ancient, collectible cultural objects of archaeological as well as aesthetic interest. The book will serve various purposes for different readers. For students and academics new to this field of study it can be a one-stop-shop introduction to the topic, amenable for use as a textbook in a field that has been populated by literature that is either research monograph, edited collection, polemic, or popular journalism. For those more long in the tooth in the field of illicit antiquities studies, the book provides a summary of much of the theory, method, and thought that has come out of the Trafficking Culture research programme, which was funded by the European Research Council from 2012–16, and which has continued as an ongoing programme of collaborative research among the authors of this volume. We are hopeful that graduate students may find in these pages inspiration in the application of particular research methodologies or theoretical directions, and that there is enough detail here that they will have the tools to build upon our research in their own work. Perhaps most importantly, the book is not only a progression of an avenue of thinking about research method and theory in the study of the illicit antiquities trade, but it steps into the domain of international policy. In this respect we use our research findings to bring new thinking to the policy debate around controlling looting, trafficking, and illegal and unethical purchasing of stolen antiquities around the world. These propositions, being clearly evidence-based—in stark contrast to much of the policy discussion in this field, and its outcomes—should push forward into more productive space the question of what to do about this particularly destructive global crime problem.

The book is structured as a movement from 'source' to 'destination market' along the paths that illicit antiquities take. We begin in Chapter 1 by identifying and explaining this analytical structure of source-transit-market and setting the scene for the discussion that follows by identifying the main players, and thinking about the roles they play.

Chapter 2 problematises this apparently easy split between source, transit, and market, by using evidence generated in our project to look at the fuzziness of the boundaries between source-transit and transit-market. This chapter also introduces the problem of the antiquities trade as a grey market (Mackenzie and Yates 2017). In the sense in which we use that term here, a grey market mixes legal and illegal goods in such a way that it becomes hard to tell the difference. Further, some legal goods in the market are in fact 'legalised' goods, because their illegal origins have been over-written by the operation of law, such as where good faith purchases in some jurisdictions start a legal clock running that can in quite short order give good title to the purchaser, or at least time-bar a claim from the dispossessed original owner, even though the chain of transactions is tainted by theft along the way. It is due mainly to this quality of the 'greyness' of the market that we often choose to refer to 'illicit' rather than 'illegal' antiquities in the book, since the former term encompasses a more realistic and socially accepted interpretation of wrongdoing. Even if at times the law chooses to sanitise title to an object, where there are destructive origins to its emergence on the market we may very well want to question the ethics of a market in such goods.

In Chapter 3 we explore the possibilities around thinking of the illicit antiquities trade as a 'transnational criminal market', comparable to other versions of such systems like global trafficking in wildlife, drugs and diamonds. Some of these other transnational criminal markets have apparently more coherent modes of regulatory control over illicit activity than antiquities trafficking does, and we break down the types of control into four categories or modalities that can be applied in turn to our particular field of enquiry in this book. This gives some broad scope for reflection on the place of antiquities trafficking in the more general scheme of contemporary transnational organized crime, and sets up a more specific discussion in later chapters of the seemingly most productive ways to approach regulation of the illicit antiquities trade.

In Chapter 4 we come to one of the core dimensions of the issue as we see it: the issue of the circulation of information in the antiquities market. In that chapter we draw attention to the nature of, and restrictions on, information circulation, and the type, texture, and meaning of the information that does circulate (and by corollary, that which is suppressed). Through various steps we will move in the book towards a deeper exploration and understanding of this transnational criminal market as a communicative system creating, sustaining and maintaining a global trading network in both legal and illegal goods.

In Chapter 5 we move to another core dimension of our analytical framework for the illicit antiquities market: the conceptualisation of illicit market activity as white-collar crime. In that chapter we explicate the links between the kinds of 'information entrepreneurialism' we see in the antiquities market and the basic premises of core branches of white-collar crime theory. By 'information entrepreneurialism' we mean the ways in which trade actors twist, obscure, and suppress knowledge of the illicit histories of trafficked objects in their attempts to sell them for profit. The ways these kinds of enterprising communication practices are put into action in the market can be understood as part of a now reasonably well-understood process of narrative work undertaken by white-collar criminals, both individuals and corporate actors. In the Appendix to the book, we present three case studies of information suppression or omission in provenance write-ups by institutional actors, which continues this theme of white-collar criminality. White-collar crime, after all, very often operates behind a veneer of purported legal compliance, while behind the scenes the cogs of the market are spinning to achieve sales without substantive legal or ethical safeguards being implemented to exclude illicit material from the sales network.

Following our suggestion in Chapter 4 that the destination market for illicit antiquities can be better controlled by doing one or more of: reducing the circulation of illicit material, restricting the circulation of criminal money, and improving the circulation of (the right kind of) information in the market, in Chapters 6 and 7, we consider possible regulatory mechanisms for achieving these goals. The market has favoured the idea of 'autoregulation', proposing that trade in antiquities is essentially self-sanitising. The argument is that objects with long and clean provenance histories will sell for more, which will over time systematically exclude illicit material from the trade. We examine this premise in Chapter 6, debunking it by using statistical evidence painstakingly gathered from trade data over a period of years.

If autoregulation doesn't work as advertised, and in effect amounts to no regulation, what then of the market's second-favourite option: self-regulation? In Chapter 7 we review how effective self-regulation seems to have been as a market control, and conclude that on its own it is not a strong prospect. We propose to place it in a framework of 'ethical consumption markets' however, where external observer bodies review market compliance with standards that they have also helped to set, making the results known to consumers who are then more able to make ethical consumptive choices. So ultimately, in Chapters 7 and 8, our thinking about the market as a white-collar criminal trading platform, the market as a global form of transnational crime, and innovative forms of regulation as the most productive way to explore crime control in this field, coalesces around a series of propositions about practical crime reduction measures in the context of economic and cultural types of influence on the destination market.

As mentioned, as well as the clear policy orientation of this text, it is also intended to be a primer and demonstration of theory and method in researching this particular illicit trade. With this in mind, several of the chapters are effectively methodological worked examples of approaches to research that can be replicated, expanded, or amended by others interested in studying illicit commodity markets. For example, Chapter 5 demonstrates a socio-legal approach to theory-building in this field, using court documents to uncover the normal routines of unethical behaviour in trading institutions. Chapter 6 shows how statistical methods can be applied to auction catalogue data in order to test the theory of autoregulation mentioned above. Chapter 2 contains insights based on the qualitative methods we have used—primarily ethnographic fieldwork—and in doing so reveals some of the possibilities in designing studies around that method in this field. Chapter 3 uses a comparative method to group similar cases of trafficking activity together and probe similarities and differences to produce a range of policy-relevant observations. The appendix to the book illustrates, in three of the case studies provided, how a forensic approach to the documentation and commentary surrounding the trade can be used to track objects by reconstituting their provenance histories based on published sources.

In all of these methodological 'worked examples' we have endeavoured to make explicit the links between theory and practice in our research: essentially that the theoretical dimensions of our work emerge directly from, and are always in conversation with, the findings of the robust methods we employ to study our object. Our hope is that this open and reflexive correspondence between theory and method in the book will engage other researchers to critically develop the approaches we have set out here in their future work, while also making it clear that our proposed contributions to the policy discussion in this field are the product of well-worked qualitative field research and quantitative analysis. In a policy arena where undeserved resonance seems often to be accorded to somewhat abstract, emotional and aspirational regulatory discussions, sometimes unduly influenced by vested trade interests, we suggest that the main contribution of this text is to produce a balanced, rational, and empirical review of the field, and to develop directions for the future accordingly.

As part of the Trafficking Culture programme, we have constructed and continue to maintain a website (https://traffickingculture.org) where the reader can find a wealth of supporting information in the form of academic papers and an encyclopaedia of specially-written case studies. It offers a range and depth of supplementary support to the evidence and arguments expressed in this book.

# ACKNOWLEDGMENTS

Simon Mackenzie thanks the European Research Council for the funding that supported the Trafficking Culture project, awarded under the European Union's Seventh Framework Programme (FP7/2007-2013) / ERC Grant agreement n° 283873 GTICO. Neil Brodie acknowledges the support of Arcadia while writing some of his contribution. Complementing the ERC grant, Donna Yates' fieldwork and research was also funded by The Leverhulme Trust, the Core Fulbright U.S. Scholar (Bolivia) Programme, and the University of Glasgow. She would like to thank the following for their support during her field research: The United States Embassy (La Paz), ICOM Bolivia, the National Institute of Culture and History (Belize), the Maya Research Program, Kathmandu Metropolitan City, ImPACT! Productions, the Rabindra Puri Foundation, and the United States State Department Cultural Heritage Center.

# 1

# THE STRUCTURE OF THE GLOBAL MARKET IN ILLICIT ANTIQUITIES

## Actors, drivers, mechanisms

The social construction of the illicit antiquities trade has grown around the basic concepts of supply and demand. Demand for antiquities, mostly but not exclusively, comes from more economically and politically secure states, inspiring a supply of antiquities to be sourced from less secure states, in violation of the law in one or both locations. Buyers of antiquities, then, are willing to pay a price that is high enough for looters and sellers of antiquities to risk a violation of the law. This fair but simplistic construction masks an intricate network of social, political, and economic mechanisms that maintain the antiquities market (including its illicit component) in its current form; govern how various actors negotiate their involvement in the trade; and, underlie the specific decisions made in heritage policy formulation at all levels.

In this chapter we will consider the illicit trade in antiquities as a form of transnational crime, moving the locus of crime from a single incidence of theft at an archaeological site, to the entire trafficking network up to, and including, the final point of sale. During its movement, the antiquity itself undergoes a complex series of negotiations and transformations. As the object changes hands, it experiences a degree of 'cleansing' and 'conversion'. Starting as an archaeological artefact, it then becomes loot, then contraband, then a commodity, then finally a collectible object of artistic or historical interest. The structure of the path through which the antiquity moves is designed to facilitate this transformation with each node in the trafficking chain, from the initial looter to the final buyer, contributing to the eventual acceptance of the illicit piece as socially acceptable within a museum, auction house, or private collection.

That a looted and illegal antiquity can, through this process, become a legal commodity based on the transnational nature of the crime is a nearly unique feature of the illicit antiquities trade. Most other illicit commodities remain illegal through the course of their smuggling and are almost always illegal at their point of final sale. The processes of smuggling arms, narcotics, ivory, endangered animal pelts, or people does not remove the illegality of the commodity being smuggled, nor do these smuggling chains lead to a nominally open and elite public market, which claims deceptionless sale. To labour the point, perhaps more than is necessary: the Metropolitan Museum of Art is not in a position to spend $1 million on 50 kilos of trafficked cocaine, to put it on public display, to then defend the purchase in the newspaper as a 'public good', and only turn the cocaine over to the authorities 30 years later without anyone facing punishment. It has done so for an illicit ancient Greek vase—the Euphronios Krater, described in the appendix of case studies at the end of this book.

To understand how this is possible for antiquities, one must understand construction and maintenance of market drivers at the demand end of the antiquities trafficking chain, as well as the social pressures and restrictions at the supply or source end of the chain. From this we can develop a framework for the middle space that connects the two through the consideration of antiquities trafficking as transnational crime.

## Source

### Context, context, context

At source there are two types of antiquities: those that are known and those that are unknown. Known antiquities, such as those that either have been previously excavated by archaeologists or those that have never been 'lost' (e.g. ancient items in an active temple) are comparatively easy to consider within normal conceptions of ownership and protection. They are documentable, possibly securable, and their recovery following a theft is facilitated by the fact that they have clear owners to claim them. Their theft, importantly, represents a loss of property, but may not involve a loss of *context*, a concept that will be discussed below. For the most part, our consideration of antiquities in this volume will focus on previously unknown antiquities: artefacts discovered at their point of looting that cannot have been recorded, cannot have been secured, and whose origins are obscured by the acts of looting, trafficking and illicit sale. We also refer frequently to antiquities in a grey zone between these two poles of 'known' and 'unknown', for example in relation to pieces of temple statuary violently removed from architectural remains, which may have been recorded by archaeologists at some point and which have rested unsecured in the context of the surrounding structures, perhaps in a remote location such as a jungle or desert. Although technically 'known' there may be precious little in the way of official documentation of these objects, and when they are stolen this is to the detriment of the overall heritage structures they relate to.

When thinking about the sources of previously unknown antiquities, it is important to understand the basics of archaeological context before moving into a larger discussion of source communities and source states. These objects were made at some point in the past by humans who eventually stopped using them. They may have buried the artefact in a grave, tossed it in a rubbish heap, sunk it accidentally with a ship, or it may have dropped out of their bag as they staggered home drunk. They may simply have deserted a decorated monument or a building. There are myriad reasons why an antiquity may have been abandoned. Following this abandonment, this *deposition*, a series of *post-depositional processes* affect the antiquity. Other objects are deposited around it both on purpose and by coincidence. Floors are built over it. Rivers flood, covering it with alluvium. Later people dig near it, burying other things. Ultimately, all of these activities—these natural and human interventions—leave traces which tell the story of the antiquity in space and time. The mosaic of all of these traces is the antiquity's archaeological *context*. It is from reading the relational information embedded in this context, not simply through studying individual objects, that archaeologists assemble what we know about our past. Once an antiquity is removed without record from its place of deposition, that context is irretrievably lost. Field archaeology, then, is the process of recording that context for study before it is destroyed. The removal of previously-unknown antiquities from their place of deposition (which usually can be summed up as 'the ground') without employing proper archaeological methods represents a grave loss to our knowledge of humanity. Because knowledge of the human past is considered to be valuable not only to science but to the construction and maintenance of modern identity, there is a drive to protect archaeological sites from destructive incursion: from natural forces such as erosion, from human building and development, and from looting to feed the market for antiquities.

Looting itself is a difficult term to define. In some situations, we may consider any antiquity's extraction at an archaeological site, performed without use of proper archaeological methods of excavation and recording, to be looting. However, for our purposes it may be best to consider the looting of an archaeological site to feature both a lack of archaeological rigour and the violation of a policy or law, usually with the expectation of financial gain. Indeed, most countries place restrictions on the excavation of archaeological remains, reserving the practice for accredited professionals who seek permits, and limiting the transferability of antiquities after their removal from the ground, although the nature of these restrictions vary from country to country. Looting, then, is excavation outside of these established norms, almost always with artefact extraction as the primary goal of the activity. Following this extraction, the looter may keep the antiquity for themselves, or may sell it onwards. The moment that the antiquity is removed from the ground, the sanctity of the site has been violated, and thus even if the object is later recovered, archaeologists are unable to reconstruct its context. Furthermore, the context of antiquities not removed during the looting incident may also have been damaged or destroyed. The looting of an archaeological site is always destructive.

## Poverty, insecurity and vulnerability

To try to understand why someone might choose to destroy an archaeological site by looting it, we must consider the market, and indeed this is something we will do at quite some length in this book. Destination market actors are not only culturally elite, they are moneyed, and antiquities are rare. If demand for antiquities is created by an elite need to outwardly display cultured status, supply of antiquities is created by an ability to pay for this luxury. Demand on the antiquities market clearly causes antiquities supply. The illegal or illicit excavation of archaeological objects is difficult and dangerous: backbreaking labour coupled with the risk of injury or death. Added to this physical risk is legal risk: looters face the possibility of arrest, fines, jail time, and even execution. It is from destination market funding that looters at source find their motivation.

Generally speaking, antiquities 'source countries' tend to be comparatively lower income than antiquities market countries, and many of the most famous seats of ancient culture are among the states with the lowest levels of infrastructure and development. Even within wealthier 'source countries', major archaeological sites, at least those that are most often exploited, tend to be concentrated in economic-ally poorer regions. There is no set reason why this should be the case, although the history of post-conquest and post-industrial power dynamics and population concentrations could certainly be considered. Suffice to say, the modern remains of the ancient Maya are in modern Guatemala, Belize, Mexico, Honduras, and El Salvador; the modern remains of the Inka are in Peru, Bolivia, and Ecuador; the modern remains of the Khmer are in Cambodia and Thailand; the modern remains of the ancient Egyptians are in Egypt, Sudan, and Ethiopia; the modern remains of the Nok are in Nigeria. Looters, then, are residents of these countries who experience the acute pressures of economic vulnerability and insecurity and their decision to loot may be in response to these pressures.

During the 1990s and into the 2000s, a body of research focused on the idea of 'subsistence diggers' as people who looted archaeological sites due to the extreme limitations of other economic options (Staley 1993; Matsuda 1998, 2005; Hollowell 2006). This concept has been much discussed and much challenged within archaeological circles, but with notable exceptions the con-sensus is that many looters can be classified as being in or near poverty. While it may be difficult to substantiate the idea of large numbers of people living off the proceeds of looting alone for any length of time, we find it helpful to move away from the idea of 'subsistence digging' to a concept of nested and related 'subsistence economies' in which looting antiquities might form part of a larger survival strategy including licit, illicit, and illegal activities (see Chapter 2). Take for example, the extensive ethnography of looting in Guatemala's Petén region conducted in the late 1990s by Sofia Paredes Maurey (Paredes Maury 1999). By joining a group of *chicleros*, men who seasonally harvest the gum of the chicle tree in northern Guatemala, she was able to document how they supplemented their meagre incomes with the looting of Maya sites that they chanced upon during their deep jungle work. The same *chicleros* might also illegally take birds or xate palm for the market. They might harvest chicle illegally. They might work in some minor support capacity for the drug and people smuggling cartels that move through the region. They loot opportunis-tically to get by.

There is also evidence that people turn to looting when times get tough and, perhaps, see archaeological sites as a source of income during extreme economic lows. In other words, they turn to looting when all other options fail. This has been observed in research into the spread of looting in Egypt gleaned from analysis of satellite data (Parcak et al. 2016). This research linked the start of an observable increase in looting, not to social unrest in 2011, but to economic recession in 2008, although unrest exacerbated an already precarious situation. This linkage of looting to extremes of economic instability has been observed in Iraq post-2003, and in other conflict locations (Brodie 2015c). While looting of archaeological sites has been linked to armed conflict, perhaps it would be more accurate to say that looting antiquities is observable as a by-product of the economic disruption associated with conflict as felt by the most economically vulnerable.

## White-collar looters

It should be acknowledged that not all looters are economically disadvantaged or are engaging in the source end of the antiquities trade for survival. There are several contexts where the typical looter can be considered as an economically advantaged or white-collar actor. These individuals tend to resist the designation 'looter', but if we continue to employ the definition of a looter as someone who removes artefacts from their original context in violation of local policy and archaeological norms, they must be considered.

The most often-cited example of these white-collar looters are illegal metal detectorists: hobbyists who use these devices to locate metal artefacts at archaeological sites in violation of local law, primarily but not exclusively in Europe. As metal detecting requires expensive equipment and significant free time, detectorists are usually middle aged, middle class individuals (Thomas 2012). They are also usually white and male. In some countries, the use of metal detectors and the extraction of antiquities is legal, within limits: restrictions are placed on where detecting can take place, what permissions are required, what types of objects can be extracted, and who ultimately owns the antiquities found. Detecting outside these regulations, called nighthawking in the UK, is illegal and is as destructive as any other form of archaeological looting. Similar demographically to metal detectorists are hobbyist 'pot hunters' in the American southwest. They engage in a long tradition, often running through generations of families, of searching for Native American pottery and other artefacts, often on tribal, federal, or otherwise protected land in violation of the law (Goddard 2011). Both illegal metal detectorists and pot hunters may sell the antiquities that they find, or they may keep them as part of their own private collections. These individuals have little in common with casual looters operating in the subsistence economies of economically disadvantaged countries.

Another type of white-collar looter to consider are the individuals or companies that target historic and ancient shipwrecks. While the complications of the law of the sea related to salvage are beyond the scope of this volume, the illegal removal of items from protected underwater heritage sites has resulted in many lawsuits, for example *Mercedes Shipwreck–Odyssey Marine Exploration Inc. v. Unidentified Shipwrecked Vessel.* While some of these relate to actions of individual divers, scuba diving itself is an elite activity that requires equipment and training, and the removal of wreck artefacts may be approached as a hobby, albeit an illegal one, by divers. On a larger scale are specialist salvage firms who operate at the edge of state and international regulation of underwater activity, and who target their actions at shipwrecks that are thought to have been carrying valuable cargo, for example Spanish Colonial vessels carrying gold and silver from the Americas. Because they are backed by investors who expect to share in proceeds from any finds, commercial salvage firms have historically had more money and better equipment than academic or national underwater archaeologists and have been denounced by the same as looters. Several prominent cases where salvage companies have been punished for illegal extraction of artefacts from wrecks support this formulation. Some undersea salvage firms have made agreements with the states who govern the waters they seek to explore, with an arranged split of the objects that result from the expedition going to the state and the company in whatever shares have been agreed (Alder and Polk 2002).

## Source actors

At the source end of the antiquities trade there are three main types of actors: looters, local brokers, and facilitators. *Looters*, as discussed previously, are people who physically extract antiquities from their context within archaeological sites. While they may engage in other trafficking-related activities, they are the ones that perform the necessary task of locating antiquities and extracting them. In doing so, they take on a significant risk of being caught by guards or police, as many forms of earth movement are difficult to hide, and they may risk injury or death, usually from being buried alive during a hole collapse. Research indicates that in most instances they receive significantly less than the final sale value of the antiquities they extract, often less than 1per cent (Brodie 1998).

While still in the source country, looters may sell their antiquities on to local, regional, or national *brokers*. These are early stage intermediaries who serve to move the antiquities physically away from their site of looting, consolidating them for further sale. These brokers may 'run' in regions, passing through to collect antiquities that locals have collected for sale. Others might operate antiquities-related or other shop fronts in local markets and are known by locals as reliable buyers. Brokers may also coordinate the targeted looting of sites, such as was observed by Matsuda (1998) in Belize. Brokers also form a key link in the movement of antiquities abroad, at times organising transport of antiquities to borders and ports (Mackenzie and Davis 2014), planning the initial or complete route that the object will take to its final market, bribing or otherwise interacting with facilitators (discussed below), and preparing the potentially false documents that the antiquity requires for movement. At times there may be no distinction between looters and brokers and at times there may be no distinction between source-end brokers and the transit-phase brokers discussed below.

Finally, *facilitators* often play an instrumental role at the source-end of the antiquities market. Here we conceive of these facilitators as actors who neither extract nor physically move looted antiquities, but who, through their actions, allow looters and brokers to operate. This usually takes the form of corruption or negligence on the part of individuals in a place of public trust: archaeological site guards, police, civil servants, elected officials, customs agents, inspectors, regulators, or even at times archaeologists or museum staff. These individuals, by way of their privileged position, may look the other way while sites are looted; neglect to inspect certain homes or vehicles; issue spurious excavation or export permits; or otherwise knowingly allow source-end antiquities looting and transport to take place in violation of the law.

## Transit

Between initial extraction from the ground and final sale, looted antiquities pass through a transit phase where they are moved through physical space away from the act of looting and towards an elite and often open market. During this process, the antiquity is transformed from contraband into a cultural commodity as it becomes further divorced from its original context. This transit phase has been the least studied and most poorly understood component of the illicit trade in antiquities (Mackenzie and Davis 2014; Tijhuis 2006). Here we offer an overview of the idea of a transit phase for antiquities, who participates in this phase, and what role it plays in transforming illicit antiquities to elite market commodities.

### Key actors

Part of the difficulty that researchers and regulators face in approaching the transit phase with regard to antiquities is that there is no clearly defined boundary between on the one hand transit and source, and on the other hand transit and destination market (see Chapter 2 for an in-depth discussion of these interfaces). Certain key actors seem to transcend the boundaries at both ends, making them difficult to classify within existing models of crime and difficult to target with local policy at any particular point. Generally speaking, transit phase actors can be divided into three groups: brokers, transporters, and facilitators. These perform related, but usually more complicated and transnational, functions as brokers and facilitators at source level.

In the transit phase, *brokers* play a key role in moving antiquities through transit countries and in providing the pieces with the types of documentation required to sell them on the market. They also act to obscure the origins of the piece, creating a situation where later stage sellers can plausibly deny knowledge of the illicit origins of the antiquities they buy. Transit brokers may funnel antiquities from multiple sources and multiple countries to the market through a series of specialised transactions, as part of, or working alongside organised criminal groups. Their role is largely organisational and transitional, and they may perform this organising function for other illicit and illegal commodities as well; their networks may not be specialised for antiquities. Some of these individuals style themselves as antiquities dealers and collectors in their own right and may engage in supplying antiquities to the local markets in what we consider to be transit countries or in establishing collections there, but at least a portion of their focus is on moving antiquities from source countries further up the chain to more elite sellers. At this phase, we might see both white-collar brokers and those who we might characterise as organised or violent criminals, yet there is a clear movement towards white-collar actors as antiquities move away from their illicit sources and towards the elite market.

This trend towards non-violent and white-collar crime as antiquities near their ultimate market is facilitated and perhaps characterised by a type of broker, which we have termed the *Janus figure*. These brokers form a key node in the trafficking chain. Janus figures are transit brokers who operate at the cusp of the market phase, interacting with market sellers and buyers, as well as with lower level brokers, facilitators, transporters, and even looters. Like the Roman god Janus with one face directed back at the past and the other towards the future, Janus figures see both the black market and the open market: the illicit, destructive, smuggling and organised crime end of the antiquities trafficking chain, and the culturally lauded, exclusive and elite end of the antiquities trafficking chain. They interact with each; they have one foot in each world. They serve as the lynchpin, the vital connection that allows an antiquity looted by the world's poor and moved by smugglers to enter our most elite cultural spaces, transforming them from contraband to commodity. Janus figures almost always operate a publicly acceptable front business within the antiquities trade and may style themselves as antiquities collectors in their own right. They may be the most difficult actor within an antiquities smuggling network to replace.

While some brokers transport antiquities themselves or arrange for the objects to move unaccompanied via shipping or the post, in some situations we see *transporters* who serve the functional role of moving antiquities from one location to another with particular focus on moving the objects across international borders and navigating any checks related to import and export. These may be low-paid 'mules' hired to move antiquities through points of the smuggling chain where risk of detection is highest, or they may be vehicle, plane, or boat owners who are willing to move antiquities or other illicit objects for a price. There may not always be a clear distinction between transporters and brokers.

*Facilitators* during the transit phase mirror and at times include facilitators at the source stage. They, too, can be characterised as individuals who in their official capacity are able to smooth the journey of illicit antiquities from source to market by way of wilful negligence or corruption. During the transport phase, objects may be cleaned and restored as they transition to their final market, for example, or they may be shown to experts for authentication and comment. Again, though these facilitators do not move the antiquities physically, they create the environment through which the antiquities flow and they allow for the transitioning of the pieces to elite markets, supporting the maximisation of profit for buyers and sellers.

## Jurisdictional issues

The actors who move antiquities from source to market are aided by global and local structures, which help mask illicit trafficking of not just antiquities, but other commodities as well. The key weaknesses that facilitate the movement of illicit antiquities mostly relate to the social, political, and legal differences between the multiple jurisdictions that an object might pass through while it is being trafficked. All transnational crime exploits at least some of these weaknesses and it is perhaps helpful to see antiquities trafficking within that wider context.

While some states have strong export and import controls with trained staff in adequate numbers who are not corrupt and are able to effectively identify contraband that is being routed through their jurisdiction, other countries do not. Actors operating in the transport phase of the trafficking chain are able to identify the different features of state export and import regimes and route illicit commodities through locations with weaker regulation, poor staff training, or corruptible officials. These attractive points of through-movement for antiquities have been referred to in the literature as 'transit ports' or more evocatively 'portals' (Polk 2000). Through these portals, illicit items mingle with licit items and often gain paperwork, a false back story, and a degree of legitimacy which will allow the item to be moved to a location with a stricter import/export regime where they gain more paperwork and more legitimacy. In some cases antiquities are moved through multiple transit ports before reaching their ultimate market: e.g. Peru to Bolivia to Canada to the US for Peruvian material (Kirkpatrick 2002).

Historically, looted antiquities have often been routed through free ports, famously the Swiss free port in Geneva (Watson and Todeschini 2007) where they may be held for some time at physical and then temporal distance from their initial act of looting. Having passed through the minimal controls required to enter the free port, antiquities can then be hoarded until they are inserted into the public market, their origins obscured by statements that they come from, for example, an anonymous Swiss collection formed over 100 years ago. Considerable effort has been made to make the Geneva free port hostile to illicit antiquities trafficking, but it is clear that antiquities still flow through other free ports such as Hong Kong and Dubai.

The picture is further complicated because there is generally a lack of obligation on the part of one state to enforce the export restrictions of another. An antiquity may have been exported from its source country illegally, but this may not prevent it from being legally imported into a transit state. The transit state, then, likely will not devote time and money to the detection of items that they do not internally consider to be contraband. If for some reason a looted antiquity is detected in a transit country, in many circumstances, states will consider ownership claims based on conceptions of ownership from different jurisdictions, but this may preclude previously unknown antiquities looted from states which have a blanket claim of ownership on all archaeological material. Without records for the antiquity in question as having been located within its borders, source states are often unable to meet the burden of proof they are required to provide as claimants.

Even in cases where transit countries wish to collaborate with a source country for the prevention of antiquities smuggling, structural differences between the jurisdictions may act as an impediment. Laws and policy related to investigation, information sharing, and collaboration may prevent effective communication across international borders, leading to information loss and protracted processes, as do linguistic barriers. Transnational cases often get bogged down in the logistics.

## Transit as a transformation process

Ultimately the transit process serves both a physical and a transcendental function. Antiquities are moved from point A, their supply, to point B, their demand, to maximise profits for various actors. However, during that process, the objects are transformed from illegal black market contraband to culturally acceptable, publicly tradable, elite commodities. The further away that the antiquity moves from where it was looted, the further it moves, conceptually, from the stain of crime. The black market artefact is effectively legitimised and enters a vast grey market, its illicit origins obscured by distance and by the process of passing into progressively more elite spaces. Transit as a conceptual space describes the zone in which a connection is made between actors and markets, which are quite vastly socially and culturally separated from each other: the rarefied circuits of consumption of the international art world, and the trenches of looters digging for treasure in the source countries. As we will see, the conceptual space of transit also disconnects the consumptive routines of the elite from perceptions of criminality at source. Therefore, in this sense, the transit phase is a one-way system, allowing objects to transition from source to market but not allowing the interest of the market in the origins of objects to reach all the way back down to the source. The transit stage connects, and at the same time disconnects, allowing for plausible deniability and a discourse of justification to evolve in the market around matters that are, in essence, unjustifiable.

## Destination market

### Background

The contemporary antiquities trade has its foundation in the market response to the Enlightenment practice of collecting tangible cultural objects (e.g. fine art, antiquities, ethnographic 'curios') as a representation of one's own intangible quality of being cultured. The ideal of collecting the splendours of Greece, Rome, and West Asia as part of a 'civilising' grand tour, or the curious products of decidedly non-European cultures during a Colonial or scientific jaunt, gave way in time to buying these items at European public auctions or selling them in the same venues during times of financial distress. Yet even the clear commoditisation of the transfer of cultural goods did not dim the cultural capital associated with collecting and connoisseurship. To own the past was to own knowledge itself, along with beauty and progress, an obvious social goal of the eighteenth and nineteenth century European and US elite.

The historic antiquities market was institutionalised, naturally, in a form that served its primary customers: individuals and organisations that were wealthy enough to buy antiquities or to have some to sell. Key pervasive features of this market, which appear archaic from a regulatory standpoint or nonsensical from an economic standpoint, can be attributed to extensions of Enlightenment/post-Enlightenment views of class, wealth, and discretion. For example, the common practice of offering an antiquity for sale with no ownership history and thus no reasonable way for a buyer to determine either the legality or the authenticity of the piece seems at first glance to be against the consumer's best interests. If one accepts the ability of consumer preferences to police market practice, buyers should favour antiquities dealers that offered more extensive information about the origins of the antiquities they have for sale, thereby reducing buyer risk. However, within the context of eighteenth and nineteenth century society, assurances of anonymity in the market allowed cash-strapped gentry to unload the family collection without a public declaration of financial insolvency, just as it allowed more moneyed buyers to purchase antiquities for sale without appearing vulgar. The stigma of having profited from the misfortune of another member of their social class could be averted through the auction house or antiquities dealer serving as proxy and being in a position of personal trust.

That said, the contemporary antiquities destination market is a neoliberal simulacrum of the historic market, having experienced the same corporatising shifts and expansions that other previously-small and niche markets have undergone in the later nineteenth and through the twentieth century. Major auction houses are now multinational businesses, which deal in everything from antiquities and art to wine, rare cars, and real estate. Antiquities dealerships may operate multiple premises in several countries and since the late 1990s, have moved many of their storefronts to the internet, expanding the once-regional nature of their customer-base. Antiquities buyers themselves are increasingly international, with strong indications that in recent decades large numbers of antiquities bought in traditional European contexts such as auction houses or dealerships have moved to the Gulf region and to East Asia (Yates et al. 2017). The conversion of the internet into an antiquities marketplace allows for buyers who would have historically been excluded from the market to now participate in the collection of antiquities by creating a vector through which low cost artefacts can be sold to low-end consumers. An ancient coin for sale at £25 on eBay is several orders of magnitude away from a Greek statue being offered at an estimated price of £25 million in a London auction house, but both attract antiquities buyers, and both represent the modern antiquities market.

Although wealthy and landed Europeans are no longer perceived of as the only, or even the primary, buyers of antiquities in the modern market, the general market structures and opaque practices designed for this customer base remain. The result is an entirely modern market with wholly capitalistic corporate actors that function behind a screen built around our society's maintained conceptions of the confluence of class and culture. Shielded by our general perceptions of these arbiters of art, taste, and culture as providing a societal good (however poorly defined that good may be), antiquities sellers and buyers operate in a largely unregulated space with minimal government or professional oversight, reducing both the consequences they face for bad actions and in fact the likelihood that those bad actions would even be detected.

## Actors

The contemporary destination market is composed of white-collar actors with persistent, if shifting, business and trust relationships with each other. Broadly speaking, the market for antiquities can be broken down into three groups: sellers, buyers, and facilitators. While we will necessarily somewhat reify here the roles that these actors play in the construction and maintenance of the trade in antiquities, it is important to note that the divisions between some of these categories are arbitrary: any of these actors may take on multiple roles within the market at any given time.

## Sellers

The primary destination market actors for the sale of antiquities are private and largely specialised antiquities *dealers* who sell directly to public customers and to each other. Dealers, especially those at the higher end of the destination market, tend to develop long term business and even social relationships with their customers, specifically acquiring objects to suit the tastes of specific buyers, providing expertise and guidance towards the growth of private collections, and serving as a gatekeeper to the market so that an air of class and exclusivity is maintained. They play a role that has emerged from the Grand Tour era, acquiring antiquities from a number of sources, consolidating them into a traditional storefront or gallery space, and marketing them to potential buyers. The contemporary ideal is that the antiquities are sourced through legitimate channels, free of the taint of illegality and with certain authenticity, with the buyer trusting that a 'reputable' dealer will have conducted an adequate amount of research to prove that any object for sale is not illicit. In theory, this would mean that the dealer only acquires antiquities that can be shown to have left their country of origin before relevant local laws went into effect, for example a statue collected in the eighteenth century, or before a 'best before' date or 'threshold' suggested by a relevant ethical code, often 1970, 2000, or 'more than twenty years ago'. It is worth noting that these dates have no legal relevance. In practice, the number of well-provenanced, legal, and/or ethical antiquities available for acquisition and resale at any given time is insufficient to sustain most dealerships. This means that nearly all dealers must be willing to sell antiquities of dubious provenance based on unprovable assumptions or assertions about their ownership histories. Many will acquire antiquities that they suspect may have been recently looted and trafficked, and some will knowingly and directly source looted antiquities from looters, traffickers, and intermediaries.

Moving beyond the traditional gallery, antiquities dealers have increasingly offered antiquities for sale via the internet, both through popular platforms such as eBay and through digital storefronts on their own websites. There is some indication that dealers in high-end antiquities use their storefront websites as advertisement, attracting interested new customers who find their business via keyword searches, and as a point of continued contact with existing customers, rather than as a vector of primary sale. For elite, expensive pieces, dealers report that buyers remain drawn to the experiential aspects of antiquities buying, wishing to see potential purchases with their own eyes, to touch them, and to see if the antiquities bring them visceral satisfaction. An online storefront boasting expensive antiquities may serve as an enticement to visit the dealer's gallery. Sales of antiquities entirely completed online, without prior buyer/dealer or buyer/antiquity contact mostly seem to occur at the lower end of the market with great amounts of lower quality or more common antiquities being sold for small sums. This appears to indicate that the personal trust relationship between seller and buyer remains important on the antiquities market. Buyers are unlikely to risk much money on objects from unknown dealers, and unknown sources, with a risk of purchasing fakes rather than illegality being the main influencing factor (Yates 2015).

It is worth noting that those who deal in small, low cost, unprovenanced antiquities may in some cases be actively involved in either the looting or trafficking of those objects. The anonymity factor of dealing online allows dodgy dealers to directly access an interested customer base. Indeed, one common aspect of antiquities sales via dealers is that transactions through them are usually understood to be private. Most buyers of antiquities, with the exception of some museums, are under no obligation to reveal the dealer who sold a piece to them, outside of a court order. Dealers are, likewise, not obliged to reveal who they sold an antiquity to unless they are forced to do so by a court order. Dealers may or may not choose to reveal what they know of the ownership history of antiquities that they offer for sale, and in subsequent chapters (in particular the Appendix) we will present evidence that in fact the antiquities sales community is selective in making relevant information public, declining to mention problematic episodes in an artefact's history where this may deter buyers.

As well as dealerships, antiquities are also bought and sold through *auction houses*, both via large multinational auction corporations such as Christie's, Sotheby's or Bonhams, and the smaller national or regional houses that may specialise in certain types of art objects including antiquities. They style themselves as a form of intermediary, connecting sellers to buyers via a professional platform, with the understanding that they are not the owners of the antiquities they sell, rather they are working as agents for their consignors. This styling can be misleading: for example, in some circumstances auction houses assume ownership of some antiquities, e.g. due to prior agreement to buy the pieces from their owner should they fail to sell, and eventually resell the objects via their own platform. That said, most antiquities offered by major auction houses have been consigned either by private sellers (see below), or other antiquities dealers.

The volume of antiquities that pass through auction houses is small compared to that of private sales via traditional or online dealers, however due to the deceptively public nature of most auctions (e.g. the publication of auction catalogues; the display of objects offered before and during the sale; the publication of prices realised), they have garnered much of the attention of scholars attempting to study and quantify the antiquities market. In fact, auction sales are only marginally more public than sales via dealers. Houses are not obliged to report either the consigner or the buyer of any given antiquity, nor are they obliged to reveal the provenance of any object for sale. Antiquities are regularly sold via major auction houses accompanied by no ownership history, and little indication of current owner beyond clichés such as 'property of an anonymous Swiss collector'. This makes external audit of the legitimacy and legality of the antiquities offered nearly impossible, and means that the auction houses themselves are able to make decisions about the antiquities consignments they accept with only superficial public scrutiny. In the event that an auction house is found to be dealing in illicit or illegal antiquities, and provided that they are not, themselves, the owner of the pieces in question, they can largely avoid penalty by removing the object from sale and returning it to the consignor, claiming that they are simply an agent, not an owner. The houses are not obliged to reveal the consignor's identity without a court order.

In addition to offering antiquities for sale at public auction, auction houses may facilitate private sales. This practice, which is increasingly being acknowledged as part of the business model of both major and minor auction houses, can involve serving as an intermediary agent between a seller who wishes to sell an object privately and a buyer who does not wish to compete in bidding. They also may encourage and organise the further sale of antiquities between two parties that have previously connected via public auction, or help a seller disperse antiquities that are deemed to be of too low value or, perhaps, too questionable in provenance history, to appear in the house's flagship antiquities sales. Finally, as mentioned above, in some cases the auction house may also deal in antiquities that they themselves own, in essence serving as a traditional dealer.

Finally, *private individuals* may engage in antiquities dealing, particularly those who are active collectors themselves who either choose to liquidate part or all of their collection or who, through their association with the collecting world, find opportunities to make extra income through sales. In some instances, these dealers may themselves be the source of the antiquities they sell. This is often the case for metal detecting finds in the UK and Europe, or projectile points in the US, and in some instances both the taking of the antiquities and their sales are legal. Dealing in antiquities for these actors, then, is either a component of a greater hobby, or is a temporary situation due to availability of the product, rather than a long-standing career or livelihood.

## Buyers

It would be misleading to paint *private antiquities collectors* with anything but a broad brush. They can range from one-off purchasers who, for whatever reason, decide to buy one antiquity and never engage with the market again, to serious collectors who spend a lifetime amassing what amounts to a private museum; from a child who spends their saved allowance on a common Roman coin to a billionaire who spends millions on a rare Greek bronze statue. They may be motivated by the enchanting form of an antiquity, experiencing it as an art object. They may be drawn to buying due to an interest in the ancient past. They may buy some ancient objects out of a sense of nationalism or spirituality. They may consider an antiquities purchase to be a business investment. They may simply think that a particular antiquity might suit the interior design of their home. Yet nearly all of these buyers share the desire to privately possess ancient objects: to personally own them. The exceptions to this rule are buyers specifically purchasing antiquities for direct donation to museums or for the purpose of repatriation: in other words, buyers who feel strongly that an object currently on the market really belongs somewhere in particular, although not in their hands. Like dealers, private antiquities collectors are often willing to engage in what can be characterised as a grey market (see Chapter 2), with significant risk of engaging in illegality, either by choice (Mackenzie and Yates 2016) or because of a lack of awareness of the illicit nature of the origins of many antiquities on the market.

Antiquities are also purchased by public institutions such as *public museums*, however, severe cuts to heritage and arts funding have limited the ability of many venerated institutions to participate in the antiquities market as they once did. While most public museums rely on donations from private collectors to increase their antiquities collections, they still from time to time either buy antiquities at private auction or purchase them through dealers. In theory, museums are bound by professional codes of ethics to conduct thorough and meaningful provenance research prior to antiquities purchases, to prevent the accession of looted or otherwise illicit objects into their collection; in particular, to prevent the spending of public funds on stolen goods. In practice, museums do not always achieve an adequate level of scrutiny and due diligence due to some combination of seller deception, staffing shortfall for research, inadequate understanding of the law or ethical standards, negligence, and indifference. Purchases above a certain amount must usually be approved by the museum's board of trustees. Some museums, however, provide small budgets to antiquities departments for purchases at curatorial discretion. In some places, museums are required to make the details of any purchases public as a condition of receiving public funds or for tax purposes. However, the reporting burden is often limited to the amount paid to whom, with further information about either the ownership history or paperwork provided with the antiquity only released if the museum chooses to do so. Unlike public museums, *private museums* and other private organisations and foundations may have significant financial resources and operate in the market like wealthy private collectors. They too usually have to approve major purchases through their boards of trustees, but their curatorial departments, at least historically, have had access to significantly more funding for purchases than their public counterparts. Finally, antiquities are bought by other dealers, for various reasons: to increase their own stock, on behalf of a client (so another buyer), or for their own personal collection.

As previously discussed, antiquities buyers, particularly private individuals functioning at the high end of the destination market, tend to develop long-standing relationships with the antiquities dealers they buy from, with representatives from auction houses that they buy from and sell through, and with the museums that, at times, benefit from their antiquities donations. These ongoing connections take the form of trust relationships built upon the reputation of both the buyer and the seller within the narrow art world. Buyers, by and large, respond to dealer reputation, which is, among other things, built on the social assumption that the dealer would have performed adequate due diligence on an antiquity for sale to ensure it was genuine and that good title could be obtained for it. In many cases buyers outsource this responsibility to antiquities sellers, and rarely commission independent evaluations of potential antiquities purchases if they have a prior relationship with the dealer. This means that only entities with a financial stake in the transaction are involved in the determination of the saleability of the object.

## Facilitators

The sale of antiquities, illicit or otherwise, on the international destination market is facilitated by actors working in a professional capacity and profiting both directly and indirectly from transactions. For the most part, these facilitators fall into two categories, which we have already mentioned in the sections above on source and transit: those who increase the value of the antiquity through their actions or expertise, and those who insulate the buyer from threats to their ownership of antiquities.

In the first category there are a number of professionals who work directly with dealers, auction houses, and at times buyers, to convert an antiquity to an ideal state, both physically and intellectually. *Restorers* and *conservators* stabilise fragile antiquities that require reassembly, treatment, or simply cleaning. They are particularly well placed to determine if an antiquity is illicit as in many cases, they will be the ones removing dirt and encrustations: evidence that the object had been recently removed from the ground. They are also in a position to notice suspicious volumes of unknown antiquities coming from unlikely sources. While some may refuse to work with this material, citing professional ethics, few report the work they turn down to the authorities. Others consider their allegiances to be with the preservation of the object while accepting payment for their work.

*Scientists and Science Consultancies* interact with and facilitate the trade in antiquities particularly around issues related to proof of authenticity. Depending on the material that a potentially ancient object is constructed of, scientific testing may lend credence to the assertion that the piece is genuinely old: radiocarbon dating for antiquities made of organic material, thermoluminescence testing for antiquities made of ceramic, and various types of surface and tool mark analysis for objects made of stone. Sellers and potentially buyers hire private labs, some of which historically have been located within universities, to conduct these tests, potentially increasing the saleability of an unprovenanced antiquity. These tests may be conducted at the request of the potential buyer or, increasingly, are conducted as a matter of course by a dealer or auction house and advertised alongside the antiquity as a selling point. In many cases, destination market actors are the primary customers of these labs.

In a related capacity, *experts and connoisseurs* also serve as destination market facilitators. This may happen directly, where they take the role of authenticator or valuer of the object, hired usually by the seller but sometimes by the buyer to lend their expertise to the determination of authenticity and value. It may also occur indirectly, through legitimising the object in question via academic study and publication. Within archaeological circles, expert participation in the antiquities market is considered to be ethically dubious: several prominent journals will not publish images of, or research on, unprovenanced antiquities and there is increasing professional backlash associated with accepting money for the authentication of privately held antiquities. That said, there are many ways for experts to participate privately in the authentication and valuation of antiquities, and the larger auction houses retain experts in-house for these purposes. The difficulty in obtaining well-paying work in the arts and heritage sector is sometimes cited as a reason why experts may agree to authenticate for the destination market.

The second category of facilitator includes those who insulate buyers from threats to ownership of antiquities, and work to mitigate risk within the antiquities trade at the behest of sellers or buyers who employ them. *Lawyers,* some of whom specialise in issues related to antiquities and other art objects in collections, may facilitate the market by assessing prospective purchases for plausible legal issues, developing contracts and sale agreements, negotiating the donation or resale of the antiquities, and formulating tax-related strategies to either shield these art assets or maximise tax relief for the placement of the antiquities in public collections. They may also be hired to reduce public relations damage following an antiquities-related scandal. Their key roles, then, are to mitigate the chances of their client facing civil suit or criminal charges for receiving illicit antiquities, and to maximise the monetary and social return on the disposal of antiquities within a collection. They are key actors in performing due diligence before an antiquities purchase, a concept that will be discussed further later in this book. *Insurers,* like lawyers, are also employed to control risks involved in acquiring antiquities by protecting dealers and buyers against the damage or theft of these assets, and in some cases providing specialist policies like title insurance, to protect buyers against the possibility their supposed good title in an acquisition turns out to be defective (Tucker 2011).

## Key drivers

When considering the key drivers of the destination market for antiquities, it is perhaps useful to do so within the framework offered by Pierre Bourdieu's concept of cultural capital. Simply put, Bourdieu asserted that of three incontrovertible forms of capital (social, economic, and cultural), cultural capital represents internalised cultured-ness, civility, and social standing (Bourdieu 1986). While social capital (who we know and how we can action those connections) and economic capital (or wealth) can be converted into cultural capital, the conversion is not direct; we can only gain cultural capital through an expenditure of time and effort in the correct environment. This cultural capital can exist in an embodied state, inherently within us, or externally as how we act and the physical objects we interact with, create, and enjoy. Bourdieu offers the collection of art and the appreciation of its aesthetic and historical qualities as an example of cultural capital. Thus, appropriate interaction with the antiquities destination market, the creation of an antiquities collection, and the appreciation of that collection serves to represent the collector's embodied cultural capital: their place within the upper echelon of the cultural component of our social human experience, a position of power and respect.

The association of antiquities with cultural clout is a byproduct of the Enlightenment era social project of binding the achievements of the ancient civilisations of Greece and Rome, as well as the 'Biblical' civilisations of West Asia and North Africa, with the foundations of European exceptionalism. The Grand Tour emerged as a sort of 'gap year holiday' through which wealthy, western European elites gained cultural capital by visiting and pondering the crumbling 'Classical' ruins, to experience the perceived seeds of the greatness with which they were to govern the world. The antiquities that came back with these newly-initiated, acculturated Europeans therefore became powerful symbols of the process. A man with antiquities was a man who had experienced the world and who was justified in dominating it (and they were usually men). That antiquities collection largely began during the era of conquest, colonialism, and empire is no coincidence.

As time moved forward, collection of antiquities beyond those cultures cast as 'European' emerged as another symbol of cultural status. Just as an Attic Greek vase might symbolise the owner's embodied links to Greek intellectual greatness, the ownership of an object from far outside the European cannon might represent other culturally-rewarded features. Antiquities from beyond the Classical or Biblical spheres, so everything from the Americas, Asia, Oceania, and Africa, were cast as primitive examples of an earlier stage of human existence, relics of a distant past that, through civilising forces, Europe had evolved from. Owning and appreciating these objects, often through Enlightenment and Post-Enlightenment concepts of science, further affirmed this sense of European cultural greatness by incorporating them in an accepted cultural evolution that placed European culture at the pinnacle. These antiquities, taken from their original contexts and moved into European collections and forced to be judged by restrictive European standards, served as part of the social and cultural apparatus that could purport to justify brutal conquest as a civilising mission. It is at this time that the regressive terminology for these types of antiquities was developed: primitive art, tribal art, etc; terms which are still used today.

More can certainly be said about the influence of the rise of contemporary art movements on the collection of antiquities and the cultural value that this continued to place on the act of collecting, but at its core, the modern antiquities destination market is driven by much the same forces as in previous generations: the social rewards we place on collecting the past and the cultural significance we place on appreciating art. Because of the relative scarcity of antiquities, their cultural value is represented by increased financial value and those who typically engage in the higher ends of antiquities collecting are wealthy. Thus, financial gain and the social standing gleaned from supplying the wealthy with antiquities or facilitating their antiquities consumption, can be seen as a key driver of other destination market actors and the continuation of the trade.

# 2

# INTERFACES AND ANTIQUITIES SMUGGLING CHAINS

## Blurring on the margins of 'source', 'transit', and 'destination market'

In the previous chapter we discussed the basic antiquities trafficking stages of source, transit, and destination market, considering the key features and stakeholders in each, and constructing a generalised framework for the illicit movement of looted antiquities onto the market. Yet, the evaluation of this model in real-world settings results in the blurring of distinctions between these stages. When looking at the actual movement of antiquities through space and over time, it is difficult to determine where source ends and transit begins, and similarly where transit ends and destination market begins. Interesting things happen on the edges of source, transit, and destination market, with the interfaces between each creating grey areas within the antiquities smuggling chain. It is at these blurred margins and these important interfaces that we find both the unique and defining features of the illicit trade in antiquities and the external structures that the trade depends upon.

To explore the features of these interfaces, the Trafficking Culture Project (2012–2016) conducted fieldwork in locations throughout Latin America, South Asia, and South East Asia, including: the La Paz Department of Bolivia in 2013; Central and Western Cambodia and the Cambodia/Thailand border region in 2013; central Belize and the Belize/Mexico border region in 2014; the Kathmandu Valley of Nepal in 2014 and 2015; and the states of Yucatán, Quintana Roo, and Campeche, Mexico, in 2015. This was supplemented by information gathered during fieldwork by project team members in Belize (2003), Guatemala (2003), Thailand (2002), Cambodia (2003–2015), Egypt (2005), Bolivia (2004, 2005), and Ecuador (2007), as well as desk-based research focused on the global market for Latin American and South/South East Asian antiquities.

Within this body of work, Latin American and South/South East Asian countries were generally conceived of as being both source countries for marketable antiquities (e.g. the popular cultural outputs of such famous ancient and historic cultures as the Maya, Chola, Olmec, Inka, Khmer, Malla, Aztec, etc.), and being a region of transit, with antiquities flowing through multiple countries along trafficking pathways, which they may share with other illicit commodities in the region. The movement of looted Latin American or South/South East Asian antiquities into the regional flows of illicit goods is instrumental to their laundering and then onward sale on an international market. How such movement takes place is closely related to the larger, more systematic challenges that Latin American and South/South East Asian countries face concerning stability, economic development, and security. These barriers to effective regulation of the illicit trade in Latin American and South/South East Asian antiquities form the substrate of the source–transit and transit–destination market interfaces.

In this chapter we will take a closer look at the interfaces of the source and transit phases and of the transit and destination market phases of the antiquities smuggling chain. Using case studies from our fieldwork in Latin America and South/South East Asia, we will unpack these interfaces as key components of antiquities trafficking networks. We will conclude with a discussion of greyness in the antiquities market, particularly in relation to greyness at interface points.

## Exploring the source–transit interface

In Chapter 1, 'source' was described as the site of disinterment or location of theft of an antiquity, strongly coordinated to the place where an antiquity was deposited in the ancient past. Transit was defined as movement away from that point of initial discovery or theft, into small or large, simple or complex networks that move antiquities physically and conceptually into destination market spaces. Yet the distinction between source and transit is, at best, undefined and is perhaps better described as undefinable. In certain circumstances we may wish to define transit as everything that happens to an antiquity from the moment it physically leaves the ground in an illicit way. In others we may wish to define source as everything that happens within an antiquity's country of origin, saving ideas of transit to represent transnational movement, involvement of organised criminal groups, or another set of criteria. Acknowledging that hard definitions of antiquities source and antiquities transit are not possible and not desirable, an exploration of the undefined space between the two is useful for understanding both the lack of definition between the two and how degrees of instability and uncertainty in the countries in which antiquities trafficking operates helps to shield this type of trafficking. Indeed, the source–transit interface can be seen as a locus of necessary and exploitable uncertainty within the illicit trade in antiquities.

Uncertainty and vulnerability at the antiquities trafficking source–transit interface cannot be evaluated in isolation. The issues and pressures associated with the transition from looting to transnational movement of illicit antiquities is not simply an 'archaeology problem', existing only within that sphere of research and policy. Rather, in low income source countries, such as those in question, it is more useful to consider the conditions which make the illicit trade possible as a development problem. The looting of archaeological sites and the movement of antiquities into market flows is one small element of the pressures and strains source countries face. In other words, continued issues with the securing of archaeological sites and the prevention of antiquities smuggling is a symptom of the systemic challenges that low-income countries face. In this section we will place the interface between looting and early-stage trafficking in Latin America and South/South East Asia within this greater context, focusing specifically on: (1) issues related to policing; (2) ineffective regulatory regimes; (3) lack of confidence in the authorities; and (4) dependence on other illicit economies.

## Problems policing the source–transit interface

Low-income Latin American and South/South East Asian antiquities source countries provide an indicative example of the policing challenges that are faced in attempting to secure sites or prevent looted antiquities from entering trafficking streams. Speaking broadly, archaeological sites in these countries are numerous and they can be remote. For example, Peru's tens of thousands of known archaeological sites are spread throughout deserts, jungles, and high mountains, as well as located beneath major urban centres. The physical presence of guards or other policing staff at most of these sites is not only financially impossible, it is physically impossible as many archaeological sites are uninhabitable. Even if full on-site protection was possible at all known sites in Peru, archaeological sites which had not yet been detected by authorities would still be vulnerable.

Remoteness and forbidding landscapes are also factors that prevent policing at the interface between source and transit when antiquities make the initial move into transnational illicit commodity streams. Many Latin American countries find it difficult to police borders. Considering Peru, again, the country is bounded by a large sea border to the west, a desert to the south, a jungle to the north and northeast, as well as the high Andes and the massive Lake Titicaca to the east, allowing localised border permeability. Furthermore, corruption at official check-points along the country's border has been a perennial issue, allowing for the illicit transfer of a multitude of illicit commodities, antiquities being no exception. Cambodia has similar border geography and permeability, with its land border with Thailand in places being mountainous and forested, and in other places being open for business, including the corrupt sort (Davis and Mackenzie 2015).

The policing and protection of sites and operations against early stage trafficking in low-income Latin American and South/South East Asian countries are not only limited by geography and scope, but by financial strain. In some of these countries, the authorities lack sufficient funding and sufficient numbers to address most crime, and the prevention of antiquities looting and smuggling falls low on lists of police priorities. Belize, a country which housed a portion of the ancient Maya civilisation, provides an illustrative example of the pressing concerns of an understaffed police force. According to the World Bank, in 2017 Belize had an overall unemployment rate of 11.4 per cent and a youth unemployment rate of 16.6 per cent. The Statistical Institute of Belize placed the percentage of the population living below the national poverty rate at 43 per cent in 2010/11. UNODC's data places Belize's homicide rate at around the seventh highest in the world and incidents of rape, violent crime, and burglary rates are also high in Belize. The population has historically held the police in low regard due to increasing violence and a perceived failure of the police to respond to and investigate crimes.

Very few crime or justice studies have focused on Belize and the academic evaluation of policing in the country is limited. An exception is a pilot study conducted in 2004 (Hanson et al. 2007). At the time it found the Belize police had a staffing shortfall of 13.4 per cent as well as a budgetary shortfall. The police lacked basic resources: police station parking lots resembled salvage yards, vehicles were scarce and barely operational, and the Maritime Unit of this long-coasted Caribbean country had only one functioning boat. Poor infrastructure was an issue, specifically a critical lack of roads (as well as the poor condition of existing roads); and having some of the most expensive public utilities in the region discouraged various types of monitoring and policing, as well as development.

Belize shares long jungle borders with both Mexico and Guatemala. Because of the density and remoteness of the jungle, as well as Belize's small population and small police and defence forces, these borders are relatively open. Interviews with Belize police conducted by Hanson et al. indicate that police check-points are easily avoided 'by simply walking through trails in the jungle', a situation con-firmed by our own observations in the region in 2003 and 2014. This, coupled with its position between South America and the US, has increasingly led Belize to become a strategic point in the international trafficking of all sorts of illicit goods, including narcotics and persons. Reports indicate that many of the criminals operating on Belize's borders were former Central American paramilitaries, hired into the cartel support infrastructure and that they are 'commonly found better armed than the police' (Hanson et al. 2007: 252).

Against this backdrop, it is understandable that, with the limited funding and, indeed, limited police officers that Belize can maintain, the looting and early-stage trafficking of antiquities is not regularly prioritised. Indeed, much of the on-the-ground protective and preventative work related to Belizean antiquities is conducted by archaeologists with the country's National Institute of Culture and History and Belize Police's Tourism Unit, the latter evidencing the country's economic dependence on the cultural tourism industry; when the looting and destruction of archaeological sites is cast as an economic threat, it may move up the list of police priorities.

Corruption is a problem well known to global illicit markets (e.g. van Uhm and Moreto 2018) and it is no surprise therefore to find it in the case of antiquities trafficking too. Cases of corruption in the illegal antiquities trade range from the fairly clear-cut to the more ambiguous. In terms of clear-cut corruption, we can look to the multitude of cases in which holders of public office have abused their diplomatic status in order to play a direct role in antiquities trafficking networks. The more usual cases are ambiguous however. These are the cases of everyday corrupt actions and decisions which happen as routine in many source countries, which have low-paid public servants and cultural practices that normalise payments for service. Such instances include, for example, bribes to customs agents that take the form of 'fees' paid for expediting the export of a shipment, or a 'fine' paid as on-the-spot penalty for an infringement which is then overlooked after the money has changed hands, or the 'processing fee' for a cross-border shipment, which includes an understanding that this particular box will not be opened to check its contents. The ways that corruption can affect antiquities trafficking, particularly in source and transit countries, are myriad, and in addition to these customs examples we could equally illustrate, although readers can probably very well imagine, the extended landscape of participants in such *quid pro quo* routines including police officers, site security guards, museum personnel, archaeologists, authenticators and academics.

## Aspirational regulation

Regardless of geographic and financial barriers, policing is only as effective as the policy and regulation that underlie it. If policy is poorly constructed, it will likely also be poorly implemented. If policy is beyond the possible and disregards on-the-ground realities, policing will not work. Most major antiquities source countries can be classified as 'lower-income' or 'developing' and public resources for both heritage preservation and antiquities crime investigation are limited. Although these countries often enact tough anti-trafficking laws with stiff penalties, as is the case with many countries within Latin America and South/South East Asia, when faced with the logistical and financial difficulties inherent in lower income countries, such laws prove nearly impossible to enforce. These laws may conform to international standards and may evidence a nuanced understanding of the issues related to antiquities looting and trafficking, however implementing them in an effective and consistent way is best described as something the source country aspires to, rather than what is possible given the resources available.

In Bolivia, for example, all pre-Conquest archaeological remains were declared property of the state in 1906 and the export of these objects without state permission was prohibited. In 1909 the government declared that all excavation of archaeological remains required an official permit, forming the core of a regulatory regime that effectively bans the transfer, export, and commercialisation of antiquities. Following these early measures, Bolivia expanded its policy to include a mandatory public registry of all archaeological objects including any held in private hands which, too, were considered the property of the state, as well as numerous procedures to deal with preservation and antiquities policy compliance. At the time of writing, the on-paper regulation of antiquities looting and trafficking in Bolivia is strong: all excavation of archaeological remains must be carried out by a credentialed archaeologist with a government-issued permit; all chance finds of archaeological material must be reported to the Ministry of Cultures; all ancient and many historic objects are cultural property of the state; export of these objects from Bolivia is prohibited without a government issued permit; theft and trafficking of antiquities is considered an aggravated offence, which carries tougher penalties under the penal code.

Yet despite this clear interest in preventing looting and trafficking through tough regulation, the policy has been aspirational at best. It does not reflect the actual resources that Bolivia, which has been ranked among the poorest countries in the Americas, is able to devote to antiquities-related crime. Take, for example, the mandatory public registry of dealers in antiquities that should, under the law, be considered cultural property of the nation and subject to export and transfer restrictions. While this registry system exists on paper, the system represents a mandate that an under-funded ministerial department in a developing country is unable to meet. Few people voluntarily register antiquities in their possession, a complete dealer list has not been compiled in years, and archaeological store rooms, even at major sites, have not been inventoried. An exception is the register of antiquities legally held within museums and churches that is maintained by the Ministry of Cultures. The files concerning objects in these known heritage structures are extensive which has helped in the recovery of stolen objects in a number of cases. That said, as is so often the case, the success of that particular registry appears to be associated with the continued institutional presence over several decades of individuals who have dedicated themselves to this particular task.

For another example of legal aspirations resulting in unfunded and poorly monitored mandates, consider antiquities record keeping in Belize, which is also mandated by local law. Here a well-trained, credentialed, and devoted but small archaeological public body is stretched too thin to meet many of their own record-keeping needs and requirements. Digitisation and processing of antiquities-related records was a point of concern during interviews conducted for the Trafficking Culture project, but a lack of staff time and the equipment needed to accomplish this task was a barrier to reaching a level of compliance that they felt was vital. The lack of ability to devote staff time to combing records, compiling data, and reporting on long-term trends and results was described as hindering effective use of policy towards, among other things, targeted investigations and prosecutions. Interviews with government-employed professionals conducted in 2014 indicated that in presentations and internal documents, they were still using looting, trafficking, arrest, and seizure numbers from as far back as the early 1980s and that the last time such numbers were compiled was 1999 by an external Master's student for their thesis. That said, Belize has made a big push to get citizens to voluntarily register archaeological objects in their possession as mandated by law, a focus on compliance that has not previously existed, again, due to the expense of maintaining such records and of pursuing people who have not complied.

By and large, internal legal mandates within Latin American and South/South East Asian source countries to train, maintain, and heavily fund numerous different policing, documentation, and heritage preservation groups in an effort to fend off the inevitable effects of international demand for illicit antiquities are left underfunded in the face of other problems related to poverty and violence. This erodes confidence in preservation authorities, and the public in source countries perceives antiquities protection law as being unenforced. This space between the law and enforcement at critical junctures in the source-transit interface can allow actors in the network to operate with impunity.

## Lack of confidence in the authorities

Compounding the issues related to difficulties in policing antiquities trafficking on-the-ground in source countries are the relatively weak state institutions that are meant to either administer policing agencies or to mete out state level justice for violations of the law. This gives the impression that the laws related to antiquities in source countries are unenforced and crimes related to antiquities will go unpunished, further leading to a continued eroding of public confidence in the authorities' ability to address these issues.

Bolivia, for example, is like many antiquities source countries in this respect. Police protection and state-level justice remains unavailable to most Bolivians. In 2012, nearly half of Bolivia's municipalities did not have a judge, 77 per cent did not have a prosecutor, and 97 per cent did not have a public defender. Bolivian confidence in the police is one of the lowest in Latin America: only 38.9 per cent express confidence in their police force, on par with Mexico (39.9 per cent), another antiquities-rich source country whose police force has one of the worst reputations in the world. Furthermore, 44.8 per cent of Bolivians reported that they felt insecure: on par with Haiti at 44.2 per cent (Ciudadanía and LAPOP 2012).

Thus, in many source countries like Bolivia, much of the population is unable to access state-level institutions. Although the law is clear and antiquities theft and trafficking penalties are steep, few criminals are ever apprehended. Those that are can languish in judicial limbo for years or be let go simply because these justice systems have significantly more criminal cases than they have the capacity to deal with, and antiquities crime is considered less pressing than more traditional or violent crimes. A key element in our international system for antiquities trafficking prevention, security on the ground, depends on the financial and organisational stability of countries that are rarely financially and organisationally stable.

Although the looting and trafficking of antiquities is considered a distinct crime under Bolivian law, and a form of aggravated theft under the penal code, Bolivia at the time of writing, like many source countries, has neither a cultural heritage police task force, nor a dedicated point-person to coordinate antiquities theft and looting cases between various government and security agencies. When a case of theft of documented cultural property is reported, a warning is issued to Interpol and to Bolivian Customs from the relevant body within the Bolivian Ministry of Cultures. This notice contains details of the theft as well as photos and descriptions of the items that were stolen, if available. It is unclear to what degree customs agents are made aware of these reports. As of the time of writing, there is no database of stolen antiquities that is available to anyone outside of the Ministry of

Cultures, which primarily keeps paper files regarding thefts. When archaeological objects are stolen from the ground, or evidence of looting at an archaeological site is detected, no warning is issued. It is unclear if any central records of incidents of archaeological looting are kept. Archaeologists are often unaware of the scale, scope, and focus of antiquities crime within the country.

Facing what is perceived as a failure of the state to respond to threats against heritage, many Bolivian communities feel underserved and insecure and a limited number of Bolivian communities have turned to fatal lynching to deal with anti-quities theft, as well as other crimes (Yates 2014, 2017). The lynchings happen in poor communities where the police are either not present or are seen as criminals themselves. These poor communities are also the primary targets for antiquities theft with the majority of recent thefts of antiquities occurring in Bolivian churches located in small, poor, rural, indigenous villages that are, by many accounts, outside of the reach of the state-level authorities. Accounts from villagers of state-level intervention following thefts of antiquities include complaints that it took multiple days for the government or police to send investigators to look into reported crimes. Government-level investigators agreed that response time was poor due to the inaccessibility of many of the sites in question, particularly related to poor maintenance of rural roads, and due to staffing and budget shortages.

One example of a cultural heritage theft ending in a fatal lynching occurred in early March 2012 when two men were lynched in the village of Quila Quila after they were allegedly caught robbing Colonial-era paintings from the local church. They were 'tried' by the community, beaten, strangled, and buried behind the church they were said to have robbed. A multi-day standoff between the community and the police followed, leading to an assurance that the community would face no charges if they handed over the alleged thieves' bodies (Yates 2014). Fatal and near-fatal lynchings related to cultural property theft have also been recorded in Peru, Guatemala, and Mexico, all also source countries that struggle with ineffective state-level security and justice. The poor reach of the authorities within these countries and the general lack of confidence in them allows for and, at times, necessitates the growth of informal and illicit economies within these countries, which antiquities form a small part of.

## Dependence on other illicit markets and nested subsistence economies

One of the most common external non-regulatory responses to looting and early-stage antiquities trafficking in Latin American and South/South East Asian countries is a call to educate the population about the non-monetary value of heritage so that they will refrain from looting it. Beyond the paternalistic sentiments inherent in insisting that foreign entities can or should teach indigenous people what they should care about, our fieldwork and related research indicates that educational intervention may have little effect on the core motivators of looting and source-end trafficking of antiquities. All of the countries we conducted source-end fieldwork in, with the exception of Mexico, were on the low to very low end of world income rankings, with high rates of poverty and low GDPs. Some were struggling with the continued social effects of recent armed conflict and major natural disaster and the regions of these countries most affected by poverty and insecurity are also those with the largest concentrations of archaeological resources. Less developed areas tend to have more intact archaeological sites than developed or urban areas, possibly because they have not been destroyed by centuries of subsequent intense human activity. People in these areas may look to archaeological looting as a stopgap measure during times of particular economic strain. They may also practise looting as one of several interrelated subsistence economies that characterise daily life on the world's economic peripheries. That these activities may be ingrained in the local experience as a means of navigating harsh financial circumstances makes them difficult to police and certainly difficult to combat through educational programmes which do not address the factors that motivate individuals to loot.

Belize provides just one example of economic pressures experienced by communities living near vulnerable archaeological sites. At the time of writing, antiquities looting and trafficking in the country rests within a regionalised collection of illicit economies. Although antiquities looting specialists may have existed in the past, looting and trafficking in the present is opportunistic. Individuals or groups are willing to commit a number of different illicit activities (e.g. animal poaching, smuggling consumer goods across the border, land encroachment, illegal logging, laundering money for narcotics cartels, etc.) because they see them as viable alternatives to other activities with limited risk of being caught or severely punished. People commit these low-cost crimes if the opportunity arises, especially when the consequences of committing such acts are minor and the crimes are perceived as victimless.

This can be seen historically in the region through the so-called 'subsistence diggers', recorded in Paredes Maury's work in Guatemala and Matsuda's work in Belize (Paredes Maury 1999; Matsuda 1998). While the 'subsistence diggers' observed by Matsuda were primarily focused on archaeological looting, he does connect their activity to illegal migration into Belize as well as overland transport of other illicit goods. Paredes Maury's ethnographic study focused on looting conducted by poor chicle gum collectors in rural Guatemala who would loot archaeological sites to add to their meagre income as they moved through the jungle during their legitimate work. She noted that families living in these areas also supplemented their income by poaching endangered animals, participating in illegal logging, and supporting the narcotics trade. Discussion of antiquities looting as one of many opportunistic illicit activities is common in the Belize/Guatemala/Mexico border regions. Belizean forestry workers considered archaeological looting to be equivalent to macaw poaching, reporting that people caught trapping macaws were sometimes the same people who were observed illicitly digging for antiquities. In 2014 Special Constable Danny Conorquie of Belize's tourism police was murdered in an ancient plaza at the deep-jungle Maya site of Caracol while tourists looked on. The men who killed him were not antiquities looters, but were xate palm poachers from Guatemala, illegally taking plants for the illicit trade in bouquet flowers. Conorquie and his colleagues, having found the Guatemalans at the archaeological site engaging in what can be seen as botanical looting, confiscated the poachers' mule, which resulted in fatal retaliation. In 2003 a Trafficking Culture team member observed locals, who both looted archaeological sites and were employed as archaeological labourers for international projects, poach an endangered jaguar at a heavily-looted archaeological site on the Belize/ Guatemala border. In 2014, while interviewing an ex-looter during a car ride along the Belize/Mexico border, our informant helped a woman illegally cross the border with a load of illicit meat for her shop, bribing the remote border guard during a break from describing the local, vulnerable archaeological sites.

Another example of overlapping and intertwined illicit economies can be found in our fieldwork along the Cambodian border with Thailand (Davis and Mackenzie 2015; Mackenzie and Davis 2014). Here, following the routes of antiquities traffickers, we came across multiple other illicit flows, including illegal trades in timber, wildlife, and gemstones, and the stories we gathered from participants in the antiquities trafficking routes involved intersections with other illegal trades like drugs and prostitution. The regional poverty, looseness and corruption at the border, and local enterprising spirit combine with limited conventional employment opportunities and a rich source of natural resources ripe for exploitation. It is the ideal mix of ingredients for cross-border illicit trade; highly profitable and, other than the violence which regulates many organized crime markets, low risk.

Within these spaces where many personal economic choices relate to subsistence and survival, we find a key feature of the source–transit interface: a population willing to integrate antiquities looting and early-stage trafficking into other nested subsistence economies, utilising existing flows of other commodities, and making the source–transit interface part of everyday life at the periphery.

## Exploring the interface between transit and destination market

As discussed in Chapter 1, antiquities are often moved through one or more other countries as they travel from their source to what we have in this book termed their destination market. We might simplify these two phases by associating 'transit' with movement of the antiquity through space, time, and jurisdiction and associating 'destination market' with actions that cause the antiquity to come to a stop somewhere. The interface between transit and market, then, can be seen as actions and circumstances which cause an illicit antiquity to leave a state of transition and flux, and enter into a more stable state. Yet the separation between transit and destination market is indistinct. Some important actors involved in bringing illicit antiquities to market appear to bridge the gap between transit and market, occupying an undefined space between the two and engaging in activities that relate both to moving an antiquity and to stopping it. In destination markets, too, antiquities may flow to and from brokers, dealers, and collectors, entering and leaving semi-permanent placements within collections, only to be re-sold, shipped transnationally, and transitioned again. At times we might see the transit and destination market phases of antiquities trafficking to be circular rather than linear, with antiquities entering into alternating periods of movement and rest. At other times we might see the two phases as overlaid, with no distinction made between the two: the idea that all monetary transactions and commodification of antiquities evidence 'the market'. Still further, we may wish to create a divide between transit and destination market in antiquities trafficking based on the nature of the actors involved, singling out the market phase as composed of so-called white-collar criminals.

Ultimately the transit–market interface serves to launder antiquities through various means, converting what was originally a black-market product into a public commodity that can be conspicuously consumed by elite actors who do not associate their actions with crime. Thus, at the frontier between transit and destination market, we find actions and conditions that obscure the illicit origins of antiquities so that plausible deniability can be constructed for dealers and buyers and so that elite actors are shielded from the consequences of engaging in an illicit or illegal trade.

Shifting back to our regional focus on Latin America and South/South East Asia, fieldwork conducted by the authors and by other researchers in this field reveals a complicated interplay of actors and conditions at the margins of the transit and market phases. The result of this interplay is the divorcing of actual provenance and history from antiquities, and the maintenance of obscurity and doubt. Within the space between transit and destination market, we find intermediary actors with sophisticated knowledge of existing regulatory regimes who are able to exploit weak points in policy and protection for personal gain. These exploitations, some illegal and some not, form the foundation of the international trade in antiquities and allow for enough 'reasonable doubt' and 'plausible deniability' to enter destination market transactions to allow for open consumption of illicit antiquities. In this section we will explore four aspects of these exploitations at the transit–destination market interface: (1) issues related to state borders, ownership, and jurisdiction; (2) destination market-end policy loopholes that are exploitable by transit actors; (3) the role of the dealer in shifting destination market taste in response to policy changes; (4) destination market interference in the provenance history presented about an antiquity for sale.

Our fieldwork primarily approached Latin American and South/South East Asian countries as 'source' and 'transit' locations, further exploring the idea that some aspects of the transit–destination market interface take place within the region. However, there is a strong internal market for antiquities within these regions, with large antiquities collections formed by private collectors within all of the countries investigated. Furthermore, it is clear that some of these countries serve as primary destination market locations for objects originating elsewhere in the region. This internal illicit/illegal trade functions much like the trade in Latin American and South/South East Asian antiquities further afield and, in many instances, serves as a feeder for more international markets in this material, supporting the loop-shaped model for transit to destination market to transit discussed previously. That said, some of the particular features of the in-country or in-region transit–destination market interface are not specifically discussed here and represent a promising area for future research (Byrne 2016).

## Shifting borders, questions of ownership

At the interface of the transit and destination market phases of antiquities trafficking, borders are a vector for laundering and exploitation. Actors that move antiquities from source into destination market take advantage of jurisdictional differences and uncertainties to construct false provenances or, more commonly, to promote enough uncertainty about origins that antiquities consumers feel that it is unlikely that a source country will be able to assert ownership.

One way this presents in the case of Latin American antiquities specifically, and antiquities more generally, is a de-emphasis of country of origin at the destination market. Rather than being sold as Mexican, Peruvian, Belizean, or Ecuadorian, etc, Latin American antiquities are presented on the destination market categorised by ancient culture and/or style. Some of these culture names or styles are only used by the destination market, having been rejected by academics or their distinctness called into doubt by actual archaeological research. All of these labels imply that an antiquity came from a specific country with many of them being place names that have been reused as culture names. Yet these names are not associated with context or provenance, rather style, and they may at times be used to shield the true origins of an antiquity; ancient borders are not the same as modern ones and the introduction of doubt through the application of a geographically opaque name is a particular feature of the market for antiquities, especially in the case of Latin America.

Take, for example, the term 'Coastal Tiwanaku' which can be observed as describing Andean objects for sale at major auctions in the United States of America. On face value, the term is meaningless: the ancient site and modern village of Tiwanaku is in Bolivia, however Bolivia has no coast. The implication to a knowledgeable buyer is that the piece came from either the southern coast of Peru or the northern coast of Chile where the ancient Tiwanaku had some sort of cultural influence, but as it is reasonable to assert that the piece came from any one of three countries, no one country could prove that they are the owners to the satisfaction of a court.

Indeed, the mismatch between ancient and modern borders, and a transit–destination market interface that emphasises obscuring movement, forms a formidable barrier to recovery of Latin American antiquities, shielding buyers and later-stage intermediaries from loss. An unprovenanced Maya vase that appears on the international destination market may have been looted in Mexico, Belize, Guatemala, El Salvador, or Honduras, and it is usually unclear which should claim ownership of such a piece. Although regional variation in Maya pottery styles exist, the Maya traded such material in ancient times and a pottery style can be found quite a distance from its point of origin. Trafficking networks that cross through more than one of these countries may further obscure the precise point of looting. The market allows for this uncertainty of origin by, again, emphasising the generic term Maya and stylistic terms such as 'Codex Style' or 'Holmul Dancer Style', the latter being a style that is known to span the Belize/Guatemala border region but with a location name, Holmul, that implies the piece is from Guatemala.

The result of this managed uncertainty at the interface of transit and destination market is a deadlock for repatriation claims. It is also a signal to buyers that the very fact that a piece is unprovenanced may protect a purchaser from return requests by countries of origin. A particularly open-ended Latin American example of this can be observed in the public label associated with a Maya Stela in the De Young Museum in San Francisco. Acquired in 1999, the museum lists the stela as 'National Patrimony of Mexico, Guatemala, or Belize', indicating that once any of those countries can prove it is their property, negotiations for return might begin, but implying that the museum's purchase and continued display of the piece was ethically sound due to the uncertainty.

The interface, then, between transit and destination market around borders takes the form of a market which rejects the need for provenance information, and modes of transit which purposefully obscure obviously-illegal origins; a market that does not ask questions and a transit stage that does not force questions to be asked.

## Exploitable policy

Another exploitable feature of many antiquities transit–market interface locations is a policy disconnect among multiple jurisdictions and between policies that are focused on either regulating transit or regulating the destination market. In the case of policy differences between multiple jurisdictions we see disparities between, for example, the export controls of transit countries and the import controls of market countries exploited for particular weaknesses with, as discussed in Chapter 1, transit ports serving not only to shield the true source of illicit antiquities, but also to facilitate the movement of the piece into market locations by allowing the acquisition of legitimate paperwork or through the exploitation of reduced trade controls. Perhaps just as important to the maintenance of antiquities trafficking networks is what can be characterised as an internal failure of market countries to regulate at the transit–market interface, with policy regimes targeted at art and antiquities markets failing to 'join up' with policy regimes targeted at transit-related activities such as illicit import. The failure to join initiatives and the, at times extreme, separation between governance related to illicit import policy implementation (often placed within customs and/or policing) and arts and art market policy implementation (often placed within ministries of culture or the equivalent) can create significant exploitable loopholes.

One example of this can be seen in the use of trafficked antiquities to exploit tax loopholes in market countries, particularly with regard to exploiting government-sponsored incentivisation schemes to encourage donation to arts institutions. Extreme examples of this transit–destination market interface practice can be seen for Latin American antiquities trafficked to Australia and for South East Asian antiquities trafficked to the United States.

In the first case (see Yates 2016), in 1979, a Costa Rican antiquities dealer, who has since been convicted of multiple felonies in the US and elsewhere, and a consortium of 22 Melbourne-based business people, were attracted to vulner-abilities in Australia's 1978 Cultural Gifts Programme, which encouraged collectors of antiquities to donate art and antiquities to private institutions for tax deductions and exemptions. The group paid the dealer $1.2mil AUD for a number of small Latin American antiquities, all of which were likely to have been looted and traf-ficked, had the pieces appraised at $3.7mil AUD, and immediately donated them to the National Gallery of Victoria, all within a very short span of time, gaining tax breaks to the tune of $2.5mil AUD more than they paid for the pieces. Enquiry into this deal in 1981 revealed that this loophole was being widely exploited, and resulted in a major amendment to Australia's tax code in 1982.

Turning to South Asian antiquities and to a more recent case, in 2008 a multi-year federal investigation in the US found that for years two antiquities dealers in California were able to place recently-looted Thai antiquities into major museums, earning tax breaks for collectors (see Yates 2016). Taking advantage of US tax deductions for 'in-kind' donations to museums and using money from various investors, the dealers would buy antiquities cheaply in Thailand and illegally import them in to the US. They would contract appraisals which valued the pieces at well above what was paid in Thailand, but just under $5000 USD, the threshold set by the US Internal Revenue Service for increased scrutiny of a museum donation. They would then arrange for the pieces to be donated, ostensibly by the investor who fronted the money to buy the piece in Thailand, to one of several high-profile museums in Southern California. The investor-turned-donor, or the dealers themselves, would then receive around $700USD in tax savings per donated piece.

In both cases, it is clear that in creating an arts-focused donation incentivisation scheme in the destination market, policy makers did not consider how connected market-end museums and collectors are to the transit and illicit import of antiquities, and failed to anticipate how the scheme could be exploited.

## The role of the dealer

A key figure at the interface between transit and destination market for illicit antiquities is the dealer. As discussed in Chapter 1, dealers at the cusp of transit and destination market can be characterised as 'Janus figures', participating in both illicit transit and elite markets for antiquities, and serving as a transformative node at a particularly sensitive point in the antiquities trafficking chain. Beyond the dealers who have direct dealings with the obviously illegal side of the antiquities market, prominent sellers of antiquities, including auction houses, play a key role in laundering illegal, illicit, and unprovenanced pieces for the market.

Dealers promote and support a culture of secrecy in the market around provenance. They do not of course call it 'secrecy': it is 'privacy' in the market's preferred narrative, justified as (a) necessary to competition (in the protection from identification of one's possibly lucrative sources of antiquities), and (b) important to client confidentiality and the desire to respect the interests of a sometimes-affluent clientele in not being named in transactions. The impression one gets is that the dealer network services a market that yearns for a bygone era where transparency and security had yet to become the norm in high-value financial transactions, and business could be conducted without pandering to such supposedly vulgar concerns. In many respects it is this ingrained and normative culture of secrecy that destroys the capacities of the market for the autoregulation we discuss in Chapter 6, since a market that has for so long thrived in this context cannot really be expected to prioritise the licit object over the illicit when it is built on a platform of communication protocols that obscure this form of knowledge. In Chapter 7 we show how this culture of secrecy also erodes public confidence in business claims of self-regulation.

Dealers are also market-makers in that they have historically been direct educators of client taste through the conversations and edifications that surround the transaction process. Clients have looked to dealers to inform them on matters ranging from the historical importance of artefacts to their aesthetic qualities and importance. In these respects, dealers have been arbiters of style and can 'help' clients to see the worth of some types of objects that may not hold obvious aesthetic appeal. In this way the look of an object and its meaning become fused in a way that affects client desire: certain types of antiquities can become more valuable to collectors, and more craved, because what they mean to history, including art history, affects how they are perceived.

This leaves dealers interested in making a good living with a clear incentive to educate their client base to appreciate objects which the dealer is able to supply. While international and domestic policy shifts may make some antiquities harder to come by, this does not seem to have diminished collectors' desires to own things from prohibited regions—in fact it may even add to the allure of rarity, which would be a counter-productive finding for cultural heritage protection policy. What is also observable though is the efforts dealers go to in order to encourage the appreciation among collectors of objects that are coming out of source countries in significant volume via largely unregulated streams. In participating in these flows there is serious money to be made, and the trend-setting aspect of dealerships in identifying what will be 'the next big thing' can be implicated in this process, which can then become a self-fulfilling prophecy.

## Destination market interference

The final category in this illustrative list of a selection of the exploitations market forces can make of the interface between transit and destination market in the trafficking flows of illicit antiquities is wilful mislabelling or misrepresentation of objects as they appear in the destination market. In the appendix we outline a series of evidence-based assessments of this practice whereby auction houses sell objects advertised under provenance histories that simply ignore problematic aspects of the item's past. This has been noted to occur, for example, when an artefact has passed through the hands of a notorious illicit antiquities dealer. In the Sotheby's Duryodhana case discussed in Chapter 5, this kind of destination market interference is also notable. In that case a catalogue was produced, and an art history sales pitch was prepared with accompanying PowerPoint including slides that called the statue 'easy to live with' and suggested that 'this is your chance to buy the best'. Nowhere, of course, were the question marks around the legitimacy of the statue noted. Naturally, marketing material is designed to promote sales in this as in any other market, but there is also a sense of responsibility lost here, in the deliberate arrangement of the content of marketing copy to sell rather than to genuinely inform.

In these destination market errors, we can perhaps begin to see the blending of the transit and destination market stages we have noted above. Where destination market actors receive illicit antiquities knowing of their illegal origins, or suspecting at least, and where high-end internationally-mobile antiquities dealers insert antiquities into chains of supply in destination markets after receiving them in the source or transit phases, we can identify the fuzziness of these analytical boundaries between the three 'phases' of the antiquities market we have identified: source, transit and destination market. This reminds us that the separations are analytical tools, in the sense of heuristic devices to aid understanding of the rhythms of this illicit market.

## The antiquities market as a grey market

Destination market actors (e.g. dealers, collectors) discussing illicit and illegal behaviour in the antiquities trade often refer to the existence of two exclusive antiquities markets: the legitimate market, conceived of as formed of legally transferable antiquities, and the black market, conceived of as being the marketplace for illegal and illicit objects. When confronted with illegal behaviour within the 'legitimate market', destination market actors often either portray that as the work of a few bad apples, a rare occurrence that does not reflect the market as a whole, or they indicate that the person in question was tricked (Mackenzie 2005b). Yet the weight of research indicates that we should reject the idea of two separate antiquities markets in favour of a model that styles the trade as a mix of legality and illegality along the source, transit, destination market, chain. In other words, that the antiquities market is a 'grey market' (Mackenzie and Yates 2017).

Emerging from the antiquities source–transit and transit–destination interfaces is the idea of the antiquities trade as a grey market with the notion of 'greyness' encompassing most of the actions and behaviours we have observed at these important, transformative points in the trafficking chain. Here we will reflect on greyness in the antiquities market, asserting that said greyness performs an important structural element of the maintenance of the trade.

### Defining grey

Definitions of greyness in markets, generally, take on two forms. The first definition portrays greyness as the difficult-to-assess zone between two extremes, often conceiving of it as the space between what is clearly legal, moral, or appropriate, and what is clearly illegal, immoral, or inappropriate. Actions fall into the grey area because the law, ethical codes, or societal norms do not provide specific guidance on the subject. However, the implication is that right and wrong will eventually be determined once the situation is clarified. The second definition of greyness is predicated on the impossibility of clarification, seeing greyness as a state in which the legal/moral/appropriate and the illegal/immoral/inappropriate, become irrecoverably mixed. Like black and white paint mixing to form grey, in this conception of greyness right and wrong become inseparably mixed and indistinguishable. The results are neither entirely clean or entirely tainted.

Is the market for antiquities grey? We argue yes. With these two general ideas of greyness in mind, and focusing on the interfaces between source and transit, and transit and destination market, we will consider three main manifestations of greyness in the antiquities trade: the market as grey, the commodities (antiquities) as grey, and the actors as grey.

## The market as grey: tainted sources

Because there are few sources of completely licit antiquities, sourcing for destination market consumption is focused on areas of relative weakness, where the reach of the authorities is limited or compromised. In this sense, antiquities exploitation mirrors the situation of other commodities, with illicit economies growing on the peripheries of social, political, or economic strain. In recent decades, several regions that house monumental, marketable ancient cultures have experienced major conflict: Iraq, Cambodia, Guatemala, Afghanistan, etc. At the same time, these regions have experienced significant looting and antiquities loss. The loss of licit income streams due to conflict, disaster, or economic decline appear to serve as an impetus to looting, coupled with a situation where, due to the same factors, the ability of the relevant authorities to protect archaeological sites is diminished.

The global market itself can be characterised as grey, in this case at the source—transit interface around the idea of mixed supply streams at source. Both sellable (but perhaps illicit) and unsellable (obviously illicit/illegal) antiquities come from the same source: the destruction of archaeological sites, often in areas and by people facing extremes of economic strain. Nearly all antiquities available on the market were produced by the destruction of heritage; there is almost no other option. Nearly all antiquities available on the market have at least some degree of illegality or criminality in their past; they are at least illicit if not illegal. Finally, a sizable proportion of the antiquities available were fed into the market in situations of significant economic strain or conflict. Although differences in trafficking routes and collection histories may render some of the pieces on the market less of a risky acquisition than others, obviously illegal and ambiguously illicit antiquities all come from the same tainted source. In other words, the antiquities that are purchasable without consequence on the market came from the same places, and in the same questionable circumstances, as the antiquities that are not purchasable. Greyness on the market, then, can be seen as stemming from this questionable source for both illicit-but-sellable and illicit-but-unsellable antiquities, and the effort made to shield buyers from knowledge about such sources.

## The objects as grey: False provenance and transit ports

Plausible deniability is a requirement for antiquities purchases on the 'high' end destination market. Elite or otherwise respectable consumers within destination market countries are, by and large, not interested in acquiring antiquities which are directly linked to illicit activity, partially because such pieces are considered an investment risk, but primarily because antiquities consumers do not consider themselves to be criminals. For a looted antiquity to enter the destination market it must carry with it a believable enough legitimate-sounding story for it to be conspicuously consumed. Thus, generally speaking, much of the middle section of the antiquities trafficking chain, between the source–transit and the transit–destination interfaces, is designed to facilitate the creation of such a back story.

The peregrinations of antiquities through space and time, through transit ports and warehouses, through low-level local sales and the likes, relate to the need to construct an acceptable false provenance for the pieces, and to allow them to gain both paperwork and distance from the initial site of theft and illegal export. Exploitation of weaknesses in various ports of transit facilitate this story-creation and paperwork gathering, with antiquities often passing through multiple locations, following a path that is illogical until one develops a nuanced understanding of the import/export regimes and antiquities legislation of each jurisdiction. The end result is looted antiquities openly for sale on the global market accompanied by false provenances that are just believable enough to shield the buyer from questioning the ethics and legality of their purchase. That looted antiquities must be rendered openly consumable by elite, 'upstanding' buyers is a nearly unique feature to this illicit market. It is here that greyness at the transit–destination interface around both the creation of false provenances and the obscuring of true provenances becomes vital to the maintenance of the illicit trade. Antiquities with true, legitimate provenance and antiquities with false provenance are indistinguishable on the market.

Again, returning to the concept of greyness, we can consider decisions made throughout transit and, in particular, at the transit–destination interface as serving to grey the antiquities themselves, resulting in products that are grey. Although the black market antiquities may have been sufficiently cleaned for sale, the stain of illicit origins cannot be fully erased, rendering the black market object a shade of grey: not completely clean. While the process of false provenance creation may 'launder' a looted antiquity, obscuring enough of its illicit origins to allow it to be openly bought by antiquities consumers, we cannot say that those cleaned antiquities are now legitimate; their illegal past is still there, just unknown, and in some jurisdictions gaining good title to the piece may never be possible.

## The actors as grey

White-collar actors play some of the more complicated roles in the trafficking and commodification of illicit antiquities and, as discussed in the previous section, much of their engagement with the destination market depends on their ability to avoid being labelled as a criminal, either by society or by their own internal self-evaluation. As such, to both satisfy their own desire to engage with the destination market, and to avoid outward and inward identity crisis, destination market actors either find themselves or place themselves in a position of moral ambiguity, where right and wrong are subject to interpretation.

This can manifest in practical ways, for example with 'creative compliance', as discussed in Chapter 5. Actions that follow the letter of the law while violating the law's intent place white-collar actors in the antiquities market in just such a morally ambiguous position. While their actions may not be illegal, it cannot be said that they are fully compliant with norms of ethical behaviour. The Australian museum donation tax loophole described above can be seen as an example of creative compliance at a point of moral ambiguity on the part of market actors. A well-intentioned policy designed to encourage donation to public museums resulted in illicit imports and inflated valuations, but also in donations to public museums. Museums opting to accept donations made by people seeking unintentionally generous tax breaks no doubt justified their actions by considering the perceived public good of preserving the antiquities in a professional setting, and being reassured that no actual laws were being broken. Indeed this sort of re-alignment of what qualifies as good behaviour can be understood through Sykes and Matza's (1957) techniques of neutralisation, a concept we will return to again in Chapter 5. Through employing various outward and inward narratives to justify participation in an antiquities market tainted by crime, right and wrong can become indistinguishable in certain contexts for destination market actors (Mackenzie 2006, 2007, 2013).

Also within the antiquities market, we observe a tendency for destination market actors to avoid regulation under the guise of an ability to self-regulate (see Chapter 7). That white-collar participants in the antiquities destination market are perceived of, generally, as upstanding and law-abiding, even public-facing individuals or organisations, may result in softer regulation and reduced oversight of the trade. Yet regulation runs counter to the trade's interests, and attempts to encourage voluntary self-regulation have been largely ignored. For example, in 2008 the Association of Art Museum Directors launched an online 'Object Registry' through which museums were meant to publicly report 'New Acquisitions of Archaeological Material and Works of Ancient Art'. Ten years later, only 1117 objects had been posted to the database from 26 museums: significantly fewer objects and museums than would be expected for that period had all acquisitions been reported. A search in December 2017 for objects listed by The Cleveland Museum turned up only a tunic and a vessel from Peru and not a trafficked Roman sculpture of Drusus Minor, purchased in 2012 at auction and returned to Italy in 2017, nor a Maya pot with a questionable history, purchased at the same time, nor a Wari hide pouch purchased at Sotheby's in 2011, to name a just a few. Instead of truly self-regulating, the only new acquisitions that The Cleveland Museum had placed on this public database devoted to museum purchase transparency at the time were two objects that have unproblematic provenances. Objects without legitimate provenance were purchased by the museum after 2008, they just were not presented on the public database.

Moving back, once again, to the concept of greyness, in this formulation, where market actors are forced to confront or, rather, avoid truths about antiquities' origins at the edge of the transit–destination interface, we can consider the actors, themselves, as being grey due to the blurring of the rules of ethics during market engagement. Within the antiquities trade, laws and codes of ethics say one thing while otherwise law-abiding market actors who, importantly, do not consider themselves to be criminals, do another. In some cases, the appropriate legal or moral course of action may not be obvious to actors due to the previously discussed greyness of the market and/or the product: in these cases, the consumer might be unable to distinguish between tainted and untainted objects on the market. In others, the individual's greyness manifests in manipulations of their moral balance sheet (Mackenzie 2006) such that even if an object's illicit status is known, trade is excused, justified or rationalised. This form of moral greyness within market actors is poorly understood, and is rarely addressed in regulation or policy.

## Towards a map of antiquities trafficking as transnational crime

This chapter has shown that the analytical framework developed to study the global market in illicit antiquities—source, transit, and demand, or as we have called it destination market—is useful but that a close look at the boundaries between these phases reveals intersections and overlaps that caution against a model of these three steps which is too reified. It should hardly be surprising, given the argument we have outlined about the 'greyness' of the market overall, that we find comparable greyness in the interstices between the stages of market flow that have been developed, after all, by researchers mainly as a heuristic and explanatory tool rather than as an incontrovertible truth in the nature of this illicit trade. So, with a suitably improved and nuanced view of the shape of the illicit antiquities flows affecting various regions of the world, we can move on to consider what in fact we really mean by this often-stated idea that what we are dealing with here is a transnational criminal market (Polk 2000; Campbell 2013; Mackenzie 2007, 2013). The implications of such a view will be outlined in the next chapter.

# 3

# THE TRADE IN ILLICIT ANTIQUITIES AS A TRANSNATIONAL CRIMINAL MARKET

The illicit market in antiquities, considered on a global scale, has been called a 'transnational criminal market' (Mackenzie 2013, 2007), and the case studies and discussions of globally moving objects provided throughout this book give a good indication of the reasons why this conceptual analytical terminology seems applicable here. In this respect, it sits alongside other transnational criminal markets (TCMs), such as trafficking in diamonds, wildlife, people, and counterfeit goods. Only rarely has the illicit trade in antiquities been explicitly compared to these other examples of TCMs (e.g. Mackenzie 2015; Mackenzie and Yates 2016), and never has this comparison been comprehensively analysed. The examples of literature where such comparison has been made tend rather to involve an offhand reference to a TCM presumed to be analogous in some respect, such as where discussion of illicit antiquities turns to talk of an outright ban 'like the ivory trade', public stigma 'like the fur trade', or conflict-fuelled resource extraction 'like blood diamonds' (Vlasic and DeSousa 2012). These references are indicators of the frayed end of a much longer thread that needs to be pulled. It is important to do better and more rigorous comparative work across TCMs in an attempt to draw lessons for the illicit antiquities debate about 'what works, what doesn't and what is promising' (Sherman et al. 1998) for crime reduction in this type of broader international cross-border criminal trading area. In this chapter, we begin to do some of that work, sketching the outline of a framework for the interpretation of TCMs, and then considering the general lessons that we can learn from observable patterns of successful or unsuccessful interventions in these other TCMs from a crime prevention perspective.

## Elements of an analytical framework for comparative work on TCMs

TCMs operate as flows which tend to move from low income countries to richer countries. The richer countries in this model provide a market, and therefore a demand, for the resources which are extracted from the poorer countries. For antiquities, this is a pattern of movement we have already noted on several occasions in this book: see in particular Chapter 1. Antiquities flow from low income countries like Cambodia, Thailand, Peru, Nepal, and in some cases from mid-range economies like Greece and Italy, to trading centres in the world's most affluent cities like New York, London, and Paris (Brodie et al. 2001) and more recently trade and collection has spiked in Middle Eastern hubs like Dubai. Diamonds, by comparison, flow along routes such as South Africa to Antwerp (Siegel 2009). Human trafficking flows along routes such as Eastern to Western Europe; from the ex-Soviet states to the Netherlands, France and the UK (Lee 2011). These are simply examples but they serve to illustrate the general proposition that TCMs are powered by economic drivers in which the pull factors are financial means and consumer desires, and the push factors can include local instability, scarce legitimate opportunities, and cultural norms that provide justifications or excuses for the wrongdoing in question.

The flows are not always from poor to rich in TCMs. Examples can be found where the direction is reversed, such as the TCM in luxury vehicles which can be taken from affluent owners in higher income countries and trafficked to meet a demand in lower income countries (Clarke and Brown 2003). Regarding antiquities, some source countries are also destination market countries, for example while the UK and the USA are major destination markets for the world's cultural heritage, they are also the sources of various types of antiquities, like Roman items found in the UK or Native American artefacts from the USA. Still, acknowledging these complexities in the permutations of the relationships between source and destination market locations, in general terms the ideal type of the TCM can be fairly and accurately described as a flow from 'producer' to 'consumer' countries with the latter usually being wealthy enough to finance the demand.

Many TCMs are functional providers of status goods to consumers in higher income countries. Status goods are those in which the transaction to buy and sell is not only concerned with the objects themselves, but in addition the symbolic value that the chattel in question implies (Bourdieu 1984, as discussed in Chapter 1). So, for example, diamonds are imbued with a social meaning beyond their physical existence as polished carbonite mineral fragments (Naylor 2011). Decades of deliberate public relations work, funded by major diamond traders like De Beers, have created in the social imaginary clear links between the minerals and positively-valenced emotions: love, commitment, indulgence, affluence. Other status goods trafficked by TCMs include some forms of wildlife, for example where large cat species are acquired as 'status pets' in some locations. The world of counterfeit goods is littered with the names of major fashion houses (Mackenzie 2010), and any visitor to most world cities will be no stranger to stalls selling fake Gucci handbags or Rolex watches.

Two further observations follow from this identification of TCMs as products of and symbolic reinforcers of global inequality. First, if we identify demand as a significant driver of TCMs, and we aspire to regulate that demand in order to control the harmful effects of these trades, we have to ask what is the incentive of destination market governments to intervene. The international nature of TCMs means that while the drivers of demand are normally centred in the destination market countries, the harmful effects of the market are most often felt in the source countries (Mackenzie 2007). Conflict diamonds, looted antiquities, wildlife poaching, and so on, produce harms which do not for the most part practically trouble the distant countries providing destination markets for these illicitly obtained goods. In fact, where illicit goods infiltrate public markets in the legitimate versions of these items, the market countries may substantially benefit from their role at the receiving end of TCM chains of supply. The cultural milieu of London's art trade, or the diamond bourses of Tel Aviv, Antwerp, Johannesburg and New York, are matters of considerable pride for those cities and sources of not inconsiderable tax dollars for the governments that preside over them. The financial and cultural attractions of providing regional homes for these international trades weigh against the moral imperative to undo criminality and harm in source countries, which are too easily put out of sight and out of mind.

Second, and following this question of the problematic incentive structure for effective global governance of TCMs, it is not only governments who have vested interests in supporting the continuity of the illicit trade that benefits 'here', and harms only 'over there'. The national and global policy debates around the ethics and legality of TCMs are hugely influenced by the vested interests of trade actors, whose often impressive livelihoods are financed by, and therefore premised on, the continuation of the trade (Efrat 2013). Antiquities dealers' associations such as those we mentioned in Chapter 2 function, among other purposes, as lobbying organisations and are seen by the governments of destination market countries as legitimate participants in commissions of inquiry into the question of the form and function of effective regulation (Mackenzie and Green 2008). Major diamond traders lobby and effect influence on trade rules in a similar way. Indeed, De Beers established the World Diamond Council to have a single organisation through which to focus trade influence on the regulatory developments in the Kimberley Process. Logging corporations put pressure on attempts to regulate illegal timber cutting, negotiating concessions for industry and softer or more specific rules, which are then able to be circumvented (Global Witness 2000).

A key conceptual reference in this book is the idea of 'creative compliance' (McBarnet 2003), which we discuss at some length in Chapter 5. An important point about governance in TCMs is that if creative compliance and active reception are mechanisms of manipulating the law governing an illicit activity once it has been put on the books, then the precursor to this manipulation is exerting influence on the formation of those restrictive trade laws in the first place. To achieve a clearer view of the influence of industry on the formulation of policy and law all the way through the process from the formation and exploration of policy ideas, to the development of those ideas into pragmatic legal statements at committee stages and debates, to the interactions of trade actors with those laws once they are put into force, we should add to our understanding of creative compliance a discussion of *performative regulation*.

The notion of performative regulation was coined by Mackenzie and Green (2008) to explain the reluctance of destination market governments to take substantive measures to control the trade in looted antiquities coming into their jurisdictions. Instead, it was observed that governments *performed* regulation by passing pieces of symbolic legislation which looked like they were 'tough on crime' on the surface, but which contained fatal internal flaws rendering them unlikely to achieve significant results. Mackenzie and Green saw an example of performative regulation in the UK's *Dealing in Cultural Objects (Offences) Act 2003*, which established a single offence: various types of dealing, handling and receiving of cultural objects 'knowing or believing that the object was tainted', with 'tainted' meaning essentially, for our purposes in the present study, 'looted'. At the time of these academic investigations into this piece of legislation, the advice from law enforcement and indeed the general impression among observers of the illicit trade was that this law would hardly ever be used.

It is only in the rarest of cases that the prosecution would be able to prove that a dealer knew or believed that a cultural object was tainted in this manner. A growing weight of research shows that the subtle mechanics of conducting illicit trade in the antiquities market involves dealers making efforts to avoid putting themselves in a position where it could be proved that they knew or believed an object had a tainted origin. Some clearly have this frame of mind, and can be proven to have it by witness testimony or a very persuasive set of surrounding circumstances: the convicted dealer Giacomo Medici who was at the centre of the cases reviewed in the Appendix might be one example. The convicted New York dealer Fred Schultz might be another (Gerstenblith 2003), although the legal interpretation of his level of knowledge is not clear cut. Schultz was a former president of the National Association for Dealers in Ancient, Oriental and Primitive Art in New York who in 2003 was convicted, fined, and sentenced to a significant jail term for his part in an antiquities trafficking operation. Sections of the antiquities dealing community complain that he was 'duped' by his accomplice and supplier Jonathan Tokeley-Parry, in effect suggesting that they think Schultz did not know or believe the Egyptian objects he was trafficking were tainted (Mackenzie 2005b). In the legal case, the New York court essentially developed a test of constructive knowledge, different to the UK situation, in which it was prepared to say that even if Schultz had not known the antiquities were tainted, because of his professional expertise *he should have known*, and this was enough to found the knowledge element of the claim against him (Gerstenblith 2003).

Another example can be seen in the case of Marion True, who endured a five year lawsuit in Italy in which the Italian prosecutor Paulo Ferri alleged she had knowingly received looted objects as curator of antiquities at the J. Paul Getty Museum in the USA for many years (Brodie and Bowman Proulx 2013). The lawsuit eventually became time-barred and was therefore struck out. Even Ferri, the renowned cultural heritage crime prosecutor, could not over a five-year period of investigation (plus the investigations in the years prior to the claim being raised) gather enough persuasive evidence of dirty dealing to make the case against one of the most public and well-known figures in antiquities collecting circles. What hope, therefore, might there be for the more day-to-day, less visible, dealings in the art world to render up clear evidence of the *knowing* acquisition of looted artefacts?

Sadly, dismal predictions for the application and effect of the UK law have been proved right, and it has been hardly ever used. Dealers often construct purchase scenarios in which they have an element of 'plausible deniability'. For example, they may ask for a seller to sign a document saying they are the true owner, which will give the dealer who buys the object some 'insurance' should there be any future investigation of the deal. In our research we have been told stories by active members of the antiquities trade about how dirty business is done. A dealer might say to a client who offers them clearly looted material that, in order to buy items, the dealer would have to know that they were from an old collection, inherited or suchlike, and the seller would have to produce a letter to say as much. When the seller leaves, and comes back the next day with the same material and a hastily constructed letter vouching for its provenance, the dealer accepts it (Mackenzie 2013). Scenarios like this sit alongside many other examples of the construction of plausible deniability, including a general 'don't ask, don't tell' approach to trading, which has long been the norm in this market. This approach has only recently been put under pressure by increasing legal and diplomatic interest in the illicit antiquities trade. In all of these permutations of sale and purchase routines, where reasonable doubt has been created around the question of what the dealer knows or believes, laws which require strict proof of those mental elements will fail to attach. So why do such practically useless laws exist?

The answer in the *performative regulation* study to the question of why such laws exist is that they serve a purpose for both the government that supports and implements them (the impression that they are doing something about this particular social problem) and also to the constituency of dealers they govern (soft regulation that those in the market can live with, as a perceived better alternative to serious intervention). Alongside the 'why' question about these toothless legal events, is a 'how' question: *how* do laws like this come to exist? To answer this question, the 2008 study looked to the history of the development of the UK law, and found that a type of trade lobbying was responsible for stripping the teeth from the law as it was conceived, developed, and then drafted. Key high-level dealers were invited on to the panel which looked at legal reform possibilities (Palmer et al. 2000), and one even invited themselves onto the panel on the presumption that it could not function effectively and with due authority in this particular marketplace without their presence! From the start, therefore, the process of policy-making was conceived as a mediation between a trade that has significant social, cultural, and economic power in London (and indeed elsewhere), and the legitimate interests of government in regulating the harmful effects of entrepreneurial free market profiteering. In this context, the resulting performativity of the regulation is not very surprising (Mackenzie and Green 2008, 2009).

We can see that across market/transit countries, there are varying levels of legal and policy engagement with the issue of looted antiquities. Internationally, some jurisdictions have legal regimes that are less hostile than others to particular TCMs. Some jurisdictions in fact provide positive benefits to TCMs. As electricity finds the path of least resistance, so TCMs appear to develop routes for their flows, which filter through these soft jurisdictions. In the case of antiquities, for example, Belgium has for many years had a reputation for indulging illicit traders in antiquities with short limitation periods on purchases of stolen property, in effect providing a title-laundering service for traders in looted artefacts who chose to arrange their transaction to take place in that country. Before it joined the 1970 UNESCO convention and tightened up its laws, Switzerland had the same reputation in the art world. Hong Kong has long been perceived to provide a useful transit portal for antiquities looted in Asia (Murphy 1995; Polk 2000). Hong Kong has had few controls on imports and will give export papers to items leaving, with the result that antiquities looted in China can be run through Hong Kong, acquiring export documentation and thus a veneer of legitimacy, which will help eventual import into a destination country and placement on the market.

Looking comparatively across other TCMs, similar examples of soft jurisdictions can be found. China currently provides a ready market for illegally obtained Cambodian timber, ostensibly preferring high levels of access to luxury woods to the implementation of effective and ethical regulation (Global Witness 2015). In third country organ transplant tourism, the donor and the recipient travel to a 'third country' where neither of them resides or has links, purely to benefit from that jurisdiction's less stringent legal and ethical approach to organ transplantation (Lundin 2015).

How do we theorise these weak points in the structures of global governance of particular TCMs? We can find a useful language to think and speak about this issue in the idea of *the space between laws*. Michalowski and Kramer developed the idea of the space between laws to summarise the jurisdictional problems that occurred when corporations acting transnationally caused harm in a host country which would have been a violation of criminal, regulatory or civil law back home, but which in the event was not considered a legal infringement in the host country because of its different legal system (Michalowski and Kramer 1987). This may be the case for some TCMs, for example dumping toxic waste overseas, but for many TCMs the situation is comparable but with the jurisdictions reversed. In the case of trafficking antiquities, it is legal infringements in the source country which may for various reasons not be recognized in the destination market country (O'Keefe 1997). The issue is therefore one of legal wrongs committed overseas which filter their way into higher income countries but which those countries then decline to 'see' in their laws. This, therefore, is a kind of 'space between laws', similar to, and developing out of the Michalowski and Kramer interpretation. Current developments in various jurisdictions signal some movement towards shutting down these spaces, or at least narrowing the gaps with regards to antiquities. We have seen legal developments in major market countries including the UK, Germany, Switzerland, and most obviously the US with its energetic and imaginative use of the law against Frederick Schultz, mentioned in the paragraphs above; Sotheby's auction house in relation to the Cambodian statue of the Duryodhana; and Nancy Weiner, the Manhattan gallery owner, both these latter being cases we will discuss later in this book (see Chapters 5 and 6).

The point of the *spaces between laws* thesis was essentially that the authors perceived Western 'transnational corporations' exporting harm to lower income countries. This is, in effect, precisely what the TCM in antiquities does, along with many of the other markets we can compare it to. Western consumption of illicit commodities, where it drives production at source and where that production is harmful, is a process of the globalisation of harmful effects caused by consumer markets among affluent world communities. Michalowski and Kramer consider the answer to the spaces between laws to be a move towards judging international conduct by international standards, whether these be global human rights norms, UN codes, or other transnational moral and legal systems.

Where national or international regulatory structures are documentary in some degree, as of course they always are, TCMs create pressure for corruption and document fraud. Antiquities are deliberately mislabelled on customs import forms as 'handicrafts', as was the case in the massive decades-long illicit international trafficking network alleged to have been run by Madison Avenue dealer Subhash Kapoor. The dealer Robert Haber, acting for US collector Michael Steinhardt, misdeclared the value and origin of an ancient gold phiale, which the US government ultimately confiscated (Mackenzie 2005b). Steinhardt argued this was a simple error by the shipping company in having interpreted the question about origin as requiring only an indication of the last port before entry into the US (which was Switzerland) as opposed to where the antiquity actually came from in the first place (which was Italy, who wanted it back). A similar series of misstatements formed the basis of the seizure of a *Tarbosaurus bataar* skeleton on attempted import into the US in 2012: Great Britain (the exporter) was listed as the country of origin on the Customs Entry Form rather than Mongolia (the country of origin), a huge understatement of value ($15,000 as opposed to $1m), and a description of the item as 'reptile' and 'lizard' fossils rather than dinosaur.

Several TCMs display evidence of re-using licences or certificates for multiple items. For example, in Israel the licensing scheme which allows a legitimate local market in antiquities has been shown to be a sham, exploited by dealers who take advantage of the fact that descriptions on licence documents which allow the sale of one particular artefact are so vague as to allow the re-use of that documentary authority many times over (Kersel 2006). In South Africa, the one-licence-per-person to shoot a single rhino is a system abused by game hunting tourists who ship in Thai prostitutes who are paid to apply for licenses that are then used by the hunter to allow the killing of multiple animals (Hübschle 2016).

Document frauds such as these can be thought of as one of the usual effects of formality in matters of regulatory design. It has long been observed that where regulators require formal responses, they will get formal compliance but not necessarily substantive compliance (Haines 1997). So, for example, in the regulation of conflict diamonds where the global system of control depends on diamonds being secured in sealed and certified crates at source to vouch for their legitimacy when they enter the market, the matter of possible corruption at that point of sealing and certifying the crates becomes of the utmost importance to the rest of the regulatory system. Comparably, in the case of antiquities trafficking, importers and exporters will manipulate processes of formal documentary regulation to their advantage, dealers will fake provenance histories for antiquities, pot-hunters will tell lies about where they found buried artefacts, institutions will drop incriminating periods from their published provenances (see the Appendix) and shift their geographical descriptions of the likely origins of objects to suggest they do not come from illegal dig-sites but from neighbouring regions where they would be less likely to be received by market observers as incontrovertibly looted (Brodie et al. 2013).

Formal compliance without substantive effort to meet the demands of the spirit of the regulation is a predictable and destructive aspect of global regulatory systems. This problem serves to displace policing problems rather than resolve them, in the sense that rather than policing the problem, enforcement agencies have to police the actual manifestation of the problem plus the documentary gerrymandering that goes along with it. Where the latter is the product of responses to legal requirements for certain documentary evidence, regulators have to be wary they are not creating more problems than they are solving.

How do regimes of governance grow around TCMs? It is useful to note, for example, that both trafficking in wildlife and trafficking in diamonds have significant global regulatory apparatus in the forms respectively of the CITES convention and the Kimberly Process (CITES 1975; KPCS 2003). Human trafficking has its own protocol to the 2000 UNTOC convention (United Nations 2000), and as such is a priority policy area for UNODC and for the law enforcement agencies in most countries. Illegal logging and the associated trade in timber is regulated in various regional formats, including significant rules and guidelines at the EU level (Mackenzie 2015). Looted antiquities, by contrast to these more coherent and focused regulatory regimes, have had more of a patchwork approach to control. Treaties with stiffer requirements than the 1970 UNESCO convention suffer low sign-up rates precisely because of this (e.g. UNIDROIT 1995). National laws at the level of the state are not harmonised or developed with reference to any clear international overarching structure, leaving the antiquities trafficking world map drawn with significant ongoing looting in source countries and an under-funded, poorly co-ordinated, and fickle response from transit and destination market countries.

Perhaps the most salient lesson to learn about the growth of global governance regimes around particular TCMs is that of leveraging expert opinion and public anxiety. In the so-called 'War on Drugs', for example, we see the fusion of domestic criminal and health issues in the US with national security concerns that through political work has elevated this TCM to one of the great global threats of our age (Beare 2003). Whether it deserves this accolade, considered alongside other harmful TCMs and global challenges, is debatable and of course this pseudo-War has been widely criticised as counter-productive. The comparable 'War on Looted Antiquities' launched in response to the depredations of Islamic State of Iraq and Syria (ISIS) is open to a similar set of criticisms.

Drugs, after all, are an example of a TCM where a significant portion of the overall harm is caused in the consumer country. There are certainly harms also occurring in drug producing and transit states, but there is enough harm felt in the destination market states for illegal narcotics to be placed high on the policy agenda. This is generally not so for antiquities, as we have observed, though the public alarm occasioned by terrorist organisations such as ISIS profiting from the antiquities trade has brought the problems much closer to home and forced them onto the policy agenda. Whether this will result in more sustained and effective action against the destination market, or will instead pass as a short-lived moral panic remains to be seen. Meanwhile, the unmasking of the harm caused by the trade in destination market countries—a warping of the presumed integrity of the social and cultural fabric—may contribute significantly to the punitive emotions of the public and the sense that something must be done (e.g. Brodie and Bowman Proulx 2013; Felch and Frammolino 2011).

Another point about the governance regimes of TCMs across the board is that there is not nearly as significant a critical mass of activist non-governmental actors in the antiquities market as there is in other TCMs (Mackenzie 2015). The illegal wildlife trade is a good example of the opposite end of the spectrum to the trade in illicit antiquities in this regard. Voices critical of the illegal wildlife market have managed to produce a raft of impressive interventions, making research the centre of widely received and impactful publicity campaigns. In the diamond trade, critical NGO actors are enshrined in the regulatory process as the third point on the triangle that includes the regulators and the trade. By contrast, critics of the illicit antiquities trade tend to exist as 'lonely prophets' (Loader and Sparks 2010), often employed in archaeology departments which do not see their work as core to that discipline. Some therefore lead rather thankless academic lives, fighting against an iniquitous and harmful global economic system of commodification and consumption of heritage from within academic roles that may not recognise the importance of what they are doing (Brodie 2015a). From these positions, they try to put pressure on various high-level political actors and systems in a context that is clearly very challenging.

Our project, Trafficking Culture, is exceptional in its level of funding and the capacity it has therefore had to appoint staff and enjoy the backing of a large European funding body with significant political influence. Our funding has now ended, however, as is the case with all grant funded projects, and while we retain our activity as a cross-institutional centre for research and policy development in this field, we now do so in more constrained financial circumstances than before. Still, we are lucky in many respects to have been able to establish our network and develop the working routines necessary to conduct long-term empirical and analytical team-oriented project activity. Many other researchers in the field do not have such opportunities.

Sources of supply in TCMs are sometimes severely constricted. In wildlife trafficking, certain species are in danger of extinction. In the diamond market the source of supply seems to be more controlled by De Beers and the difficulty of maintaining stable legitimate access channels into areas suitable for mining than by the availability of rough diamonds in their natural settings. In the case of antiquities, the sources of supply are severely constrained. As discussed in Chapter 1, there are limited legitimate sources of freshly excavated antiquities which could be made available to the destination market. All source countries regulate discovery and excavation in some way, and very few will allow finders to keep or export their discoveries, or give permits to archaeological digs which would allow foreign excavators to keep objects found and export them to sell on international markets. Really the only examples of these kinds of arrangements are where (a) governments do a deal with a marine salvage company to excavate an undersea wreck in territorial waters—something which has in the past been arranged to involve a splitting of the objects found so the market can in that case receive genuinely and certifiably legal artefacts (Alder et al. 2009) or (b) in countries which permit it, like the UK and the US, where landowners or people operating with their permission find artefacts on their land which fall outside the category of objects controlled by the government. Even in the case of (b), however, if the landowner is allowed to keep or sell the object, export from the source country may not be straightforward. For the most part, the circumstances in which the majority of the significant source countries for antiquities around the world would grant a licence for the export of antiquities for sale are so rare as to mean that in theory the international market is dealing only in recirculating objects. In practice, it is dealing in recirculating objects and also those which have been illegally obtained and clandestinely exported, mixed together in the grey trade.

It is the constricted nature of the supply of the objects which flow through TCMs that makes those objects so rare, desirable, and valuable. From this observation comes regular calls for source countries to 'open up' and allow a licit internal and export trade in antiquities, on the premise that releasing the floodgates of supply will diminish the economic imperatives of traffickers, reducing some of the pressure from which black markets are formed (Merryman 1988). Effective regulation may well have to involve thinking about these global flows in terms of metaphors of pressure, tension, or strain and how to relieve it—we will think about this perspective on illicit trade in Chapter 5 when considering Merton's work on strain and the various interpretations scholars have made of that work since.

However, the risk of acceding to the transparently self-serving calls of various markets to decriminalise trade flows so that they may achieve profits, is that the pragmatism of such crime reduction strategies overwrites the concerns related to ethics and social harm which were the forces pushing countries to criminalise the relevant market activity in the first place. In other words, legalising criminal activity does not make it right. Source countries are caught in a 'damned if you do, damned if you don't' conundrum in these arguments for less regulation and more open borders. If they deregulate, the international market will surely extract the resource in question, although perhaps the source country will be able to exercise some level of control over when and how this extraction will take place. It is not clear, however, whether in the face of such attempts to control extraction, the black-market activity that previously persisted would dry up. On the other hand, if source countries retain or expand their system of regulatory controls, they will continue to be accused of being instrumental in generating the social and economic forces that create and sustain black markets. These arguments are not specific to the trade in illicit antiquities of course—a legalization debate has been going on in relation to the international drugs trade for some time, *mutatis mutandis*.

It will be clear from the discussion so far that in many TCMs a search for the 'causes of crime' reveals two main prospects, which are not mutually exclusive. The first diagnosis of what causes illicit antiquities trafficking, as with many of the other comparable TCMs, is poverty and opportunity in source countries. Social dis-organisation and strained political resources in source countries facilitate the criminal extraction and movement of illicit antiquities through an incapacity of states to effectively police the issue and diminished forms of informal (i.e. non-state) social control on illegal digging and black-market activity. But if those are facilitating factors, the motivation for the crime is often thought to be found in people suffering poverty looking for ways to resolve their situation, even if only temporarily, as we outlined in Chapter 1. Accepting this is the case in some, but by no means all, examples of the phenomenon (Brodie et al. 2013), our research generates a picture of an interconnected global economic system in which economic issues at source are only part of the picture. The other, and in our view more significant, part of the picture is the consumer capital markets in more affluent world cities, which generate such significant demand for cultural heritage as a saleable commodity. This demand creates economic forces that reach into source countries and provides a financial context to the decisions actors are making locally, promising rewards for looting.

These push factors and pull factors constitute the shape of the market. The push factors here, manifesting in the source country, include poverty, need, and capacity to exploit unguarded local resources. The pull factors, manifesting internationally, include global market demand, collector devotion to art collection, investment value in consumer nations, and the social alchemy involved in the possession of chattels which imbue symbolic status upon the bearer of these objects.

## A typology of crime control methods in TCMs

A review of the available crime control, prevention or reduction methods in the variety of TCMs available for study leads to the proposition that transnational crime control can be thought of as situational, social, legal or economic. The basic premises of these modes of governmentality are sketched in Table 3A below:

**TABLE 3A** A typology of crime prevention philosophies for the regulation of TCMs

| Situational | Social | Legal | Economic |
|---|---|---|---|
| **Changes to:** | **Changes to:** | **Changes to:** | **Changes to:** |
| Physical environment | Social environment | Legal environment | Market environment |
| **Affects:** | **Affects:** | **Affects:** | **Affects:** |
| Opportunities | Motivations (usually normatively) | Choices (usually rationally) | Financial interests |

The assumptions of each mode of regulation about the drivers of criminal activity, and therefore their theoretical propositions about how to reduce or prevent crime, are quite different. Identifying these governing logics can help us to assess the likely fit with and effect on the illicit antiquities market of policies based on each philosophy.

Situational crime prevention (SCP) is the practical policy-facing perspective that emerges from criminological theories like rational choice theory and routine activities theory. SCP comprises opportunity-reducing measures that: (1) are directed at highly specific forms of crime; (2) involve the management, design or manipulation of the immediate environment in as systematic and permanent a way as possible; and (3) make crime more difficult and risky, or less rewarding and excusable as judged by a wide range of offenders (Clarke 1997).

SCP therefore manifests primarily as a form of environmental criminology in the sense that the term was used prior to the onset of a new 'green criminology' (e.g. Brantingham and Brantingham 1981; Bottoms and Wiles 2002). SCP recommends changes to the physical environment, to make crime harder to achieve (so that it requires more effort) as well as riskier in terms of the likelihood of detection and/or apprehension. In recommending these target hardening measures to the physical environments in which crime happens, SCP affects opportunities to commit crime, reducing them, or making them less attractive. The situational crime prevention perspective has been applied to a number of TCMs, including trafficking wildlife (Lemieux and Clarke 2009; Wellsmith 2010; Pires and Clarke 2011; Pires and Moreto 2011 Ayling 2013; Pires et al. 2016; ).

'Social' types of crime prevention constitute a very broad category but they can be grouped together in the sense that they take as their object issues of offender motivation, and aim to reduce the motivations of offenders or potential offenders through thinking on the level of 'the social' about why people may want to commit crimes and therefore what can be done about it, in terms of social structural changes. Into this category would fall social bonding theories, social structural strain theories (see, for example, Chapter 5), and a wide range of theories all of which consider the social environment of the offender rather than the physical environment of the offence. As we have seen, the latter is for situational crime prevention. In social crime prevention, the effect regulators aim to have is on norms, values, beliefs, commitments, attachments, and the like, as well as structural issues resulting in forms of social exclusion, such as poverty and relative deprivation, schooling, parenting, and employment opportunities. The underlying philosophy is therefore about changing people for the better, and aiming to do so by changing their social environment for the better.

Legal approaches to crime prevention are essentially based in the theory of deterrence (von Hirsch et al. 1999). The criminal justice system responds to crime by punishing those who break the law, and underpinning the sense that this process of punishment may reduce crime are propositions about specific and general deterrence, in other words where either the offender themselves (specific) or observing members of the public (general) are deterred. The theory is based on three propositions: those of certainty, celerity and severity (Marshall 2002). Certainty proposes that the likelihood of punishment should be certain enough in the mind of the person at the time they are considering committing the offence to put them off doing it. Celerity requires that the punishment follow relatively swiftly on from the commission of the offence, so that the relationship between the offending behaviour and the penalty is clear enough to the offender (in the case of specific deterrence) and/or the public (in the case of general deterrence). Without such celerity, the punishment can lose its deterrent effect, as by the time it comes around, the censure of the original rule infraction may have become considerably weakened. Finally, severity requires that the penalty should be serious enough to deter a would-be offender who is rationally weighing up the benefits to be obtained from crime against the pain to be incurred if caught. Without adequate severity, a certain and swift 'slap on the wrist' is unlikely to deter.

Last, we can consider economic types of crime control, which involve thinking about TCMs as markets first and foremost. We are thus looking here for a 'market reduction approach' which goes beyond the version of the more specific market reduction approach that was developed in relation to the UK's stolen goods markets (Sutton 1998; Sutton et al. 2001), and has been recommended as something to be adopted and adapted in combatting the TCMs for wildlife (Schneider 2008) and antiquities (Mackenzie 2011b). That market reduction approach is premised on the networked connectedness of buyers and sellers within market contexts, the importance of fences as key brokers, and the effects of targeted police crackdowns on the capacity of the criminal elements in a market to do business undisrupted. Building on this market-oriented crime prevention analysis, we might consider other ways to intervene in market settings to leverage the financial interests at stake, for example. Where buyer demand is investment-oriented as well as about consumptive enjoyment of commodities, one might look to depleting the investment value of criminal goods. Campaigns against conflict diamonds, ivory artefacts, and unprovenanced antiquities are examples of attempts to do this. As another example, currently in some countries wealthy owners of antiquities and works of art can obtain significant tax relief if they donate those objects to public museums, effectively recouping the market value of the object through a deduction from their tax bill (Yates 2016; see Chapter 2). Arguments have been made that those tax breaks should explicitly not be available for looted antiquities, which would serve as an economic disincentive to the collection of unprovenanced cultural heritage, albeit perhaps a marginal one.

Out of the four options we have outlined for regulation—situational, social, legal and economic—the most powerful influencers of action may reasonably be argued to be social and economic. Why? Let us look at some of the flaws in legal and situational approaches.

The deterrent approach of the legal institutional responses of the criminal justice system is largely theoretical. Deterrence theory has been the subject of empirical study, and the results are not encouraging (Nagin 1998; von Hirsch et al. 1999). The severity of the penalty is important up to the level where it may seriously affect offender decision-making, but above this level the rewards of increasing severity may be thought to be diminishing. Even more troublesome, the empirical evidence suggests that most offenders across a range of crimes do not know the severity of the punishment they would be likely to get if arrested, charged, prosecuted and convicted, and anyway they do not feel that they are likely to be caught. So the problems for the criminal justice system in raising levels of deterrence appear to be problems of certainty and celerity rather than problems of severity. Unfortunately, raising the levels of certainty of arrest and celerity of the processes of police and court justice would be a prohibitively expensive exercise. It would likely involve massive expenditure on police and court resources, and the starting point for issues of certainty and celerity are so low that to make any serious gains the shift in process would have to be momentous. So politicians tend to settle for a penal populism in which public emotions around crime are whipped up and exploited with manifestos to 'get tough on crime' and to increase the severity of the system (Pratt 2007).

Situational crime prevention measures may be more effective, but the image of society they create and engage with is a hotbed of widespread criminal motivation, prevented from becoming actualised in offending behaviour only because of the sealing off of opportunities the environment presents (Hope and Karstedt 2003; Lee 2009)—in our case, the market environment. We should not, of course, be satisfied with a market that provides ready criminal opportunities and it does seem sensible to lock down as many as possible of the loopholes and lures which represent these opportunities (Vander Beken and Van Daele 2008). But a philosophy of target hardening which is not paired with a holistic view of the market as a joined-up transnational system seems to lead to a focus on physical heritage protection and security measures at the source end of the supply chain. All of us who work in this field of research will be aware of the temptation for new commentators, often those who have just taken over a rotating chair in an international policy organization or law enforcement agency, to call for better site protection. Situational crime prevention asks, among other things, that poor countries should harden the targets that their temples and underground tombs present: a request which is pragmatically really a non-starter as we have discussed in Chapter 2.

Social crime prevention measures would tend to be longer term, looking to structural change to affect behaviour, and economic approaches may be shorter term but require a political platform to regulate markets, which is usually hotly contested by the players in those markets, who prefer *laissez-faire* or deregulated trading zones. But overall both of these 'types' or 'styles' of approach to crime prevention seem to be promising. The types are not mutually exclusive of course, and any given regulatory field may well be made up of layers of these different types of approach, the aim being to promote a 'culture of compliance' (Johnstone and Sarre 2004)—regulatory terminology and conceptual apparatus that we will explore in more depth in Chapter 5.

It is interesting, however, if we are to agree that the legal and the situational are subordinate in likely effect to the social and the economic—in the sense of playing important supporting roles to those other styles of intervention but operating most usefully when they are not 'the only game in town'—that by far the greatest amount of activity in the regulation of the global illicit antiquities trade has been, and continues to be, legal. This is a field governed by a patchwork of international conventions, treaties, bilateral and multi-lateral agreements between countries, and associated domestic laws in the various jurisdictions which legislate on the criminal and civil implications of dealing in looted antiquities. Second to the legal activity in the regulation of the market has been situational crime prevention, in much lower order of energy and importance: essentially efforts at museum and site security in heritage-rich countries which have often been fairly rudimentary.

Aside from in the modest criminological research field around the market and in the work of community archaeology programmes in source countries there has been little discussion of social interventions, which would involve the preliminary step of seeking to understand what kinds of people are operating in this TCM, from where their motivation comes, and how it might be depleted or diverted into more pro-social activities. Local museums and community participation in archaeological programmes would be one example here, along with public awareness-raising campaigns in destination market countries. These latter are, however, virtually non-existent with the exception of the few popular books, documentary films and investigative TV shows that are produced every year by interested journalists (e.g. Atwood 2004; Felch and Frammolino 2011; Watson 1997; Watson and Todeschini 2007). Economic interventions, in the sense of market-altering financial manipulations by political actors who want to regulate the flow of antiquities by deliberately suppressing the price of looted material, are similarly non-existent other than to the extent that legal developments (e.g. the criminalisation of dealing in tainted cultural objects) may have some such effects, although our research will show in Chapter 6 the minimal effects on price evident even in the widely accepted red line provided by the 1970 standard (UNESCO 1970). This is a free market where prices are set by the forces of supply and demand rather than regulated in any other economic way.

So perhaps this analysis helps us arrive at one window into the answer to why policy has failed in this area. For the most part it has been pulling the wrong regulatory levers, and some new and inventive thinking is needed if progressive policy is going to develop which can seriously reduce the worldwide trafficking problem in looted antiquities.

## Towards more productive policy design for the TCM in illicit antiquities

We can therefore conclude this chapter by thinking about what social and economic crime prevention interventions might look like in broad measure, before turning in the next chapter to a consideration of their role in supporting the development of ethical consumption as part of a coherent regulatory approach focused on the destination market. For now, let us consider the implications of the discussion we have had about the regulatory forms developed in other TCMs and their market contexts. The range of possible social and economic interventions are broad, including high-level strategies many of which are sensible, if difficult to implement, such as development aid schemes that have the aspiration of long-term global poverty reduction, as well as cognate propositions about global economic justice (Pogge 2002). We will focus our comments on ideas which are more specific to the illicit antiquities market than these much broader policies.

Economic interventions into the market might be thought to take two overall forms: diversion of prospective looters at source, and the diminution of the value of unprovenanced antiquities in the destination market. In fact, these two forms are clearly linked, since as we have said market reduction will reduce supply through disincentivising prospective looters by removing the potential profit. Other possibilities at source involve community-building cultural activities like local archaeological and museum projects, which can have the dual benefits of reinvigorating in local communities a sense of pride and cultural value in the local heritage, so making them less likely to engage in looting due to the protective factors involved in those social bonding activities, and also possibly generating tourist revenue and associated jobs for locals, which would be an economic type of intervention. Often economic and social interventions will be overlapping, or mutually reinforcing.

Another example of an overlapping economic and social intervention might be where the trade value of objects is reduced by attaching social stigma to them. This invites comparisons to art stolen during the Holocaust, conflict diamonds, or illicit wildlife, where these types of stigmatising initiatives have been applied. For example, PETA (People for the Ethical Treatment of Animals) claimed to have cut fur sales in Europe in half between 1991 and 1999 through their direct action. There has certainly been a sea change in the social meaning of wearing fur. Once a status symbol, it is now a thing from which many people recoil in horror. Others hurl abuse at the wearer. It is hard to imagine such widespread revulsion being aimed at the collection and display of looted antiquities, but even a much less violent rejection of unethical practice in the market for cultural heritage might be powerful were it to become broadly imbedded in the public consciousness and widely felt in collecting circles.

Global treaty-based trade rules regulating import/export and trade in a way that provides harmonized and joined-up regulation among member countries, along the lines of CITES or the Kimberley Process are a tantalizing prospect for the TCM in illicit antiquities. However, these processes are not the panacea for those TCMs that they are often assumed to be, and while harmonizing or further integrating import/export control in the global antiquities trade has been raised in various respects and from a variety of perspectives (Mackenzie 2005b), there has been practical resistance to this process. That process of restricting the import into destination market countries of unprovenanced antiquities which have made it past the export prohibitions of source countries is clearly a useful way to diminish the value of illicit antiquities in the market. In this case it would therefore be considered an economic imperative, in our scheme for thinking about regulation. A global import and export system that was, like CITES, premised on seizing at point of import or afterwards those cultural goods which do not arrive with proof of authorised export would be useful. It is highly unpalatable to the market, obviously, and it would require a mechanism to deal with existing collections, and so it is not on many political agendas presently.

This type of 'prove it's legal' approach leads into a wider discussion about reversing the burden of proof: a legal intervention which would require dealers to be able to prove that an object was legally obtained, rather than the current situation in which prosecutors have to prove it was illegally obtained (Gerstenblith 2007). There are isolated examples in the TCM in antiquities of shifting that burden, such as the UN security resolutions in respect of Iraq, and now Syria, and the variety of domestic applications of those regulations in destination market and transit countries. Therefore, this kind of special treatment for certain classes of antiquities is not unprecedented, although the application of the rule more widely has so far been hotly resisted by the trade and by some governments which see it as constitutionally problematic because of the inroads it makes into the presumption of innocence.

Situational interventions into the trade might involve emphasis on 'capable guardians' at key points (Felson 1995). In the diamond trade, for example, dealers are required to keep detailed records of sales and purchases of rough diamonds and these records are monitored by external auditors. Comparable processes of external auditing of trade records are notable in their absence from antiquities dealers, who still operate in an informal zone as sole traders, in charge of their own record-keeping routines and reluctant to show them to anyone (we have asked!) let alone to an external auditor who may have the power to generate law enforcement consequences if criminal dealing is detected. These law enforcement consequences of audited bad practice can be thought of as a useful fusion of the legal and situational approaches, with the situational requirements providing a structure within which law can achieve more grip than usual. In this example, it may be significantly easier to prove a dealer has not been keeping accurate or honest records than it would be to prove they were dealing in tainted antiquities.

It is not the aim of this chapter to be exhaustive in our coverage of the range of ideas which might be useful in increasing forms of control in this TCM. Rather, the aim has been to set up a typological framework for thinking about the crime prevention possibilities: economic, social, legal and situational. Then, we can consider the wide range of comparative issues raised here when illicit antiquities are thought of as a TCM and held alongside other examples of TCMs to see how they compare. This helps work towards a framework of policy development which not only thinks of regulation in 'types' but can now see practical examples of those 'types' in the other TCMs available for study. Structured approaches to the development of crime policy like this seem to hold more potential than the less regimented processes we chart in other chapters in this book, where illicit antiquities policy is seen as responding to whichever country the media focuses on as the current 'crisis situation', while largely ignoring the systematic, longer term, global picture.

# 4

# THE DESTINATION MARKET

As we described in Chapters 1 and 2, the antiquities trade can be schematized as comprising three phases—source, transit and destination (Prott and O'Keefe 1989; Polk 2000). These phases are generally separated geographically and socioeconomically, with source markets located in poorer areas of the world and destination markets in wealthier areas, though different phases can co-exist within a single country, the most obvious example being the source and destination markets for Native American objects in the United States. The actors and agencies driving the trade through all three phases were also described in the Chapters 1 and 2, but here we want to focus in on the operation of the destination market where demand for antiquities is both created and satisfied.

In Chapter 3, we argued that the situational modality of crime control often advocated for discouraging looting at source is inappropriate because of the harsh socioeconomic realities of many of those areas. The antiquities trade, along with other illicit trades, is driven by consumer demand and will persist until demand is reduced (Naylor 2004: 11). Yet, as we describe in Chapter 8, international public policy aimed at tackling antiquities trafficking though a series of laws and normative recommendations has since the 1960s struggled with a supply-side strategy to protect archaeological and cultural sites at source and prevent material from reaching the destination market. By the 2010s, the massive, ongoing looting of archaeological and cultural sites in Syria and other countries provided emphatic demonstration that this policy was failing (Brodie 2015c, 2015d). The destination market had grown in size both materially and financially and developed sophisti-cated operational strategies and cultural logics to defend its participants from any judicial penalty or moral opprobrium. In the absence of effective, countervailing policy measures, demand for trafficked antiquities had grown with it. The destination market is a white-collar criminal trading forum—a concept we will unpack in more detail in Chapter 5, where we will investigate it as a locus of white-collar crime, describing the actors involved and the cultural obfuscations that obscure or disguise their criminality. By way of introductory contrast, however, this chapter offers an organisational or structural perspective on the market.

## The structure and organisation of the destination market

The destination market for antiquities can be construed as a mutually-engaged circulation of money, material and information. Its logic and action is to construct value and determine price, create the conditions of trust necessary for the orderly commercial exchange of objects, and to extract a monetary profit. It also functions communicatively, cognitively and discursively to insulate participants from any direct or overtly criminal knowledge of transit and source markets. At destination, the antiquities market is subsumed within the larger art market, and is subject to many of the same laws, normative constraints and informal conventions of doing business. At its centre are the transacting actors, the buyers and sellers described in Chapter 1. These actors comprise the destination market proper. They are supported by a diverse cast of facilitators, including the museum curators, conservators, critics, shippers, insurers and so on also described in Chapter 1. Together, the transactors and facilitators constitute a broader and more variegated commercial network, which for the art market generally has been characterised as the 'art world' (Becker 1982) or 'art system' (Alsop 1982). The art world acts culturally to create and sustain consensual belief in the symbolic qualities and values of art objects, and socially and materially to construct and maintain the market for their exchange. We have chosen not to discriminate between these narrower and broader conceptualisations of the destination market, though, as should be apparent, we do recognise them in our choice of terminology for the various actors involved.

We described in Chapter 2 how the entry of material into the destination market is enabled and controlled by criminal brokers or entrepreneurs, who possess the stocks of social and cultural capital necessary to work effectively across international borders (Brodie 2019). They maintain wide-ranging networks of contacts, extending upwards into the licit destination market and downwards into the illicit transit and even source phases, and are able to exploit these networks for identifying or creating commercial opportunities and mobilizing the financial, material and human resources to exploit and profit from them. They must possess or have access to the necessary cultural understandings and competencies and expert knowledge of the legal and financial systems in the different countries involved that enable them to arrange and manage transnational transactions. These criminal entrepreneurs are the Janus figures identified by Mackenzie and Davis (Mackenzie and Davis 2014: 723) and discussed in Chapter 1, offering the respectable face of reputable and trustworthy dealer to destination market buyers, while at the same time looking backwards along the illicit supply chains of transit and source. The role of these entrepreneurs is to organise the movement and sale of material onto the destination market, but also to ensure it arrives there cleaned of any evidence of trafficking, theft or forgery. In practice, this means expunging any associated information that may reveal the illicit origins of traded material and producing new misinformation about origins and previous ownership chains, which can extend to preparing fraudulent documentation. Moving material into the destination market can be a tortuous process, involving numerous criminal actors, conspiring to separate and distribute criminal components of dishonest intent and action, thereby protecting them from criminal culpability, and shielding collectors and facilitators from any knowledge of wrongdoing, or at least providing them with plausible deniability of any such knowledge.

## The discursive bubble

As we will describe in the next chapter, destination market actors justify or normalise their participation through narratives of denial and neutralisation, offering what often purports to be a moral defence of lawbreaking (offered abstractly but not personally in a way that might be incriminating). General theoretical grounding for this moral defence derives from a liberal belief in the public benefit of private ownership, but particularly from John Merryman's construction of a judgmental opposition between 'cultural internationalism' and 'cultural nationalism'. For Merryman (Merryman 1986, 2005), cultural internationalism is an enlightenment-derived belief in the benefits of universal private ownership of antiquities so that international circulation ensures their possession by those best able to care for them and allows for their study and enjoyment by the broadest possible constituency. In opposition to what he sees as an enlightened philosophy of cultural internationalism, he argues against 'cultural nationalism', which he sees as an expression of romantic nationalism, whereby a national character is imputed to antiquities and used to justify State ownership and retention. State ownership is usually imposed by poorer source countries where he argues that the necessary resources for the adequate care and curation of antiquities are not always available, and the associated export restrictions stand in the way of circulation and universal access. Thus, he argues that the aim of any regulatory regime should be to ensure 'preservation, truth and access' through international circulation and distribution of objects (Merryman 2005: 11), and diminish opportunities for the 'covetous neglect' of source country ownership and retention (Merryman 1986: 846).

Merryman's nationalist–internationalist polarity with its preference for so-called internationalism has offered a ready theoretical resource for destination market participants wishing to defend their actions. Phillipe de Montebello, for example, writing in 2007 when he was director of New York's Metropolitan Museum of Art, echoes Merryman when he says (De Montebello 2007: 33):

> Naturally, a nation state has the right to pass laws claiming ownership of objects found in its ground. It can derive national identity from such treasures. But does deriving national identity from such objects rule out other claims?

James Cuno, writing in 2008 while director of the Art Institute of Chicago, argues in similar vein (Cuno 2008: 124):

> Nationalist retentionist cultural property laws are based on the nineteenth-century idea of nationalism: that we are first and most important a national, a member of a tribe determined by language, ethnicity and place. Emphasis in nationalism is on separateness: one nation separate from other nations. Emphasis in cosmopolitanism is on commonality: we are all branches of a single family, to whom we are obliged equally. Nationalism narrows its vision of the world. Cosmopolitanism expands it.

Thus cultural internationalism, conceptually up-dated for twenty-first century consumption as cosmopolitanism (Appiah 2006), is the justification of choice for participants in the destination market. It is easily countered in material terms that antiquities do not in fact circulate internationally for the broadest possible public benefit, but instead are attracted up an economic gradient from poorer countries and communities into restricted circulation on the destination market for the cultural and economic aggrandisement of wealthier ones. International circulation can also be secured through mechanisms other than trade—inter-museum loans being the obvious example (Heilmeyer 1997). But a more insidious aspect of Merryman's 'two ways of thinking about cultural property' is that it frames the issue as one of ownership, international vs national, and excludes other ways of thinking about antiquities. It ignores, for example, the political and historical grievances of countries and peoples emerging from colonial rule and who see control of their culture and respect for their laws as inescapable components of their sovereign independence and equality on the international stage (Prott 2005; Al Quntar 2017; Brodie 2018). From that viewpoint, 'cultural internationalism' is indistinguishable from 'cultural imperialism' (Prott 2005: 228). Thus, destination market constructions of morality take place within a discursive bubble whose boundary is marked by Merryman's weighted answer to the single question of 'who owns antiquity?' (Cuno 2008). Broader questions of historical and social justice are excluded from consideration.

## Quality uncertainties

The destination market is a place of serious quality uncertainties. With some exceptions, antiquities and other cultural objects are not amenable to any externally-agreed quality metric. Quality is assigned through the consensual assessment of those with the socially-recognised learning or taste (cultural capital) necessary to offer authoritative judgment. Those judgments rely upon an accumulated body of scholarly research, which has developed techniques for constructing the typologies and hierarchies allowing the classification and comparison of what would otherwise be an amorphous conglomeration of singular objects (Beckert and Wehinger 2013: 9–10; Karpic 2010). Classification and comparison create quality gradations and provide conditions for differential price determination and market formation—put simply, 'better quality antiquities are in greater demand and thus shorter supply than poorer quality ones' (Brodie 2014a: 36). Thus quality, cultural value and ultimately exchange value are all constructed through reference to the accumulated judgment of generations of experts.

Although scholarship should not be concerned with the market profanity of exchange value, its effect on pricing is undeniable. When the Metropolitan Museum of Art's then director Thomas Hoving justified paying $1 million in 1972 for the red-figure-decorated Attic 'Euphronios krater' by saying it would 'force the history of Greek art to be rewritten' (Hoving 1993: 318; and see the Appendix), he was pronouncing a judgment about the quality of the krater in relation to previously published scholarly opinion about the already known corpus of Attic figure-decorated pottery. Such pottery is today regarded as being the artistic summit of ancient Greek ceramic production, but it has not always been so. An appreciation of Attic figure-decorated pottery as art did not develop until the seventeenth and particularly eighteenth centuries when its increasing availability from Italian tombs allowed the assembly of large collections which were made available for systematic study and publication within the emerging discipline of art history (Nørskov 2002: 35–58; Sparkes 1996: 46–50). The commercial consequences of scholarly acclaim were not slow to follow. By the middle of the nineteenth century 'excavated vases were instant treasure' (Sparkes 1996: 59), and while it might no longer be true to say that they represent instant treasure for their finders, they are still valuable commodities.

Joseph Alsop summed up well the commercial impact of scholarship when he wrote that, 'Art collecting and art history … engender an art market by Siamese-twin incest' (Alsop 1982: 139). A vicious circle is engendered, whereby the increasing availability of looted objects allows the accumulation of larger and more typologically differentiated collections, made increasingly accessible for sophisticated scholarship, which creates quality hierarchies and affirms authenticities—prerequisite conditions for market formation, further enthusiastic collecting and more illegal appropriation. It is clear that scholarly experts, living and dead, mainly from museums and universities, directly and indirectly, have provided and continue to provide what certainty about quality is possible in the very uncertain world of the antiquities market. In so doing, they have played and continue to play a central and indispensable role in constructing value and determining price, and in supporting market confidence.

## Quality judgments

To assess the quality of an individual antiquity, to investigate its artistic or historical importance and thus cultural value, market participants are reliant upon what Karpik (2010: 51) calls 'oriented knowledge', which is available from various personal and impersonal sources (Karpik 2010: 98; Brodie 2014a: 39), but which ultimately relies upon the authority of published scholarship. The literature relating to Attic pottery is as voluminous as the corpus of pottery itself, but even when made more readily available through museum exhibition and sales catalogues it is largely confined to university, museum or other specialist libraries, and so not readily available for consultation. So although published scholarship is of paramount importance for establishing the criteria by which quality can be judged, it has less utility as a means of actually judging quality. It is more a resource for training experts who may act in turn to offer judgment. Most types of antiquities have not received the long-term scholarship accorded to Attic figure-decorated pottery, and so are more resistant to the fine-grained quality assessment and comparison. Nevertheless, the general situation holds true. Quality assessments and thus price determination rest upon the work of scholarly experts.

Many collectors develop their own expertise or 'taste' through extensive handling and study of material in their possession, but many more must depend upon the advice of scholars or their interpreters and popularisers. Scholars can be approached directly for advice, but by and large only by the better-connected collectors and dealers. The documents seized by Italian authorities from the convicted antiquities dealers Giacomo Medici and Gianfranco Becchina (see the Appendix) included congenial correspondence between themselves and scholars, all profiting from a mutually-beneficial relationship whereby scholars would identify and assess new material for dealers while incorporating their findings into ongoing research. Describing his modus operandi for accessing cuneiform tablets, Assyriologist Aage Westenholz wrote:

> Most of the "illicit" tablets published here are known to me from a single dealer in London. We had made an agreement that I could take the tablets to Denmark to treat them for conservation, where I would also photograph and copy them. I would then return them the following year, bringing another batch with me home. This is what I did in the years 1999–2002. Nothing was written down by the dealer; all was done on trust. Most were subsequently sold to la Banca d'Italia, one to the Schøyen Collection, while the present whereabouts of others are unknown. I later bought two tablets from two different London dealers (Westenholz 2014: xvii).

Occasionally the lot descriptions in auction catalogues are attributed to a scholar, but even when they are not, it seems likely that auction houses would need to buy in the necessary expertise to provide reliable descriptions for all types of objects offered—particularly inscribed objects where translation is needed. Discovered among the papers of Assyriologist Wilfrid Lambert after his death in 2011 was a carrier bag marked 'Christie's' containing written descriptions of hundreds of cuneiform tablets that he is said to have 'seen' as they were passing through London in the late 1980s and early 1990s (George 2013: 285). Auction catalogues then make scholarly descriptions and quality assessments available to market participants more generally. Museums retain their own 'in-house' experts in the form of curators. Thomas Hoving was careful to take the Metropolitan's Curator of Classical Antiquities along with him for his initial viewing of the Euphronios krater in Switzerland (Hoving 1993: 310–312; and see the Appendix).

Criticism and commentary offered in print and online by scholarly and non-scholarly experts offers another potential source of advice for quality judgment. It is oriented more towards the market, explicitly considering prices, and with a greater focus on sales and exhibitions. It is potentially available to all collectors, even those of limited financial means but with the time and aptitude to seek it out. Ultimately, however, critics and commentators cannot deviate too far from a scholarly frame of reference without losing credibility and authority. Their role can be seen as that of populariser, making available and intelligible to collectors selected results of scholarly research within a market context. Reviewing a forthcoming auction at Christie's London, for example, journalist John Windsor (1998) wrote about some cuneiform tablets being offered for sale. Saying they were 'translated by a retired academic', presumably Wilfrid Lambert, he was able to work from the reproduced texts to highlight the historical interest of the tablets, reporting estimates in the range of £450 to £550 each. He went on to describe other tablets and their availability from Bonhams and London dealer Chris Martin, again with likely prices. Articles such as this one might be viewed as little more than advertisements, but they are published as critical pieces, offering the reader easy access to the work of scholarly experts and offering reassurance about the authenticity and quality of material offered for sale.

Finally, there are the dealers themselves. We have already described in Chapter 2 how dealers can advise potential customers about the quality of an object, though with the obvious proviso that their advice is likely to be biased and self-serving. They might be interested primarily in selling an object, securing or keeping a profitable client, or extolling the virtues of a previously unfashionable type of antiquity with a view to creating further demand.

## Information and provenance

The destination market is a place of quality uncertainties, but it is also a place of severe information asymmetries. Information is a closely guarded and often deliberately suppressed strategic resource. Antiquities need to be kept free from any taint of previous theft or trafficking, and likewise market participants must be protected from 'knowing' about illicit object histories. More confusion is introduced by the fraudulent creation of new misinformation necessary to bring illicit antiquities to market. Dealers might keep information about a source secret so as not to attract the attention of competing dealers, and collectors who are buying or selling might have many reasons for keeping their identities secret, including a wish not to attract the attention of thieves or advertise financial problems. Prices may be talked about to encourage a belief in market buoyancy, or kept secret. Even questions of quality and authenticity are at root questions of information. Honest and reliable information is hard to find, and becomes an object in itself of careful search and jealous possession. So although we have said that information circulates on the destination market, it might be more accurate to say that information pools behind many artificially constructed obstructions. This general scarcity of information underpins the concept of the 'grey market' that we introduced in Chapter 2, whereby licit and illicit objects are stripped of reliable information about their source and legitimacy and mixed together in an undifferentiated market churn of poorly described material (Mackenzie and Yates 2017).

## Provenance

Information searches can seek out details about the availability and comparative pricing of antiquities, about who sold what and who might be selling what, and for how much money. But a lot of energy is devoted to finding or establishing reliable information about the previous ownership and authenticity of antiquities being offered for sale. Most of what is interesting about this type of information comes packaged in the idea of provenance. Provenance means the ownership history of an object, from the time and place of its modern discovery or forgery through to its most recent location and holding. (Not to be confused with provenience, meaning its place of discovery and original archaeological context alone). Ideally, the provenance of an object should provide an unbroken chain of ownership, thus allowing a full account of lawful possession and authenticity to be established without doubt. Unfortunately, such complete provenances remain an aspiration, and are hardly ever found in practice. Most 'provenances' for antiquities appearing on the market provide little more than one or two references to previous owners, or the time and place of a previous sale. Sometimes the only thing provided is a single name, or a vaguely defined date, such as 'on the European market in the 1960s', which is hardly a step up from the 'property of an anonymous Swiss private collector' type of provenance characterised in Chapter 1.

Archaeological concern about provenance centres upon the desirability of knowing where and how an antiquity was discovered and removed from its original context—information about its provenience. When this contextualising information is not available, the utility of the object for scholarly interpretation is dramatically reduced. The absence of this information also fuels belief that the original archaeological site or monument was damaged or destroyed by the object's undocumented extraction (Chippindale and Gill 2000). For destination market participants, however, with different priorities, a different view of provenance predominates. Provenance can help establish the legitimacy and authenticity and thus monetary value of a circulating object, and the provenance itself might also enhance monetary value by demonstrating the historical interest of the object's previous owners.

## Published provenance

Figures 4.1 and 4.2 show how the two main auction houses Sotheby's and Christie's have since the 1980s endeavoured to include more provenance-related information in their catalogue descriptions, with a sharp increase occurring in the early 2000s. These efforts to publish more provenance information could well have

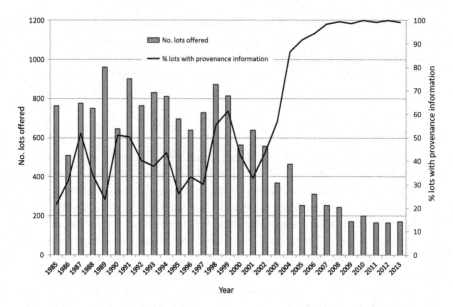

**FIGURE 4.1** Number of lots offered annually at Sotheby's New York 'Antiquities' sales, together with the percentage of lots offered with provenance information.

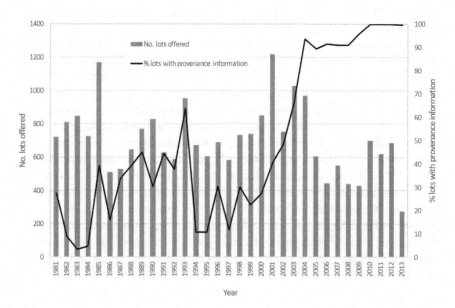

**FIGURE 4.2** Number of lots offered annually at Christie's London 'Antiquities' sales, together with the percentage of lots offered with provenance information.

been in response to damaging allegations published in 1997 that staff of Sotheby's London had knowingly engaged in marketing trafficked antiquities for Italian dealer Giacomo Medici and Indian dealer Vaman Ghiya (Watson 1997). For the first time, there was evidence to suggest that 'reputable' institutions such as Sotheby's were involved in trading illegally acquired material. In apparent response, Sotheby's announced its decision to stop holding regular antiquities sales in London and senior staff in its London Antiquities and Islamic and Indian departments were forced to leave the company (Farrell and Alberge 1997).

Since then, Jane Levine, writing in 2009 as Sotheby's Worldwide Compliance Counsel, has talked about a 'perceptible, if gradual, shift in the market toward more rigorous provenance standards', mentioning as causes the 2004 prosecution of Giacomo Medici and the trials in Italy of Robert Hecht and Marion True, the looting of Iraqi museums and sites around the time of the 2003 Coalition invasion, and the successful claims for repatriation lodged against US art museums by Italy in the early 2000s (Levine 2009: 219–220). Likewise, Elyse Dreyer, quoted in 2013 while Sotheby's Vice President of North American Compliance, stated that:

> It would not be accurate in our view to correlate or associate implementation of increasingly robust standards with any one particular piece of legislation or MOU. ...This attention [to substantiation of provenance] itself stems from many things, including increased activity by source countries to protect their cultural heritage, increased international attention to the importance of protecting cultural sites and curbing the trade in illicit material and evolving domestic case law in this area.
>
> *(Levine and de Luna 2013: 269)*

If what Sotheby's says is taken at face value, the trend towards including more provenance information in catalogue entries is a cumulative response to several incidents and processes that have acted synergistically to create a more questioning public and therefore critical trading environment on the destination market.

Levine also drew attention to the distinction between published provenance and documented provenance. What is published about an object's previous ownership in an auction catalogue might not comprise the totality of what is known about its provenance through associated documentation such as invoices recording sales transactions and less deliberate sources such as insurance accounts and family diaries and photographs. This type of provenance documentation is hardly ever made public, often for reasons of personal confidentiality, but presumably changes hands with the object as part of its documented provenance. Until recently, however, comprehensive documented provenance was not considered a necessary accompaniment of a sales transaction because customer expectations and the regulatory environment were not so well developed and market participants did not expect it to be made available (Levine 2009: 229–232; Mackenzie 2005b: 33–36).

Looking at Figures 4.1 and 4.2, there does appear to be a marked improvement in publishing provenance by the major auction houses. But the appearance is to a large extent deceptive. Tables 4A and 4B below examine the quality of published provenance information in some more detail, looking at two auction catalogues from 2013, one each from Sotheby's New York and Christie's London.

The quality of the published information is ordered into three categories. First, 'provenance information' denotes any factual reference such as a name or a date entered in a catalogue description that might offer information about the object's ownership prior to its appearance in the catalogue. Anonymising entries such as 'Swiss private collector' are not counted. Second, a 'verifiable provenance' entry includes one or more conjunctions of name and date that allow a preliminary assessment of how long an object has been on the market, and facilitate its further investigation using other sources. Christos Tsirogiannis (2015b) has shown what is possible when reconstructing a fuller provenance through further investigation of such limited information. Finally, a 'publication provenance' comprises one or more references to the object in previously published works, such as a book, sales catalogue, exhibition catalogue, scholarly paper or magazine article. A publication provenance is the strongest form of provenance as it is the most difficult to fabricate and the easiest to confirm.

Table 4A shows for both auction catalogues that although nearly all lots were accompanied by some sort of provenance information, in both cases less than 50 per cent of lots carried the most reliable publication provenance—for both catalogues, the majority of provenance entries were minimal. Table 4B looks more closely at catalogue entries listing a publication provenance. It shows that even when a publication provenance was provided, in the overwhelming majority of cases, it was for one publication only, often a sales catalogue, indicating the location of an object at one

**TABLE 4A** Provenance provision in two sales catalogues.

| | Christie's London24 October 2013 | Sotheby's New York12 December 2013 |
| --- | --- | --- |
| Total number of lots offered | 130 | 79 |
| % lots with provenance information | 99 | 99 |
| % lots with verifiable provenance | 78 | 85 |
| % lots with publication provenance | 42 | 47 |

**TABLE 4B** Provision of publication provenance in two sales catalogues

| Number of publications | 1 | 2 | 3 | 4 | 5 | >5 |
| --- | --- | --- | --- | --- | --- | --- |
| Christie's 24 October 2013, no. lots | 35 | 12 | 8 | | | |
| Sotheby's 12 December 2013, no. lots | 25 | 3 | 2 | 1 | 1 | 5 |

particular point in time. No identification or description of place of discovery was provided for any objects, and for no object in either catalogue was a full, unbroken account of provenance offered.

Thus, while auction houses claim to be making more efforts to investigate and establish provenance, and are publishing more provenance-related information in their catalogues, the information provided is only minimal, and does little to facilitate information searches. In reality, the situation in 2013 as regards provenance provision was little changed from 1993. It looks to be another example of creative compliance, with auction houses working around the strengthening normative expectations of provenance provision, meeting those strengthening expectations in form but not really in substance.

Even when available, the provenance information published in an auction catalogue might not be reliable. The careful forensic work of Tsirogiannis (2015b) has revealed not only that published provenances are limited in what they reveal, but also as we explore in the Appendix, that they might be selective, omitting incriminating associations to dealers such as Medici and Becchina who have been convicted of criminal offences related to antiquities trafficking.

It must be remembered, however, that auction sales to not constitute the entirety of the destination market. In terms of monetary value, they comprise the high-middle to high end of the market. Larger quantities of lower value material are traded by other means, since 2000 particularly on the internet (Brodie 2014c, 2015b), and here the situation as regards provenance is much worse. Of 4,032 Precolumbian objects offered for sale on the internet between 2012 and 2013, for example, only 23 per cent had any kind of verifiable provenance information (Brodie 2014c: 250–1, 257; Table 13.4).

## Falsified provenance

Sometimes stolen objects are offered for auction with a completely fictional provenance. In September 2013, for example, Neil Kingsbury was convicted of fraud for consigning trafficked Egyptian antiquities to the London auction houses Bonhams and Christie's. Kingsbury told Christie's that he had inherited the objects from his uncle who had been based in Egypt during World War II. The provenance published in the catalogue stated, 'Private collection, UK, acquired Egypt 1940s; thence by descent' (Bailey and Gerlis 2013). The crime was discovered when an Egyptologist at the British Museum noticed that one of the objects, a relief fragment of a Nubian prisoner from the temple of Amenhotep III in Thebes, had probably been stolen from a storage facility in Egypt. After his arrest, Kingsbury admitted to having bought the material in a gift shop at Luxor and bringing it back to the UK in a suitcase (Peachey 2014). Material evidence of theft allowed the police to bring charges and Kingsbury admitted to charges of fraud but not possession of stolen property.

This trial is interesting in itself as it establishes the criminal act of fabricating misinformation about provenance as fraud, but it also illuminates what might be Christie's policy of due diligence as regards the publication of provenance. First, Christie's seemingly accepted Kingsbury's false account of an Egypt-based uncle, though, perhaps at Kingsbury's request, neither Kingsbury's name nor that of his uncle was provided in the published catalogue entries. This omission could be defended as an example of an auction house respecting the wish of a consignor to remain unknown—client confidentiality. Christie's claimed to have asked the British Museum to check the auction catalogue prior to sale, at which point the stolen relief was recognized (Adam 2013), and later stated that 'This case shows how our procedures, our due diligence and the transparent and public nature of our sales combine to make our saleroom highly unattractive to those engaged in the illicit trade' (Bailey and Gerlis 2013). In fact, this statement seems to show the auction house spinning the narrative to construct a silver lining in the cloud the story would otherwise cast over the claimed cleanliness of the market, given the relative ease with which a made-up tale of prior ownership had made its way into catalogue print.

Many more identifications and recoveries of stolen objects from auction houses are known (Brodie 2014b). With some notable exceptions, most of the recoveries have been of objects stolen from inventoried collections or documented monuments, such as the Nubian prisoner relief consigned by Kingsbury, or discovered through the work of researchers such as Tsirogiannis (Tsirogiannis 2013a, 2015a) or national enforcement agencies that like Tsirogiannis have relied heavily on the evidence of images of stolen objects seized from dealers during police raids. The fact that most antiquities identified and recovered from auction sales are from inventoried collections or otherwise documented sources also suggests a much broader market penetration of illegally-excavated and thus undocumented material.

## Circuits of commerce

Foregrounding the importance of information for destination market function-ing encourages the market to be viewed as what Viviana Zelizer has termed a 'circuit of commerce'. Zelizer (2004: 124–125) emphasises she derives her understanding of 'commerce' from an older sense of the word, when it was taken to imply conversation and interchange, with 'dynamic, meaningful, incessantly negotiated interactions' among participating actors. A circuit of commerce comprises impersonal and personal (termed 'intimate' by Zelizer) relations, with gifts or other personal favours passing between participants alongside money and material. This idea of conversation and interchange captures the essence of the destination market, emphasising the importance of accessing good conversationalists—or knowledgeable informants. For Oscar Velthuis (Velthuis 2005: 40), the art market 'is a communicative market, in which gossip, word of mouth and permanent access to information are key to survival'. For the antiquities market, with its marked information asymmetries, the situation is even more acute.

In Chapter 1 we looked at the actions of antiquities dealers and auction houses operating from physical gallery spaces and the internet. These are the impersonal commercial settings of the destination market, but they do not exhaust the totality of market interactions, and invite consideration of personal (intimate) social settings, which are more important for information gathering and exchange. For outsiders, whether scholars, journalists or police investigators, information about the social settings of the market circuit are hard to access, but occasionally something is revealed.

Marion True, for example, while curator of antiquities at the J. Paul Getty Museum, found herself enjoying the company of millionaires at the villa of dealer Robin Symes and his partner Christos Michaelides on the small Greek island of Schinoussa:

> When you arrived, the peninsula would have two or three giant yachts tied up. And all of a sudden there would be fifteen or twenty people. At first, everyone would be standing around having cocktails, laughing, telling whatever news there was to tell. Then everyone went to different tables for dinner. After dinner, there might be dancing, there might be music. It was just a jolly evening ... I have to say, I enjoyed it, I enjoyed these people.
>
> *(Eakin 2007)*

Exchanging 'news' and accessing information was no doubt an important part of such occasions, but they were probably also used to arrange transactions (Zirganos 2007: 318), an aspect of what Nørskov calls the 'invisible market' of high-end deals (Nørskov 2002).

True had bought a house on the nearby island of Paros in 1995 with the help of a loan from Michaelides, which she paid off a year later with a further loan of $400,000 obtained from collectors Barbara and Lawrence Fleischman (Watson and Todeschini 2007: 288). The Getty had mounted an exhibition of the Fleischman Collection in 1994 and on 10 July 1996 acquired it through a combination of gift and purchase for $20 million. One week after the acquisition, the Fleischmans loaned True the money for her house (Felch and Frammolino 2011: 124–146). True's relationship with the Fleischmans has been characterised as one of those 'entanglements that mixes business with pleasure, friendship with money, a shared passion for art with mutual back scratching' (Felch and Frammolino 2011: 124)—a textbook instantiation of a circuit of commerce.

Michaelides died in 1999, and the Schinoussa villa was raided by Greek police in April 2006 (Zirganos 2007: 306–324). The search of the villa and its grounds lasted for a week, and the police recovered approximately 33 antiquities with an estimated market value of $1,120,000. They also recovered many photographs, including some of True's wedding ceremony on Paros. Other photographs recorded the convivial parties recounted by True, with Greek and foreign archaeologists numbered among the guests, alongside wealthy collectors Shelby White, who at the time was a trustee of the Metropolitan Museum of Art, and her husband Leon Levy. There were also 2,191 photographs of 995 objects that had passed through the hands of Symes during the 1980s and 1990s. In 2018, Symes's whereabouts were unknown.

Social gatherings of the sort described by True must be a recurrent feature of the destination market, though such eye-witness accounts are hard to come by. Another example is offered by the opening in November 1997 of the purpose-built Miho Museum twenty miles southeast of Kyoto in Japan. Among those present at the opening ceremony were the directors of the Metropolitan Museum, the British Museum and the Berlin Museums, major antiquities dealers including Robin Symes, representatives from Sotheby's and Christie's, and private collectors including George Ortiz, Shelby White and Leon Levy (Kaufman 1997). The Miho's collection of European and Middle Eastern antiquities had been largely acquired through dealer Noriyoshi Horiuchi, who purchased more than 300 objects between 1991 to 1996 with a budget estimated to have been $200 million. Horiuchi was acting on commission as an intermediary for four dealers based in Switzerland, including Gianfranco Becchina (Watson and Todeschini 2007: 294–296). In 2010, Italian and Swiss police raided warehouses belonging to Horiuchi in Geneva Freeport where they recovered thousands of antiquities (Knowles 2010).

Even an auction, which can be viewed commercially as the archetypal impersonal market setting, where exchange values are established and transactions secured, or understood sociologically as a symbolically charged arena of sumptuary competition, must also be seen as a social opportunity to acquire information, not only from the illustrated catalogue, but also through personal interactions at the viewing that precedes the auction or at the auction itself. The auction should be considered as much a process as an event, with information exchange as important as commercial exchange (Geismar 2001).

In Chapter 5 we will discuss in some detail a set of internal e-mails released by Sotheby's New York as part of the discovery process attendant upon a court case over ownership of a Cambodian statue. They too contain tantalising hints of the personal side of the auction process. On 19 May 2010, Anu Ghosh-Mazumdar (who was Assistant Vice President of Indian and Southeast Asian Art in New York) wrote that she had been visited by the grandson of the artist Camille Pissaro (who was at the time a curator at MoMA) accompanied by a 'world-renowned expert on Khmer art' who was 'very close to the Museé Guimet, which has the best collection of Khmer art in the world'. Pissaro's grandson had brought a 'client' to a viewing of the piece prior to sale, who had asked the grandson to conduct further research into the piece, and was a 'serious potential bidder'. Art fairs too are social events (Reyburn 2014).

Looking again at the Schinoussa gatherings and the Miho opening, it is dealers such as Symes and Noriuchi who play the role of the Janus figures we described in Chapter 1—bridging the divide between destination and transit markets, with the crucial function of insulating destination market participants from unwelcome information about dishonest or unlawful actions further back along the trading chain. Other than Marion True, who was put on trial in Italy on conspiracy charges, none of the museum curators or collectors at the Schinoussa or the Miho gatherings faced any formal allegations of wrongdoing despite the police actions against Symes and Noriuchi. Their defence would no doubt be 'how were we to know', really meaning 'we did not have access to the relevant information'. Whether that defence is true because Symes and Noriuchi chose not to share information, or constructed because information was shared through gossip rather than written communication, is a matter for speculation and thus not open to proof.

## Relations of trust

We have already described the close relationship between an Assyriologist and the trade in our mention of Wilfrid Lambert earlier in this chapter, and it is notable that some of the evidence used to bring True to court comprised personal letters she had written in friendly terms requesting information from convicted dealers Medici and Becchina. In one letter to Medici, for example, dated 22 January 1992, she starts 'Dear Giacomo', going on to thank him for 'information on the provenance of our three fragmentary proto-Corinthian olpai. To know that they came from Cerveteri and the area of Monte Abatone is very helpful …', before finishing with 'I send all best wishes to you and your family and hope that you have had a very happy holiday'. Olpai are small ancient Greek jugs used for pouring wine. Cerveteri is an ancient Etruscan cemetery just north of Rome. True had obviously taken advantage of her friendship with Medici to ask for information about the find spot of the olpai in the Getty collection. The answer, that they derived from Cerveteri (and must therefore have been looted) was an incriminating one for True, and helped land her in court. But the letter is a material expression of how personal relations are important for securing information. Medici might have intended the information about Cerveteri to be seen as a gift, to be reciprocated, and True enters into the spirit of the relationship when, before ending her letter, she says 'I hope that we will be able to get together and have some further discussions about future acquisitions'. Access to information and its processing into actionable knowledge are dependent upon the social and cultural capital of the actors involved, and the interconvertibility of different forms of capital means that knowledge itself becomes a commodity, something that can be transacted over the long term.

Long-term transactions must be enacted on the basis of trust. Trust encourages the maintenance of persistent personal relationships, and bolsters the importance of reputation (symbolic capital). In July 2017, for example, dealer Hicham Aboutaam of Phoenix Ancient Art initiated a suit for libel against the Wall Street Journal for allegations of wrongdoing made in an article by two of its journalists (Faucon and Kantchev 2017). The complaint claimed that the 'Plaintiff's business and reputation have been severely and immediately damaged' (Aboutaam v Dow Jones 2017).

Reputations, for dealers, are quite clearly highly valuable and worth defending. It was surprising for many observers that despite the potential reputational harm suffered by Sotheby's in the wake of Watson's allegations that its employees had been knowingly involved in antiquities trafficking, the company did not seek damages against him through libel action (Watson 1997). The failure to do so could be construed as a tacit admission, by omission, of its guilt.

In January 1985, the J. Paul Getty Museum paid its established supplier Gianfranco Becchina $9.5 million for what purported to be a Greek marble statue (kouros), with associated documented provenance. Soon after its acquisition the statue and its provenance were both denounced as fake, and the question of its authenticity has never been resolved (Felch and Frammolino 2011: 57–83). It is believed that Becchina was victim of an elaborate deception intended to destroy his reputation and standing with the Getty, masterminded by his Italian rival Giacomo Medici. If so, it worked. Going forward, the Getty never purchased from Becchina again and transferred its business to Medici (Felch and Frammolino 2011: 334 note 80).

## The antiquities bazaar

Some writers have offered a conception of marketplace activity as 'the bazaar'. Clifford Geertz observed that 'information flows give the bazaar its particular character and general interest' (Geertz 1978: 29). Information in the bazaar is patchy, unevenly distributed and its acquisition is subject to negotiation, misdirection and obstruction, so much so that information itself becomes part of the bargaining process. Geertz attributed the central importance of information to the functioning of the bazaar to a general level of ignorance among sellers and buyers about the comparative costs, qualities and prices of material being sold. For Arjun Appadurai (1986: 43) 'bazaar-style information searches are likely to characterise any exchange setting where the quality and the appropriate valuation of goods are not standardised'. These characterisations of the bazaar as an information processor are well-suited to the destination market for antiquities. It is perhaps no accident that Oscar White Muscarella (2000) refers to the 'well-appointed bazaars' of the antiquities market, where knowledge is fabricated, suppressed, revealed, and hinted at.

Muscarella is particularly concerned to show how the information asymmetries of the destination market for antiquities encourage and facilitate the entry of fakes into private and museum collections. He gives the example of a gilt-silver beaker acquired in 1998 by the Miho Museum engraved with 'Assyrianlike' scenes showing the procession of an Assyrian king with captive Elamites and carrying two inscriptions, one naming the Assyrian King Assurbanipal and another the Elamite King Ampirish. The Miho believes the beaker dates from the seventh century BC. Muscarella, on the other hand, pointing to poor execution, linguistic inconsistencies and unparalleled iconography doubts its ancient manufacture, preferring instead a date in the '1990s AD'. Or, at least, he thinks the beaker itself might be ancient, with the inscriptions and engraved decoration added after its modern discovery to increase its monetary value. The beaker has been described in some academic publications as a 'chance find', though it seems more likely that it was part of the Kalmakarra (Western cave) Hoard of more than 30 silver objects excavated illegally from the Kalmakarra cave in Iran between 1989 and 1992 (Henkelman 2003: 106–119). Muscarella shows how the bazaar-style information scattering of the destination market, with its suppression of any reliable evidence of provenance, facilitates the passage of trafficked or forged objects. He also describes how it impedes reliable historical scholarship when information about discovery and trade has been systematically expunged from the modern story of the beaker, and possibly replaced with fraudulent misinformation about its ancient use and significance.

In December 2003, antiquities dealer Hicham Aboutaam, mentioned above as proprietor of Phoenix Ancient Art, was arrested and charged with misrepresenting the country of origin of a decorated silver rhyton (ceremonial drinking vessel) in the shape of a griffin also thought to have been part of the Kalmakarra Hoard. Hicham Aboutaam is co-proprietor of Phoenix with his brother Ali Aboutaam, with galleries in Geneva and New York. The rhyton had been viewed in the Geneva gallery in 1999 by private collector and Metropolitan Museum of Art trustee Paula Cussi. Hicham Aboutaam carried the rhyton himself on a flight from Zurich to Newark in February 2000, and the commercial invoice submitted to US Customs upon arrival claimed Syria as the rhyton's country of origin instead of Iran. After importation, at the request of Cussi, three experts examined the rhyton, concluding it was authentic, with two of the experts further suggesting it was probably from the Kalmakarra cave in Iran. Reassured by the expert reports, Cussi purchased the rhyton in June 2002 for $950,000. On 20 July 2004, Hicham Aboutaam pled guilty to the misdemeanour charge of falsifying a customs declaration and was sentenced to one year's probation and fined $5,000; he also refunded Cussi her purchase payment (Lufkin 2004; United States Attorney - Southern District of New York 2004). In court, Hicham Aboutaam stated he had claimed Syria as country of origin instead of Iran because material from Iran was subject to more rigorous customs inspection (Meier 2004). A lawyer acting on behalf of Phoenix Ancient Art stated in Geneva that the rhyton had been in the United Kingdom for decades before being acquired by the Aboutaams (Besson and Campiotti 2004).

Cussi herself cannot have been concerned by the Iranian origin of the piece or its uncertain history as she proceeded with the purchase nevertheless. She wanted and obtained reassurance that the piece was genuine, and that reassurance was forthcoming from experts willing to provide the necessary information. As Cussi would not have bought the piece without this expert input, it is fair to say their contribution was vital for securing the price and sale. But they were protected from any allegations of malpractice or improper conduct by the lack of any material evidence adhering to the rhyton of illegal excavation and trafficking, despite the probable origin in Iran. Again, as in the case of Symes and Horiuchi, it was the dealer Hicham Aboutaam who was convicted of a criminal misdemeanour, not the purchaser.

The rhyton was returned to Iran in 2013, but again Muscarella believes it to be fake because of stylistic and technical improbabilities (Muscarella 2012), and questions have been raised about the evidence of authenticity produced by expert testing. When contacted by journalist Suzan Mazur, two of the experts involved, metallurgists Tom Chase and Peter Northover, suggested that while the metal might be ancient the vessel itself might be modern, and the fact that the vessel had been cleaned before their analyses meant that they could not assess whether surface condition was consistent with the rhyton's supposed age (Mazur 2013a, 2013b). Jewellery expert Jack Ogden still believed the rhyton to be genuine. The observation that the vessel had been cleaned was a new one, convenient for the market, either removing surface evidence of illegal excavation, or, for a forged or altered piece, explaining why there was no evidence of illegal excavation. It testifies to the involvement of another expert facilitator backwards along the trading chain, before Cussi's purchase, in this case a conservator/restorer. Phoenix Ancient Art does routinely use the services of two London-based conservators (Watson and Todeschini 2007: 184), though whether the gallery was responsible for cleaning the piece is not known. It is well known in studies of illicit antiquities that evidence of provenance can be eradicated and created anew through forged documentation. But here is a parallel process of materials scientists eradicating and creating actual physical evidence by working with the object itself: a further example of how provenance information is suppressed and invented at the transit–market interface.

## Towards the better circulation of information

We said at the outset of this chapter that the destination market can be construed as a mutually-engaged circulation of money, material and information. We have taken pains to demonstrate the central importance of information, and the many impediments to its circulation which facilitate the entry onto the market of trafficked or forged material. Logically, then, the criminogenic action of the destination market could be controlled by reducing the circulation of illicit material or criminal money, or by improving the circulation of information—by improving market transparency. In subsequent chapters we will look more closely at this issue of the circulation of information in the market: both the nature of, and restrictions on, its circulation, and the type, texture and meaning of the information that does circulate (and by corollary, that which is suppressed).

As we move in this book towards a more expansive understanding of this transnational criminal market as a communicative system, we will probe the ways to remove existing barriers to the circulation of information in the antiquities market. Before we do that, through a series of chapters focused on the destination market end of the chain of supply, we will look more closely at this issue of information management and communication around the antiquities trade. We will explore in more detail the manifestation of the improper 'information work' the antiquities market routinely does around its trades, which facilitates the nexus of licit and illicit markets, accepting looted antiquities into the transaction network. We turn to the first of these analyses in the next chapter, in the context of criminological perspectives on white-collar crime.

# 5

# WHITE-COLLAR CRIME AND FACILITATION OF THE CRIMINAL MARKET BY 'LEGITIMATE' ACTORS

As we have seen in the introductory chapters to this book, illicit antiquities are often inserted into legitimate supply chains, and we have noted in Chapter 3 that they have this feature in common with several other transnational criminal markets, for example diamonds and wildlife. Once antiquities have entered into legitimate trade circuits, they can be offered for sale for very high prices in prestigious venues like the large auction houses, with many being purchased by major public museums. The question arises, how much do these 'legitimate' buyers know about the illicit origins of the antiquities they buy, and how do they deal with suspicious information, or 'red flags', about illicit origin in their acts of purchase.

As we have explained in Chapter 1, those directly engaged in a transaction for the sale/purchase of a cultural object will be the buyer and the seller, and perhaps an intermediary agent acting between them, like an auction house. However, as well as these parties to the sale contract, we have already observed that there can be a range of other legitimate actors providing knowing or inadvertent support to the illicit trade in antiquities, including valuers and appraisers, authenticators, and academics who add value to objects by studying and publishing their history, or translating text inscribed on the objects. In this chapter, we will build on the consideration we have given these directly and indirectly involved groups of actors in Chapter 4, aiming here both to clarify the nature and importance of their participation in the licit and illicit parts of the trade, and to theorise that participation as a form of white-collar crime. In this task, criminological studies of white-collar crime will be drawn on to develop an analytical frame of reference for engaging with these questions around participation and facilitation, and policy implications considered.

Building around our initial scheme of supply-transit-destination market as the three phases or 'movements' of this particular market, in criminological terms we conceive of the global illicit antiquities trade as an organized criminal enterprise linking with a white-collar criminal trading forum (Mackenzie and Davis 2014). In this model, organized criminal activities extract antiquities from source countries and traffic them across borders, often through one or a number of transit countries, to cities where lucrative markets exist for their sale. This receiving end of the supply chain, where antiquities are inserted into the normal routines of the market, is where a white-collar crime analysis becomes particularly useful.

There is not a great deal of literature dealing directly with the antiquities trade as white-collar crime. Brodie and Bowman Proulx have argued that museum acquisitions of illicit antiquities are a form of corporate crime (Brodie and Bowman Proulx 2013). They recommend that some of the usual regulatory interventions to prevent or punish corporate crimes be considered as useful reference points in developing appropriate constraints for museums. Balcells has reflected on Conklin's seminal view of art crime as white-collar crime (Balcells 2015). Conklin himself used Routine Activities Theory to good effect in considering the opportunity structure of art crime (Conklin 1994). Mackenzie has worked through the main implications of thinking about trade in looted antiquities as white-collar crime, with a focus on the elements of denial and neutralization setting the context for illicit and unethical conduct by embedding that conduct in a pervasive narrative that justifies and excuses unlawful behaviour with reference to various standard tropes about the positive effects of collecting and preserving antiquities (Mackenzie 2005b, 2006, 2007, 2009, 2011a; Mackenzie and Yates 2016).

So, there is some literature that establishes a basis for the analysis of buying and selling antiquities in the international marketplace as a form of white-collar crime, but the depths of specific insight suggested by that general observation have not yet been plumbed. In this chapter we will consider the conjunction of several theoretical positions as a framework to help understand white-collar crime in the illicit antiquities trade. The main bases of this theoretical explanation are found in: (1) McBarnet's ideas of active reception, creative compliance, and 'whiter than white-collar' crime (McBarnet 1991, 2006); (2) Vaughan's normalization of deviance thesis, an example of differential association and described as 'a social psychological product of institutional and organizational forces' (Vaughan 2004); (3) some broader contextual propositions around the anomic nature (Merton 1938) of the international antiquities trade, the strain of a market situation characterized by constricted legitimate opportunities; and (4) the adverse effects on ethical decision-making of organizational structures and routines that have characterized 'modernity' and serve to distance individual choices from their immediate effects (Bauman 1989). Let us look at a case study example of a recent controversy in the antiquities market in order to illustrate what this theoretical work might look like.

In 2011, Sotheby's auction house in New York offered for sale a tenth century stone statue of Duryodhana, a key figure in the Mahabharata, at an estimated price of two to three million US dollars. In litigation raised by the US District Attorney's office on behalf of the government of Cambodia, it was alleged that this statue was one among several that had been looted from the Prasat Chen temple complex at

Koh Ker. The feet of the statue were found at Koh Ker, still attached to the plinth on which it had once stood. Another statue, part of a pair with the Duryodhana, had also been hacked off its plinth at the ankles and this one—a depiction of Bhima—was in the possession of the Norton Simon Museum in Pasadena, USA. A French archaeologist named Eric Bourdonneau had recreated virtualized computer models of the Prasat Chen temple at Koh Ker in Cambodia, showing how these two statues would originally have faced each other, surrounded by several depictions of kneeling attendants, who were watching them fight. In the time since the Duryodhana was advertised for auction, two kneeling attendants have been returned to Cambodia from the Metropolitan Museum in New York, along with the Bhima from the Norton Simon museum and, ultimately, the Duryodhana itself when Sotheby's settled the legal action.

In the course of the court case concerning the Duryodhana many documents were released into the public domain as the two parties to the dispute went through the 'discovery' processes for obtaining and lodging evidence. Among these publicly accessible documents were a series of emails sent internally at Sotheby's, between several of its employees. These emails paint the auction house in a poor light, revealing types of systematic connivance and spin that there is no evidence to suggest were other than normal operating routines for those involved. In order to appreciate the importance of this case for the progress of the field of study of trafficking antiquities, we first need to outline the linked theoretical concepts of *creative compliance* and *active reception,* which are fundamental components of the study of regulation in corporate and white-collar criminology.

## Creative compliance and active reception

White-collar criminology refers to 'regulation' as a broader concept than law, including the law but reaching out beyond it to reference the many ways in which conduct can be influenced (Braithwaite 2011). This would include ethical codes, systems of inspection and monitoring, informal social controls such as intra-market shaming or negative publicity, and so on (Ayres and Braithwaite 1992). We will look more closely at the concept of regulation throughout this book, as we work through the possibilities for developing productive policy interventions into the market (see especially Chapters 6 and 7 in this volume).

Compliance is a term used in regulatory discourse to refer to the end goal of having individuals and businesses obey the rules, so in conventional regulatory debates non-compliance has been seen as the problem, and compliance the solution, or at least the aim (Oded 2013). Based on empirical studies of white-collar criminals in action, however, Doreen McBarnet proposed that compliance, as well as non-compliance, could be 'the problem'. In her conceptualization of *active reception*, she noticed that 'law need not just be passively received, but can be actively worked on to alter its consequences, regardless, indeed, of the intentions of those making and enforcing it' (McBarnet 2006). This observation brought the question of compliance into the centre of the frame for questions about white-collar deviance: in McBarnet's framing of the question, how exactly were the 'law abiding' abiding by the law?

From this observation, the idea of *creative compliance* was developed as:

> the use of technical legal work to manage the legal packaging, structuring and definition of practices and transactions, such that they can claim to fall on the right side of the boundary between lawfulness and illegality. It is essentially the practice of using the letter of the law to defeat its spirit, and to do so with impunity.
>
> *(McBarnet 2006)*

This kind of (non)compliance was noted empirically to be the sort of thing that corporate and white-collar actors would euphemistically refer to as 'sailing close to the wind'.

McBarnet's studies construct creative compliance as a practice which is 'clever and imaginative'; an enterprising and valuable business/legal skill where 'the point is to achieve something that law is obstructing but to do it legally' (McBarnet 2006). It is a practice for which people are praised and rewarded in corporate cultures. Since the problem is one of a culture of manipulating the law, she considers that the solution must come in addressing that culture, as well as the formatting of law which might make it susceptible to being manipulated in this way:

> ultimately, creative compliance depends on a mindset in which to comply with the letter but defeat the spirit of the law is deemed clever and legitimate. To tackle creative compliance, one must challenge that culture of legitimacy, and to do that means moving from a positivist vision of law as a technical task to one in which compliance means compliance with the spirit of the law.
>
> *(McBarnet 2006)*

In the Sotheby's Duryodhana case, we can see an example of creative compliance by the auction house. The law requires 'due diligence' from antiquities traders, a much debated concept that can be hard to define but that at least requires traders to make some enquiries into provenance, and in particular to take some reasonable steps to resolve questions that may arise about lawful ownership of an object (Redmond-Cooper 1997). In the story that follows, we can see Sotheby's responding to this issue of regulatory compliance with an active form of reception characterized by creative compliance, very much in tune with McBarnet's formulation of that concept. Rather than ignoring due diligence issues altogether, the auction house paid the issues a fairly superficial form of lip service calculated to give the appearance that 'something was done' to conduct checks on the possible illicit background of the statue and whether there was a dispossessed owner of the statue who might have a better claim to title than the current seller. One is reminded in this case study of the infamous policy of 'optical due diligence' introduced at the Getty museum by Arthur Houghton, Marion True's predecessor as Curator of Antiquities. This was a policy 'intended to give the appearance of due diligence while at the same time avoiding certain knowledge of illicit trade that would either prevent the acquisition of a desired object or open the Getty to charges of receiving stolen property' (Brodie and Bowman Proulx 2013: 7; Felch and Frammolino 2011: 61). This policy from the mid-1980s is described by critical commentators in a way that foreshadows the general approach of Sotheby's as revealed in court documents concerning the Duryodhana seizure around twenty-five years later:

> First, the museum would obtain guarantees from vendors that the objects had been legally excavated and exported. Second, the museum would notify possible countries of origin of a piece prior to its acquisition, and would only proceed if no evidence of theft or illicit trade was received in response. Finally, the museum would publish all acquisitions, and if evidence emerged that the piece had been recently looted, it would be returned to its rightful owner (True 1997: 139–140; Felch and Frammolino 2011: 90). This policy might be characterized as encapsulating the principle of 'innocent until proven guilty'; in that the Getty would presume an object was on the market legitimately unless it would be proven otherwise by an authority outside the Getty. It was clearly inappropriate in circumstances where guarantees of legal trade and ownership were known to be forged and most antiquities were illegally excavated and traded clandestinely, so that it would be unlikely for authorities in countries of origin to have knowledge of theft or trafficking.
>
> (Brodie and Bowman Proulx 2013)

## The Sotheby's emails

In 2010, Zara Porter-Hill was Head of the Indian and Southeast Asian Department at Sotheby's, based in London. Anuradha Ghosh-Mazumdar (known as Anu) was Assistant Vice President in the New York division of the Indian and Southeast Asian Department. Above both Zara and Anu in the Sotheby's hierarchy, Henry Howard-Sneyd was Vice Chairman of Asian Art (Americas), Executive Vice President (North America) and manager of the Asia Division in New York. In a series of emails between these parties and some others, filed as evidence in the litigation, it is clear that the auction house knew by at least September 2010 that the statue they were to offer for sale in March 2011 was likely to have been removed from Cambodia with its feet left behind. In an email exchange on 23 September 2010 about rumours the piece may be a fake, Henry says to Zara, Anu and others:

> I have to say that if Emmy Bunker and the whole art world accept the Norton Simon one—added to the presence of two sets of feet at Koh Kher [his mis-spelling] would make me feel it is highly unlikely that the whole piece is wrong.

By 'wrong', he means fake. Therefore, it seems clear that at the highest level, Sotheby's knew or thought it highly likely that the Duryodhana they were offering, and the Bhima at the Norton Simon museum, were a pair and had been forcibly removed from their feet at the Koh Ker temple complex in Cambodia. In such a state of knowledge, one would think some serious due diligence would be the order of the day.

Emma C. Bunker, referred to in Henry's email as Emmy Bunker, is an art historian and freelancer, a research consultant to the Denver Art Museum's Asian Art Department, who has worked with Bangkok and London based collector Douglas Latchford on a landmark book recording collections of Khmer statuary (Bunker and Latchford 2003) together with other texts, *Khmer Gold* and *Khmer Bronzes*. Sotheby's consulted Bunker about the proposed sale of the Duryodhana fairly early in the process of sale, asking her to write up a sales brochure for it and give a public lecture to promote it. The legal complaint records Bunker as telling the auction house:

> I do not think you should sell the Dvarapala [she is referring to the Duryodhana] at public auction. The Cambodians in Phnom Penh now have clear evidence that it was definitely stolen from Prasat Chen at Koh Ker, as the feet are still in situ... The two Dvarapalas must have stood close together and their feet remain, so it's pretty clear where they came from.

So in fact the auction house was made aware of the view that the piece was 'definitely stolen' in that correspondence in early June 2010. Bunker subsequently softened her line after checking the issue out through what she refers to as her 'culture spies' in Cambodia, and agreed to 'write up something', suggesting to Anu that Sotheby's could proceed with the sale because the Kingdom of Cambodia's 'focus these days is to stop anything from being exported from Cambodia now, not to go after pieces that left years ago when there were no restrictions' (Email from Bunker to Ghosh-Mazumdar, 19 July 2010: produced in 2012 as Exhibit 10 in the legal proceedings).

The statue was sent off for testing by John Twilley, an art conservation scientist, to satisfy the auction house that the rumours it may be fake were baseless— rumours that were brought to Anu's attention by her clients who she refers to in an email of 23 September 2010 as 'the Chicago boys' (Exhibit 4, 2012). These clients said they had been offered the piece 'three years ago, with an ex-Latchford association' but 'they turned it down as they would not touch anything with that association' since Latchford's reputation as a significant collector also came at that time with growing speculation about his involvement in trafficking networks moving objects out of Cambodia and Thailand. Twilley has worked extensively in the field of art conservation, having served as conservation scientist at the J. Paul Getty Museum, as senior research scientist at the conservation centre of the Los Angeles County Museum of Art, and taught art and artefacts conservation at graduate level at the University of California for decades. Twilley's theory, after examining the statue but before testing samples removed from the statue, is reported by Anu in an email of 11 November 2010 as that 'the sculpture was either forcibly broken for ease of transport from the find site and then put back together later OR that the head and torso do not belong together' (Exhibit 7, 2012). At this stage therefore, if the auction house wanted to proceed with selling the statue as an original single piece, and not a composite or a fake, alarm bells should have been loudly ringing about the prognosis that it may have been 'forcibly broken for ease of transport'. If the statue was not screaming fake, it must surely at this point have been screaming loot. A subsequent technical examination of the statue on 17 February 2011 by Pieter Meyers, a specialist in Los Angeles, found that 'the head is the original head, reattached in recent times' (Exhibit 8, 2012).

Prior to this, on 28 October 2010, Henry emailed Zara to ask 'How are you getting on with the letter to Hab Touche [sp]? I think we really need to get on with things if we are to lock it in for the sale' (Exhibit 9, 2012). Hab Touch was the Director General for Tangible Heritage at the Ministry of Culture and Fine Arts in the Cambodian Government. In situations where it is likely that a particular national government may want to express a claim to ownership of an antiquity, the norm in dealers' approaches to due diligence has been to send the government a letter notifying them of the intention to sell the object, thus giving them the explicit opportunity to consider the matter and object if they wish. This was, purportedly, the point of sending Touch a letter about the impending sale of the Duryodhana in New York. Zara replies to Henry: 'The letter was done weeks ago. Anu and I both think the letter should come from you' (Exhibit 9, 2012). This is a multi-million dollar piece of cultural heritage after all, a big deal by anyone's standards, and correspondence about such a financially, artistically, and culturally important statue would seem to be appropriately issued by the upper echelons of the auction house's hierarchy. Yet Henry writes back:

> Just talked with Anu. We agreed that one of our points was that we simply wanted to be informing him out of politeness and did not want to raise this to important or "pay attention" levels. I think it much better that it come from the department... Quite nice to be from Anu if you do not feel it should be from you (Exhibit 9, 2012).

To which Zara replied 'All good points. Send from Anu'. So the letter was to be sent not by the more senior figure in the chain of email correspondence, but by the most junior, and this was apparently part of a strategy aiming to avoid raising the matter to 'pay attention levels' for its recipient and presumably also other possible readers in the Cambodian government.

Here we see the 'creative' nature of the compliance with the norm of due diligence and notification of likely erstwhile owners. The auction house is able to put themselves in a position where they can say, essentially, 'look—we sent a letter to the Cambodian government notifying them of our intention to sell the piece' when in fact that process of notification was calculated *not* to notify, if a reasonable definition of notify is to raise something to 'important or pay attention levels'.

In fact, Anu's correspondence with Emmy Bunker in July and August 2010 shows Anu asking Bunker whether an even less formal version of notification might be possible:

> Our legal department has suggested that perhaps once you've completed the essay you would like to share it with Mr Hab purely for intellectual/art-historical exchange of views. This way he will be properly informed well in advance. If he doesn't react adversely (within a time span of 7–10 days) then we will first celebrate and then immediately go ahead and prepare our museum packs....

To which Emmy replied:

> There is NO WAY that I can send what I write to Touch. If this is brought to his attention specifically, now that he is Minister of Culture, he will be forced to do something... Sending him the writeup specifically would be like waving a red flag in front of a bull. Douglas [Latchford, the collector] has already spoken with Zara on the subject and told her that she should not involve Touch in any of this (Exhibit 10, 2012).

And so, in the end, the decision was taken to go down the route of correspondence with Touch that did not 'raise the issue to important or pay attention levels'. Bunker is recorded in notes on a telephone conversation recorded by Anu as having counselled Sotheby's to 'Be prepared for bad press. You will get it no matter what you do as you're selling something so important. If you get bad press it will be from the US—from academics and temple huggers not from Cambodians' (Exhibit 10, 2012).

On 24 March 2011, Tan Theany, Secretary General of the Cambodian National Commission for UNESCO wrote to Sotheby's that 'as the pedestal with the two feet... is still in situ at the Prasat Chen temple at Koh Ker, it is believed that this statue was illegally removed from the site' (Exhibit 6, 2012) and asked the auction house to pull the object from sale and facilitate its return to Cambodia. Litigation ensued, and the statue was eventually returned to Cambodia in a settlement agreement which stipulated that it was accepted by all parties that Sotheby's was not at fault.

## Theoretical perspectives on antiquities trafficking

As outlined in the introduction to this chapter, criminological and sociological work on white-collar crime can give us the theoretical tools to support an understanding of this kind of harmful sharp practice in business settings as being normal, or at least normalized. In Diane Vaughan's propositions around the normalization of deviance we find some contextually relevant explication. In her work on organizational deviance within NASA she came to see 'history as cause' (Vaughan

1996). On the face of it this sounds rather tautological since of course the cause of anything will be found in the history of that thing, and on the level of platitude that doesn't seem to take matters of explanation very far forward. But the proposition has more sociological depth than that. Organisations develop working cultures, and most organisations operate in an environment characterized in some respects by elements of risk. Over time, a tendency can develop to accept more and more risk, if the harms associated with prior risk-taking behaviour have not materialised. In the normal course of events, therefore, organisations can be found engaging in more extreme risk-taking behaviour than a rational assessment of the risk landscape would have said was sensible. The organisation, and key people within it, have at this point become 'acclimatised' to certain levels of risk, coming to perceive the taking of those risks as normal practice, and incorrectly diagnosing the associated danger as being within the bounds of acceptable conservative practice (Vaughan 1998, 1999, 2004).

Antiquities trading businesses are clearly a good fit for this model of acclimatisation to risky behaviour. As has been well remarked upon in the literature on antiquities trafficking, the likelihood of legal sanction for handling looted antiquities has generally been very low indeed in the marketplace (Manacorda and Chappell 2011; Mackenzie 2002). At the same time the financial rewards for successfully 'fencing' looted antiquities are high (Mackenzie 2011b). A culture has clearly emerged in the market of the normalisation of this form of deviant business. Technically risky trades of antiquities with no provenance, or suspect provenance, are carried out with such regularity, with no penalty, and generating significant return, that this 'history' of trade is indeed a 'cause' of criminality in the present. In this context of a general normalised form of market deviance, the Sotheby's email correspondence perhaps becomes more amenable to a reading that sees it as normal, in the eyes of the actors involved, if not in the analysis of external critics. It is clearly a process that has involved knowingly and intentionally 'gaming' a legal and ethical system of regulation, which requires good faith and due diligence from the protagonists. When we ask 'how can people do this sort of thing?' the answer seems to be in some measure a function of the theory of organisational deviance, which can be thought of as drawing together several other key theoretical positions in criminology, including differential association and routine activities theory.

Sutherland's theory of differential association (Sutherland and Cressey 1974), an acknowledged pillar on which Vaughan developed her ideas of organisational deviance, is a type of social learning theory in which deviant norms are seen to grow and become sustained in group settings where there are a preponderance of learned definitions that are favourable to violating the law over learned definitions that are unfavourable to it. Where the original deviant impulses may have come from is less important to this view than the fact that they can be propagated in group settings, so that law-breaking comes to be seen by individuals within the group as positive rather than negative (Sutherland et al. 1995).

The theory of Routine Activities proposes that crime will occur where there is a confluence of three factors: a motivated offender, a suitable target, and the absence of a capable guardian (Cohen and Felson 1979). Routine activities has been applied to the analysis of antiquities trafficking to flag up the vulnerability of the market, characterised as it is on a general level by these three factors (Mackenzie 2009). Thinking about the white–collar crime destination market end of the supply chain, we might further observe that part of the process of differential association is the absence of capable guardians. In the deviant normative hothouse that we are coming to see established cultural capitalist institutions as exemplifying, who has the incentive or capacity to regulate processes of acclimatisation to risk-taking behaviour? Who in the conversations about tactics and strategy within the organisation could disrupt the promulgation and social embedding of norms, values and beliefs which support the kinds of compliance games we have seen in which, as McBarnet says, the spirit of the law is defeated by calculated designs over how to give the appearance of adherence to practices which represent good behaviour while actually behaving badly?

Alongside (1) creative compliance, (2) organisational deviance (and by extension differential association), and (3) routine activities, a fourth theoretical perspective to reflect upon is Bauman's review of the social effects of bureaucratic and morally-distanciating processes of modernity (Bauman 1989). For Bauman, the organisation of modern processes of production allowed individuals to separate, in their minds, contributions to the world of work from the moral consequences of these acts. Famously he has described how engineers during the Holocaust produced careful designs for vans used to effect mobile mass killings using gas. How could they calculate such horror as if it were just another industrial design? The answer is proposed to lie in the ethically numbing processes of modern work, which settle actors into a routine of making contributions to overall processes they do not see themselves as the authors of, and therefore do not see themselves as responsible for.

Parallel theories offer slightly different inflections on this core proposition. They include observations of actors 'just following orders', set within a wider literature studying crimes of obedience (Kelman and Hamilton 1989). We might also look to the theories of techniques of neutralisation and systems of accounts through which exculpatory social narratives are drawn on to justify and excuse deviant behaviour (Sykes and Matza 1957; Scott and Lyman 1968; Benson 1985). Also relevant are the effects of trust in superiors and the suppression of moral judgement of subordinates on the basis that those in charge 'must know what they are doing' (Duster 1971), which is slightly different from straightforward hierarchical obedience, although it may look similar in practice and amount to the same thing in effect (Mackenzie 2013). Finally, the sociology of denial gives us an approach to questions of moral cognition that problematises concepts of 'knowing' and 'not knowing', seeing these as being more confused and fluid in empirical form than they have usually been conceived of in law and in common wisdom, recognising that there may be things we know on one level of our conscience to be wrong, but that knowledge may be buried, ignored, overwritten, or conveniently forgotten when illicit temptation presents itself (Cohen 2001; Zerubavel 2006).

All of these theoretical ideas have, at their core, a sense that sound moral judgement is not as much of a precursor to, and driver of, action as we may have thought and hoped. Moral thinking comes out of much of the sociology of decision-making as being less a pre-choice influencing factor and more a post-choice rationalisation and ethical balancing act that involves manipulation of the facts as much as it does recognition and rational evaluation of them. In the world of licit and illicit business enterprise, where profit and status rather than ethics have traditionally been the basis for organisational development and success, finding evidence of warped or emaciated ethical thinking is not unusual.

The Sotheby's correspondence therefore looks to fit this approach to understanding the differential interpretation of social norms and values quite well. The kind of 'gaming' behaviour that has been widely observed in business across many sectors through the development of a now quite voluminous literature on compliance is, unsurprisingly, present in the market structures of the antiquities trade, where profit trumps ethics. If theories around acclimatisation to risk, differential normative association, and routine activities can help us to think more abstractly about 'how' these gaming practices can come about, we also need to consider the broader contextual issues within which individual business people and their groups operate, which can help us to see 'why' this happens. These contextual issues can perhaps best be summarised with reference to the concept of strain, and in particular viewed through the lens of Robert Merton's strain theory.

Merton's propositions about social structural strain were based around a perceived disjuncture between a given society's 'cultural goals' and the institutional means available to individuals to achieve those goals (Merton 1968). The cultural goals he saw in US society, which was the object of his analysis, were cultural in the sociological sense (as in 'of the culture') rather than the art world sense ('about cultural affairs'). He considered the cultural goals of the time to be infected by what he called a 'pathological materialism', which established unrealisable aspirations to wealth as the lodestar for a society that provided employment opportunities which were neither universally enjoyed nor for the most part a likely pathway to the pinnacle of this American Dream (Merton 1938, 1968). Merton thought that where achievement of the cultural goals was not widely available, a society should place considerable emphasis on the importance of playing by the rules, and the intrinsic value of pursuing the institutionally approved means. In the USA of his era he saw, to the contrary, an over-emphasis on a culture of winning at all costs, which was a highlighting of the cultural goals at the expense of the worthy attractions of the institutionalised means.

Among the various adaptations to the structural strain in a society constructed in this way were 'innovations': some people tried to achieve the cultural goals of wealth and success by means other than those which were institutionally approved. As such, strain theory has become an important reference point in many fields of criminology. Innovation is such an attractive option, since the normative outlook of our western societies are such that:

the person who adheres to [the methods of] hard work, education, honesty, deferred gratification, receives little social reward for it unless he or she also achieves at least a moderate degree of wealth as a result. But the person who achieves wealth, even if it is not by the approved means, still receives the social rewards of prestige and social status.

*(Vold et al. 2002)*

This arrangement only seems to have accelerated as neoliberal social, political and economic approaches have developed through the latter half of the twentieth century and into the twenty-first, where the most affluent in society seem to be working in tech companies, hedge funds, and premier league football, all of which have in common the capacity to generate incredible payouts in fairly short order by comparison with the now increasingly outdated version of a standard working life.

In the field of dealing and collecting antiquities we can see some parallels to this diagnosis of social structural strain. Here as elsewhere there are short-cuts to success, fast money to be made from 'sailing close to the wind' (McBarnet 2006), and an anomic intangibility to the ethical structures of the particular institutionalised means in this field, which resonates alongside other high-flying professions that seem to some extent to make their own rules. Antiquities buyers and traders have, in our studies, been quite explicit that while it is certainly possible to earn a good living 'playing it straight', the temptation to step around the legal rules is occasionally simply too great to resist (Mackenzie 2005a). The strain of very large amounts of money to be made from criminality, combined with a weak investment in the intrinsic value of the institutionalised means to achieve the goals of wealth and status in this field, results in innovation here, as it does in other areas of social and economic life.

Branches of strain theory have developed to extend the analysis, taking into consideration social and global developments since Merton introduced the theory. Two of these interpretations are 'institutional anomie' theory and 'global anomie' theory. The institutional anomie theory sees the particular warping of society that causes the structural strain as being held primarily in over-emphasis of the economy above other social institutions, such as family, school and politics (Messner and Rosenfeld 1994). As such, there are precious few areas of social life in which the main drivers of decisions are not predominantly economic in focus. The policy prescription, for theorists of institutional anomie, is to shore up a commitment to collective obligation in society, while diminishing somewhat the pervasive neoliberal individualism of rights-oriented self-advancement.

Through this lens, the structural strain inherent in the antiquities trade is symptomatic of a wider disjuncture between the ostensible community-facing cultural role of museum-level collection, preservation, study and display, and the economic role of the market which is more confronting: commodification, competition, careerism and, for some dealers, extravagant levels of compensation. There is no doubt much more to be written about these 'four Cs' in diagnosis of the challenges of a capitalist market in cultural heritage. But here we can simply observe that the casting of cultural pursuits such as the collection and appreciation of heritage in the form of global consumer-capital markets brings with it many of the strain-related criminogenic features that have been identified in the institutional anomie perspective in its wider critique of the economisation of everything.

The global anomie theory provides yet another extension and reinterpretation to the conceptual analysis of social structural strain. It looks to the globalisation of trade, licit and illicit, and the 'criminogenic asymmetries' which various imbalances between jurisdictions create: 'Cross-border crime is the product of criminogenic asymmetries: conflicts, mismatches and inequalities in the spheres of politics, culture, the economy and the law' (Passas 1999). Passas sees these asymmetries as implicated in the causes of crime in three ways: 'by fuelling the demand for illegal goods and services; by generating incentives for people and organisations to engage in illegal practices; and by reducing the ability of authorities to control crime' (Passas 1999). Each of these three factors is clearly on display in the international market for illicit antiquities, and indeed Passas himself has made these observations in an editorial on this field of transnational crime (Passas and Bowman Proulx 2011).

Overall therefore, strain theory and its variants provide a rich source of analytical and conceptual language which we can bring to bear on questions of motivation and method in the trade of illicit antiquities. On both the global and the more localised market level, the sources of strain that characterise dealing in the market are quite clear, and in the relationship between this perspective and the others introduced above we can begin to construct some robust theoretical scaffolding around the otherwise perplexing questions of why anyone would buy looted cultural heritage, and how they not only get away with it but have over time been celebrated in high society for their role in cultural transmission and edification.

## The Weiner complaint

At the time of writing, two of the protagonists in the Sotheby's Duryodhana case referred to above are again at the centre of an emerging controversy, in the complaint against the New York antiquities dealer Nancy Weiner. The complaint was raised at the instance of Brenton Easter, the special agent in the US Department of Homeland Security Investigations who is becoming increasingly famous for his focus on art and antiquities trafficking. It is being prosecuted by Matthew Bogdanos, an Assistant District Attorney in New York, who is similarly a familiar name for researchers in this field (see for example Bogdanos 2005). Nancy Weiner has for many years run a very prestigious antiquities dealership in Manhattan's Upper East Side, and has sold objects into collections in the world's major museums, including the Metropolitan Museum of Art in New York, the Art Institute of Chicago, the National Gallery of Australia, and the Asian Civilisations Museum in Singapore. Weiner now stands accused of using her gallery to buy, smuggle, launder, and sell millions of dollars' worth of antiquities stolen from Afghanistan, Cambodia, China, India, Pakistan and Thailand.

The complaint paints a picture of a dealer who made significant profits from what is alleged to be a systematic pattern of behaviour in buying looted antiquities from thieves and traffickers operating out of Asia, and 'laundering' the objects. The laundering process set out in the complaint has several dimensions. It includes misrepresenting provenance to purchasers, some of whom appear to have been fairly undiscerning in this regard. It includes placing objects for sale through Sotheby's and Christie's auction houses with false provenance histories, and in some cases buying them back using straw purchasers, thereby creating a chain of provenance history and also creating the impression of a stiffer demand than was truly present in the market at the time (a technique also famously used by Giacomo Medici, see the Appendix, who called it 'triangulation'). In some cases the anti-quities were sent off for restoration in a process that removed physical indications which may have raised suspicion of their illicit origins.

The complaint references 'co-conspirator #1', an 'antiquities dealer based in London and Bangkok' (hereafter CC1), and 'co-conspirator #2', 'who works as a research consultant for an American museum' (hereafter CC2). These co-conspirators have been identified as Douglas Latchford and Emmy Bunker (Blumenthal and Mashberg 2017). They are also 'the collector' and 'the scholar' referred to in the court papers in the Sotheby's Duryodhana scandal (Blumenthal and Mashberg 2017). The Weiner complaint references an email in which CC1 'told the defendant that he typically gave CC2 bronze statues in exchange for false letters of provenance'. Several specific cases of provenance fabrication and restoration with the objective of covering up signs of looting are detailed in the complaint, including a tenth century Khmer Naga Buddha valued at US$ 1.5m and two seated Buddhas from the first to third centuries, one of which Weiner sold to Singapore's Asian Civilisations Museum without any statement of provenance. In what appears to be a response to persistent questioning about the provenance of the statue by the investigative journalist Jason Felch, the museum requested further details from the dealer years later, in reply to which she 'first claimed that Seated Buddha #1 had belonged to an unnamed European collection for at least 35 to 40 years, but then stated that the owner's father had acquired the piece in India', and then switched to a third version in which the statue had been bought in Vietnam in the 1960s. The investigation of Subhash Kapoor, detailed in Chapter 6, turned up a computer disc with an image of the Buddha, and evidence to suggest that Kapoor was involved in facilitating the sale of the statue to Weiner from a trader representing Vaman Ghiya, 'the idol thief' in the New Yorker's story of that title (Keefe 2007).

There are several other such transaction histories alleged in the complaint, and we can see a pattern in the allegations in which failures on the part of institutional actors have been exploited by the dealers and experts involved, for example where auction houses and museums have not asked enough, or sometimes it seems any, questions about provenance. In the cases where provenance has been put on record, the fabrication of very thin provenance stories has been enough to satisfy what superficial requirements there seem to have been. An interesting feature of the case that follows our previous observations in this volume about the support structure for the market is the involvement of 'experts' like CC2 who is said to have provided fake provenance stories, and the restorers who in this case are said to have removed visible traces of looting and covered up restoration work on suspicious breaks in the statues with splatters of paint. We might also bring into this category of experts in our spotlight the authenticators who we saw working on the Duryodhana in the Sotheby's emails discussed above. In the research literature on organised crime, people performing services to organised crime activity in roles such as all of these various support functions to the illicit antiquities trade are called 'facilitators', and their presence in illicit markets has become increasingly recognised as functionally important—in other words, they emerge from studies of organised crime often as key players performing supporting roles that allow the illicit networked activity to be successful (Kleemans et al. 2012).

## The roles of facilitators

The importance of facilitators has been recognised in the commentary on the illicit antiquities trade for some time. It might be useful to think of facilitation as either active or passive. An example of active facilitation would be the provision of fake provenances by experts who know how to game the market in this way. Let us define active facilitation as where an illicit service is provided to support the workings of the overall criminal conspiracy, and the purpose of the service provided is precisely to support that conspiracy. A person in such a role can reasonably be taken, for analytical purposes, to be a member of the organised crime network in question.

In passive facilitation by contrast, we have a range of ancillary actors doing their business around the antiquities trade in ways that intersect with its nature as a grey market comprised of both licit and illicit objects. As we set out in Chapters 1 and 4 above, these people include conservators and authenticators. As well as in this book, Neil Brodie has previously forcefully argued in other publications and lectures that academics sometimes support the trade in this way, by studying and publishing material that may be known or reasonably suspected to be looted (Brodie 2009, 2011b). Their facilitation is passive rather than active because its main aim is not usually to provide direct support to an organised crime venture. Rather, their goal is intellectual and sometimes the more crass and self-interested career progression pathways which may result. Still, although supporting crime may not be their main aim, their effects on the illicit antiquities trade can be significant, increasing the value of objects on the market and giving them a certain type of validation through scholarly pursuits around it.

Kathryn Walker Tubb wrote about this kind of facilitation too, in her brief history of the development by the Institute of Archaeology at University College London of their policy statement regarding the illicit trade in antiquities (Tubb 2002). She described this stance by an academic department as refuting 'the contention of dealers and collectors that archaeologists and associated heritage professionals are only motivated by self-aggrandisement and self-interest, and that they will undertake work on any material regardless of provenance if it happens to be in furtherance of their own careers and renown' (Tubb 2002: 288).

Tubb also covers the case of the Oxford University Research Laboratory for Archaeology and the History of Art. Throughout the 1980s this lab provided thermoluminesence dating tests as a commercial service to dealers and collectors in ancient art, and would provide them with a certificate of authenticity which was 'a passport to a high-value price tag in galleries and auction houses the world over' (Tubb 2002: 286), although the lab made no attempt to identify and exclude looted material from its business activities. Tubb cites the documentary film which exposed these practices at the lab, *The African King*, in which 'it was... ascertained that TL dating was undertaken on a no-questions-asked basis', and 'when challenged to explain this policy, the answer [from the Director of the lab] was that you had to earn money in Thatcherite Britain [and] that this was a business' (Tubb 2002: 286).

Tubb and Brodie's work on the facilitators of the illicit antiquities trade has also included analysis of conservators (Tubb 2013). The Sotheby's Duryodhana case and the Weiner prosecution show that the services of restoration consultants are important facilitators of the illicit market. There is little empirical data on the views of these actors and their approaches to questions of moral judgement where such matters may be in tension with business imperatives and personal financial enrichment. We might suppose that the kinds of strain identified in this chapter as operating throughout the market may also be present among facilitators. They may see illicit opportunity as simply something to be exploited in the pursuit of normal business ends. This may especially be the case when those opportunities occur in a context where the facilitator is able to consider their involvement to be passive rather than active. They might do this by rationalising that if they don't engage with potentially illicit antiquities, someone else will. Or they might believe that the status of an antiquity as looted or otherwise is not their concern—they do not see themselves as the 'capable guardians' in this market system, and if they were to get a reputation for refusing to work on suspicious material, or even reporting suspicions to the police, business might dry up. So, in the ways suggested by Bauman that we have discussed in this chapter, we might assume these professionals choose to focus their minds on the technical task at hand whether that be restoring, dating, authenticating, or academically studying, and let knowledge or suspicion of the crimes to which they are a witness and an accomplice of sorts fade into the back of mind. In McBarnet's phrase, this is 'whiter than white-collar crime' (McBarnet 1991). McBarnet used that phrase to draw attention to the fact that white-collar crimes are notoriously hard to discover, but also to recognise that some (the 'whiter than' crimes) might even, when discovered, still be the subject of some dispute and discussion around whether the activities in question were actually crimes at all.

In our case, we can see that the forms of white-collar criminality we are talking about are so thoroughly integrated into the culture of doing business in the antiquities trade that they are rendered invisible, or at least extremely hard to see, not only to outside analysts but also to some of the participants in the trade themselves, who do not, or perhaps cannot, see criminality or the facilitation of crime in their actions. This seems to apply to passive facilitators just as it does to some of the actors who are more core to the illicit trade. Of course, there are also more committed criminals in this transnational criminal market whose motivations and mindsets are less abstruse and do not demand a great depth of theory to explain how and why they exploit illicit opportunities in the antiquities trade. But for others, including some facilitators and institutional actors, we have set out to construct, in this chapter, a framework in which participation in wrongdoing that is rather harder to explain, might be made sense of through a sensitivity to the processes that support or generate normalisation, rationalisation, routinisation, and economic strain.

# 6

# AUTOREGULATION OF THE DESTINATION MARKET?

In this and the following chapter we want to build upon some of the theory and evidence previously presented to examine the different regulatory approaches to the destination market, starting in this chapter with a critical investigation of the concept of *autoregulation*. The idea of autoregulation—that the market acts to regulate itself—took hold in the late 1990s and into the 2000s perhaps because of the increasing provision at auction of provenance-related information described in Chapter 4 (Figures 4.1 and 4.2). The argument went as follows: customers were starting to discriminate against poorly-provenanced and likely trafficked or faked antiquities by paying higher prices for well-provenanced objects whose legitimacy and authenticity were not in question. Higher prices for well-provenanced objects were in turn encouraging the release into the public domain of more provenance-related information, so that the market was gradually becoming more transparent, allowing the customer to be more selective about acquisitions. In consequence, trading in unprovenanced or poorly-provenanced antiquities was seen as becoming less profitable, and the market for looted objects was thought to be diminishing in size (Cannon-Brookes 1994; Borodkin 1995). Referring back to our typology of crime control methods, autoregulation would be an example of economic control, with increasing public awareness of the problems associated with the trade manifesting commercially as reduced demand for poorly provenanced material.

This economic process of crime control has been termed autoregulation to emphasise that the mechanism envisaged is something different and apart from self-regulation. We will study the idea of self-regulation more closely in Chapter 7, but for the moment we can simply note that self-regulation is conventionally understood to comprise the adoption by antiquities dealers of voluntary codes of practice and ethics (Brodie 2014a). Autoregulation, however, denotes the aggregate effect of customer preference for good provenance, with price forcing a legal market. It does not imply moral agency on the part of customers or dealers. They need not be actively selecting well-provenanced antiquities with a view to minimising the harms caused by illicit trade. Their purchasing decisions might simply reflect self-interested assessments of personal risk, with customers believing that a good provenance ensures a high resale price and dealers concerned to protect the symbolic and commercially important asset of good reputation (Prott 2000: 348; Nørskov 2002: 320–321; Levine 2009: 219–222; Gerstenblith 2012: 70; Anderson 2017: 46). The idea of autoregulation is a compelling one, as it holds within it the promise of a more transparent and legitimate market without the need for costly statutory control regulation or other kinds of government intervention. But for the same reason it invites suspicion that it is more of a rhetorical reality than a material one, advanced by market actors to deflect demands for any additional regulation or more rigorous enforcement of already established control measures (Gerstenblith 2012: 72).

Most evidence for autoregulation is anecdotal, derived from the stated opinions of dealers themselves that provenance is becoming an increasingly important determinant of price. New York antiquities dealer Jerome Eisenberg, for example, has made the connection between provenance and price a few times in his reporting of auction sales (Eisenberg 1993: 23; 2004: 26). His fellow New York dealer Robert Haber was quoted as saying in 2004 that 'Within the complex world of the ancient art market it is becoming more apparent that a good provenance has a very positive effect on the value of a work of ancient art' (Russell 2004). Likewise, ten years later, Gregory Demirjian of Ariadne Galleries was quoted as saying 'We have to be incredibly careful about provenance' (Reyburn 2014). For the auction houses, Christie's head of antiquities Max Bernheimer was quoted as saying that 'Provenance used to play second fiddle to quality and beauty, but now it is king and reigns supreme' (Page 2009). Dealers interviewed by Mackenzie in the early 2000s were mixed in their opinions. One London dealer said that 'Ten years ago I never thought of provenance. Now I'll actually pay more for the provenance of a piece' and another that 'Everybody says that now: "got your provenance?"', although one New York dealer expressed a contrary opinion when he observed that 'There are collectors that thrive on no provenance' (Mackenzie 2005b: 32–38).

## The 1970 provenance threshold

Another potential red light for the destination market was switched on in 2008 when the Association of Art Museum Directors (AAMD) adopted a new policy on acquisitions, which stated that a museum:

> Normally should not acquire a work unless solid proof exists that the object was outside its country of probable modern discovery before 1970, or was legally exported from its probable country of modern discovery after 1970.

> *(AAMD 2008: Guideline E)*

The 2008 AAMD policy raised the prospect of US art museums no longer accepting the gift or bequest of an antiquity unless accompanied by a provenance showing it to have been out of its country of origin before 1970. As such 'charitable' donations in the United States attract large tax deductions (Thompson 2010; Yates 2016), going forward it would no longer be in the financial interests of collectors to purchase unprovenanced antiquities for prospective donation and the major attractive pull of museums on the destination market would have diminished markedly.

The AAMD's introduction of the 1970 threshold was predicted to exert a chilling effect upon the market (Melikian 2008, 2010, 2012, 2013). In 2012, experienced commentator Souren Melikian confidently predicted that:

> Growing numbers of buyers feel that at some point in the not-too-distant future, the Convention will be widely adhered to. Then, costly antiquities bought after 1970 will become hard if not impossible to sell, and their commercial value will nosedive
>
> *(Melikian 2012)*

He later enlarged '... important works of art that can be proved to have reached the market before 1970 shoot to vertiginous levels, while those that cannot fail to sell with increasing frequency' (Melikian 2013). It was being more widely reported that the major New York auction houses were turning away artefacts without a secure pre-1970 provenance (Page 2009; Blumenthal and Mashberg 2012). Thus, in the public imagination, the operation of autoregulation became tied to the AAMD's 1970 threshold, with the market discriminating against antiquities without a pre-1970 provenance.

The AAMD's adoption of the 1970 provenance threshold was met by a combination of fear, loathing and not a little confusion on the part of the collecting and trade communities. At a meeting of the Asia Society in New York in 2012, for example, Arthur Houghton, who had been curator of antiquities at the J. Paul Getty Museum, offered statistics suggesting that the threshold would exclude from acquisition by US museums between 67,000 and 120,000 objects already located in the US (Asia Society 2012: 17). At the same meeting, however, Julian Raby, who was at the time Director of the Sackler and Freer Gallery of Art at the Smithsonian Institution, expressed his belief that the AAMD had not instituted 'a total ban on anything' (Asia Society 2012: 18). Objects with undocumented or incomplete provenance could be acquired by a museum provided they were subsequently listed on the publicly-accessible Object Registry (https://aamd.org/object-registry), a database constructed by the AAMD to support its 2008 guidelines (AAMD 2008: Guideline G). In February 2018, the AAMD's Object Registry listed only 1173 objects in 38 institutions, some of which were pieces of fine art related to Nazi-era cultural property claims. As we showed in Chapter 2, not all antiquities falling short of the AAMD's pre-1970 provenance requirement are in fact listed on the Registry.

The significance of the year 1970 is that it was on 14 November 1970 that UNESCO adopted the Convention on the Illicit Import, Export and Transfer of Ownership of Cultural Property. The year 1970 came to mark a watershed in museum attitudes and practice, separating off the years before the UNESCO Convention, when the problems caused by illicit trade were either not widely known or thought to be unimportant, from the time afterwards, when the problems became better known and were of mounting concern in the museums' world. Throughout the early 1970s, individual museums and museum organisations started incorporating cut-off dates or thresholds into provenance requirements to separate ethically acceptable from unacceptable acquisitions (Prott and O'Keefe 1989: 128; Brodie and Renfrew 2005). Through time, the idea of 1970 as a threshold or 'bright line' distinguishing between what would be regarded in the museums' world as objects with 'bad' (post-1970) provenance and 'good' (pre-1970) provenance began to solidify (Brodie and Renfrew 2005), and for museums, the 1970 date came to constitute a strong normative threshold (O'Keefe 2007: 156–158), as confirmed in the 2008 AAMD acquisitions policy.

A provenance threshold is a convenience for museums and collectors as it provides the opportunity and justification for abbreviated due diligence when the jurisdictional and transactional histories of an antiquity intended for acquisition are obscure. Instead of investigating and reconstructing an unbroken chain of legitimate ownership back to source, it allows ownership claims to be anchored to a simple determination of licit or illicit export before a specified date. It also protects the repose of established museum collections, particularly guarding those acquired during colonial times against claims for repatriation.

But provenance thresholds are controversial, particularly for source countries. Many countries have taken antiquities into State ownership by means of so-called patrimony laws, and are prepared to commence civil or criminal court proceedings for the recovery of illicitly-traded antiquities using appropriate stolen property laws. The date of patrimony legislation varies from country to country, but is often earlier than 1970, and is regarded by the country concerned as the relevant and legally-enforcible date underpinning repatriation claims. In 1987, for example, Turkey commenced ultimately successful court proceedings against New York's Metropolitan Museum of Art aimed at recovering the so-called Lydian Hoard, an assemblage of more than 360 precious objects that had been looted and illegally traded from Turkey sometime during the 1960s, and acquired by the Met later that same decade (Kaye and Main 1995). Turkey took antiquities into State ownership in 1906 (Blake 1998: 826), and the 1970 date of the UNESCO Convention was immaterial to the case. For dispossessed countries such as Turkey, the adoption of a 1970 threshold discriminating between licit and illicit antiquities would be akin to relinquishing legitimate claims to ownership of property stolen prior to 1970.

Thus, questions can certainly be asked about the legitimacy and perceived legitimacy of provenance thresholds. An acquisition rendered acceptable by the 1970 or any other provenance threshold offers no guarantee of good title to the collector concerned. A stolen antiquity might still be vulnerable for a recovery claim. The 1970 UNESCO Convention has now been recognised by several courts as comprising international public policy (O'Keefe 2007: 163–165), but the Convention is not retroactive and does not establish that the date of 1970 should be a legal watershed for acceptable object provenance. Thus legally, with lawful ownership in mind, a provenance threshold does not supersede due diligence, and some jurists have opined that they might be better dispensed with (Prott and O'Keefe 1989: 129). It is notable that the International Council of Museums has not incorporated a provenance threshold into its own code of ethics, which for antiquities and other cultural objects requires that due diligence 'should establish the full history of the item since discovery or production' (ICOM 2004: article 2.3).

Other than dates imposed by UN Security Council Resolutions (which are few in relation to illicit antiquities, and have been specific to crisis situations in conflict regions), auction houses, dealers and trade associations do not openly advocate a provenance threshold, 1970 or otherwise. Even UNESCO's own recommended International Code of Ethics for Dealers in Cultural Property makes no mention of a 1970 threshold. The media report in 2009 that 'major auction houses now follow UNESCO guidelines, and will not acquire or sell anything after 1970' (Page 2009) was mistaken, though illustrates the pervasive faith in the exercise and effectiveness of the 1970 threshold.

Nevertheless, it does look as though some companies at least have some internal rules about provenance. Christie's auction house, for example, claims to have adopted a variable threshold, depending upon the country of origin of an object and the date of commencement of any conflict, but with a default position that if an object can be shown to have been out of its country of origin since before 2000 it is acceptable for auction (SAFE 2016). Dealers too must take their own counsel. Phoenix Ancient Art has been quoted as saying that 'We research pieces as much as we can and if we fail to find a provenance, we put everything on the table and let the buyer decide' (Page 2009).

As we described in Chapter 4, antiquities collectors are largely dependent for advice about international laws and standards upon published sources and dealers, and to a lesser extent museum or university experts. Dealers, at least, seem unlikely to be advising customers about the desirability of a pre-1970 provenance, when they do not themselves openly advocate it. Faced with such an information shortfall, it is quite possible that the majority of collectors are unaware of the normative significance or even existence of a 1970 threshold, and in those circumstances it would exert no discernible effect on the market, in contrast to what would be needed for autoregulation to take hold.

Nevertheless, despite the apparent disinterest of dealers and auction houses and likely unawareness of collectors, there is some concrete evidence to show that the 1970 provenance threshold is not just a fictional construct and that it might be exerting a material effect on the market. In the preceding chapter, we examined e-mails from Sotheby's New York for what they reveal about the company's attitude towards regulatory compliance. The e-mails were released during discovery for a court case in New York disputing possession of a Cambodian tenth-century Duryodhana statue from the site of Koh Ker. The statue appeared as lot 27 in the catalogue of the 24 March 2011 Sotheby's New York Indian and Southeast Asian Works of Art sale with a pre-sale estimate of $2–3 million and a provenance 'Spink & Son Ltd, London, 1975'. We noted that the Duryodhana was withdrawn from sale after Sotheby's received an official complaint from the Cambodian government alleging it had been plundered during the 1970s. In April 2012 the US Attorney for the Southern District of New York filed unsuccessfully to seize the statue but in December 2013 an out-of-court agreement between Sotheby's, Cambodia and the statue's consignor secured its return to Cambodia (Davis 2015; Hauser-Schäublin 2016).

In addition to the email messages we analysed in the preceding chapter, several other messages related to an attempt by Sotheby's to establish that the statue had left Cambodia before 1970. Thus on 19 May 2010, Anuradha Ghosh-Mazumdar (Assistant Vice President of the Indian and Southeast Asian Department), e-mailed David Weldon (Senior Consultant in the Indian and Southeast Asian Department) and Zara Porter-Hill (Head of the Indian and Southeast Asian Department) that a prospective client was interested in a private purchase, but wanted reassurance that the statue's provenance stretched back to before 1970. Ghosh-Mazumdar suggested that Bangkok resident and collector Douglas Latchford might supply a pre-1970 provenance. Responding to a query from Porter-Hill, on 1 June 2010 Latchford clarified that he 'had the Guardian figure on reserve from Spinks in 1970' (Exhibit 3, 2012), thus placing the statue outside Cambodia by but not necessarily before 1970.

On 22 March 2011, Jane Levine (Sotheby's Worldwide Director of Compliance) wrote in an e-mail defending Sotheby's possession to Brent Easter (Special Agent with Homeland Security Investigations) that Sotheby's had 'identified two individuals who presently have no financial interest in the property and who personally saw the piece in London in the late 1960s'. An e-mail dated 31 March 2011 written by Craig Karch (Special Agent with Homeland Security Investigations) further described these two individuals as an academic and an art dealer—presumably Denver Art Museum consultant Emma Bunker and Douglas Latchford (Hauser-Schäublin 2016: 71). The prospective client must have pulled out of the purchase, because the statue was subsequently offered for auction. The catalogue entry written by Bunker made no mention of sightings in London during the late 1960s or any other evidence of a pre-1970 provenance. Clearly, if true, and no documentation was produced by Sotheby's to validate it, the claim of a pre-1970 provenance was not considered important enough for securing a sale or a good price to merit publication. In the event, the 1970 date had no material bearing on the court case. Sotheby's legal defence focused on the ambiguous nature of Cambodia's claim to ownership of the Duryodhana under its colonial and post-colonial law codes and the consequent US claim that the piece was stolen property (Hauser-Schäublin 2016: 73).

## Provenance and price

Evidence of an association between provenance and price is largely anecdotal, sometimes buttressed by the high prices that well-provenanced objects have achieved at auction (Brodie 2014a). More systematic confirmation of an association should be necessary before autoregulation is demonstrated to be an established process of market control and accepted into the policy toolkit. A few time-series analyses of large auction data sets have detected the appearance through the 2000s of a positive correlation between provenance and price, attributed either to the acceptance of the 1970 threshold (Kiel and Tedesco 2011) or to the deterrent impact of relevant court decisions on sales of specific categories of material (Beltrametti and Marrone 2016; Lobay 2009). But assessing the state of the destination market and imputing the operation of autoregulation to long-term auction data alone is a deceptive exercise. Auction sales comprise only a part of the antiquities market in both material and monetary terms, and auction prices can in any case be demonstrated to be determined by factors other than provenance.

Price data from Sotheby's New York has figured prominently in quantitative studies of the antiquities destination market. In Chapter 4, we demonstrated and discussed the increasing provision of provenance information in auction catalogues. For Sotheby's, it was associated with a decreasing number of lots being offered and sold but an increasing median price (Figure 6.1). On the face of it, this pattern is consistent with the operation of autoregulation, with progressively smaller numbers

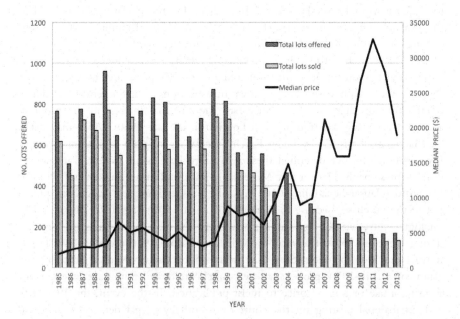

**FIGURE 6.1** Number of lots offered and sold annually at Sotheby's New York 'Antiquities' sales, plotted against the median price of sold lots. (All median prices in US dollars standardised to 2005).

of better-provenanced antiquities lots being sold for higher prices. But considering that pattern in a broader commercial context calls the interpretation into doubt. Autoregulation is not necessarily the explanatory process. Although in percentage terms the proportion of provenanced lots being offered annually at Sotheby's has increased, the actual number of provenanced lots being offered has held fairly steady. The increasing percentage of provenanced lots is because the number of lots being offered without provenance has declined dramatically (Figure 6.2).

Thus, Sotheby's has not been endeavouring to search out better-provenanced lots, or to publish more provenance information than was previously the case, it has simply stopped selling at public auction poorly-provenanced and unprovenanced lots. Nevertheless, Figure 6.3 shows that since the late 1990s, lots sold at Sotheby's Antiquities sales with a pre-1970 provenance have generally performed better than those with a 1970 or later provenance or no provenance at all. On the face of it, then, this appears to offer support to the idea that a 1970 threshold is affecting the price of objects sold at auction, as commentators have claimed.

However, Figure 6.4 breaks down the pre-1970 provenance class into three subsidiary components, and shows that over the same time period lots with a provenance stretching back to before 1946 have outperformed lots with a provenance dating back only to between 1946 and 1969. Since 2009, on average, lots with a provenance stretching back to before 1915 have commanded the highest prices at auction. Thus Figure 6.4 demonstrates that the relationship between provenance

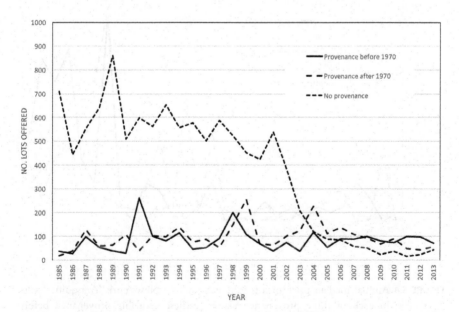

**FIGURE 6.2** Number of lots offered annually at Sotheby's New York 'Antiquities' sales in each of three provenance classes: earliest verifiable provenance before 1970; earliest verifiable provenance 1970 or later; no provenance.

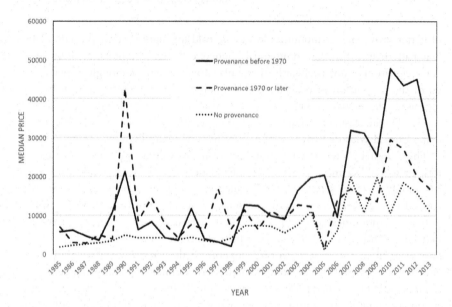

**FIGURE 6.3** Annual median price of lots sold at Sotheby's New York 'Antiquities' sales in each of three provenance classes: earliest verifiable provenance before 1970; earliest verifiable provenance 1970 or later; no provenance. (All median prices in US dollars standardised to 2005).

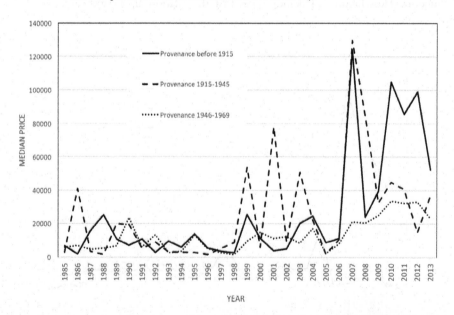

**FIGURE 6.4** Annual median price of lots sold at Sotheby's New York 'Antiquities' sales in each of three provenance classes: earliest verifiable provenance before 1915; earliest verifiable provenance between 1915 and 1945; earliest verifiable provenance between 1946 and 1969. (All median prices in US dollars standardised to 2005).

and price is not attributable to the 1970 threshold, but is instead a more general one. On average, since the late 1990s, lots with longer provenances have performed better at auction than lots with shorter provenances.

Figure 6.1 shows that from 2000 to 2013 the number of lots Sotheby's offered annually in its Antiquities sales dropped from about 600 to about 180 per year. Over the same time period, the annual (standardised) median price of sold lots increased from about $7500 to figures generally in excess of $17,000. Similar volume reductions and price increases at Sotheby's New York have been demonstrated for South American (Yates 2006), Cambodian (Davis 2011), Central Mexican (Levine and de Luna 2013) and Maya antiquities (Tremain 2017). Since 2000, Sotheby's is known to have shifted its business strategy up-market by making a conscious decision for all departments to sell a smaller number of higher-quality objects. Between 2002 and 2007, across the company, it halved the number of auction transactions and shed staff (Thompson 2008: 100). In 2004, New York-based antiquities dealer Jerome Eisenberg reported Sotheby's had announced that going forward the company would only accept antiquities or lots with a minimum value of $5000 (Eisenberg 2004: 25). This consistent picture of reduced sales volumes and increased prices across different categories of antiquities must reflect Sotheby's deliberate business strategy of moving up-market.

For antiquities after 2002, a progressively higher number of lots achieved prices higher than their pre-sale estimates, as shown in Figure 6.5. Sotheby's specialists are unlikely to be consistently and accidentally undervaluing material, and it seems

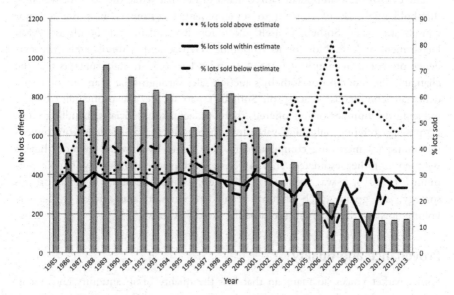

**FIGURE 6.5** Number of lots offered each year at Sotheby's New York 'Antiquities' sales, plotted against percentages of lots sold with prices above, within and below the range of pre-sale estimates.

more likely that estimates are being intentionally kept low to draw in potential buyers. 'Come-hither' estimates of this sort are an old-established auction device used to attract buyers ( Eisenberg 1995b: 28; Heath 2012: 215). Once the potential buyers are engaged in competitive bidding, the pre-sale estimates may cease to condition their willingness-to-pay.

Traditionally, auction houses profited from charging a seller's commission, effectively a service charge levied on a seller. In 1975, in addition to the seller's commission, both Sotheby's and Christie's began charging a buyer's premium—a service charge levied on a buyer. From 1975 to 1992 the buyer's premium remained steady at 10 per cent. From 1993, however, Sotheby's (and Christie's) began to increase it, and to charge proportionately more for lower-priced lots. By 2013, Sotheby's was charging a 25 per cent buyer's premium on prices up to $50,000, 20 per cent on prices between $50,000 and $1 million, and 12 per cent on prices in excess of $1 million. The auction houses have been forced to increase the buyer's premium because in a competitive marketplace they are vulnerable to potential consignors 'shopping around'. With auction houses keen to secure business, consignors can negotiate a deal to reduce or even dispense with seller's commission or to secure a performance guarantee (Gerlis 2016). In such circumstances, auction house costs then have to be recovered from the buyers, who are less willing or able to negotiate. Thus the patterning seen in the time-series auction data might be explained by Sotheby's changing its business model to increase profitability by attracting upmarket buyers and have nothing to do with company concerns about illicit antiquities.

The case of the Cambodian Duryodhana shows that while the 1970 provenance threshold might be of concern to some potential customers, it is not a major consideration for Sotheby's itself. Not for its Indian and Southeast Asian Department at least. Nor for its Antiquities Department. Cumulatively, the evidence presented in Figures 4.1 and 4.2, and 6.1 to 6.5, strongly suggests that the changing configuration of Sotheby's auction sales through time is an outcome of a deliberate commercial strategy on Sotheby's part to increase profitability by: (1) reducing the number of lots offered, thereby decreasing associated handling costs; (2) publicly offering only high-value lots, thereby increasing income from buyer's premiums; (3) increasing competition to raise prices by drawing in more buyers with come-hither estimates; and (4) charging buyers progressively higher premiums. In 2016, it was reported that Sotheby's might be about to abandon this strategy, and go in search of more reliable revenue streams offered by higher-volume lower-priced sales in the 'middle market' (Gerlis 2016).

## Provenance and quality

Some market voices do maintain that it is the quality of an antiquity and not its provenance that is the major determinant of price. Jasper Gaunt, curator of Greek and Roman art at the Michael C. Carlos Museum, has been quoted as saying that 'provenance is a crucial aspect that must be considered, but it is not the overriding factor. Beauty and importance are also significant: by far the most important aspect to consider when acquiring an object is the object itself' (Russell 2004). But it is difficult to disentangle the determining influences of quality and provenance upon price, more so perhaps because while provenance and price can be quantified for comparison, quality is a subjective attribute and resistant to objective measure.

Sometimes empirical support for autoregulation or more generally for the proposition that good provenance is a major determinant of price has been derived from exceptional performances at auction by objects with long provenances (Borodkin 1995; Gerstenblith 2012: 70–71; Brodie 2014d). In June 2007, for example, Sotheby's New York sold the 92 cm high Hellenistic bronze Artemis and the Stag for approximately $27 million. The Artemis had been acquired in 1953 by the Albright-Knox Art Gallery in Buffalo when reportedly it had been accompanied by an export licence from Italy (Gerstenblith 2012: 70–71). Not long after the Artemis sale, on 5 December 2007, Sotheby's New York sold the small, 8.3 cm high limestone Guennol Lioness, dating to between 3000 and 2800 BC, for just over $57 million. The Lioness had been found in Iraq and the catalogue entry stated that it was in the possession of New York dealer Joseph Brummer by 1931 and thus out of Iraq by the date of the country's 1936 patrimony law (Brodie and Kersel 2014: 199–200).

Both the Albright-Knox Artemis and the Guennol Lioness provide examples of how a long provenance traced back to either a licit or at least not obviously illicit acquisition can seemingly underpin an unusually high price at auction. But there are counter-examples. In April 2017, for example, at Christie's New York bids for the so-called Guennol Stargazer reached $14.5 million. The Stargazer is a 23 cm high third-millennium BC marble figurine from Turkey. The catalogue entry noted that it had been in the possession of Alastair Bradley and Edith Martin since 1966, but also that it was 'subject to a claim by the Republic of Turkey'. Turkey took antiquities into State ownership in 1906, and the circumstances of the Stargazer's discovery and export from Turkey are unknown, and therefore suspicious. Nevertheless, doubts concerning the provenance and even ownership of the Stargazer did not deter bidders on the day. Perhaps the questionable provenance did frighten some bidders and depress the price, but with a pre-sale estimate of $3–5 million the $14.5 million hammer sale price was surprising. The Turkish claim obviously did not dampen bidding.

The Christie's catalogue entry for the Guennol Stargazer dwelt upon the inspirational role played by such marble stargazer figurines for modern artists of the twentieth century, and a Christie's press release described it as 'one of the most impressive of its type known in existence'. The Sotheby's catalogue entry for the Guennol Lioness claimed it to be 'one of the oldest and most important works of ancient sculpture from the Near East in particular and the ancient world in general'. The catalogue entry for the Artemis did not highlight its artistic importance, but did develop its culture-historical context by reporting that it was 'designed for the eclectic and highly refined taste of the Roman art market in the late Republic or early Empire'. These catalogue entries referenced the high quality of the objects, judged either by aesthetic or artistic significance (formal properties of appearance, or 'beauty') in the cases of the Lioness or Stargazer, or art historical importance in the case of the Artemis (in relation to Roman culture) and the Stargazer (in relation to twentieth century art). For all three objects the auction houses were keen to impress upon bidders that the objects in question were of an unusually high quality. Thus for the Lioness and the Artemis, the exceptional price tags might be attached to their artistic significance, art historical importance, long provenance, or a combination of all three. For the Stargazer, perhaps a pre-1970 provenance was enough to calm customer concerns, because on the day the advertised Turkish interest in recovering the piece does not seem to have unduly worried the highest bidder. Arguably the bid reflected only the perceived high quality of the object because its provenance was questionable.

New York dealer Jerome Eisenberg accepted that the high price paid for the Guennol Lioness was probably because of its good provenance, but also suggested it might have been due to the attraction of 'American hedge-fund billionaires, Russian oligarchs, and Near Eastern rulers' to an 'undervalued field' (Eisenberg 2008). Eisenberg had already reported in 2005 on a sale at Christie's New York on 16 June 2006, when three Roman marble statues with provenances stretching back to the nineteenth and eighteenth centuries failed to sell. Eisenberg attributed the failure to the high pre-sale estimates published by Christie's, complaining that 'The catalogue is an excellent example of an over-reaction by the auction houses to all of the excessive fuss over provenance' (Eisenberg 2006: 44).

During the run-up to its 25 April 2017 New York Antiquities sale, Christie's specialist Laetitia Delaloye offered her thoughts on what determines the price of an antiquity (Delaloye 2017). First and foremost, she said, it is a matter of size— 'As a rule, larger pieces in good condition will sell for the highest prices, while smaller pieces are more likely to survive and are therefore more common on the market'. Then, obviously perhaps, she also highlighted the importance of condition—the extent to which a piece has been repaired or restored. A piece signed by the artist is good too, a possibility for the Attic pottery Delaloye was discussing. For provenance, she said it is the name or reputation of previous owners that is likely to add 'significant value' to a piece, and she did not mention any legal or ethical advantages of a pre-1970 provenance, or any positive effect that a pre-1970 provenance might exert upon price.

Delaloye's observation that size is important does not come as a surprise. It is known that the price of paintings correlates positively with size (Velthuis 2005: 103, 112), and a similar correlation has been observed for cuneiform tablets and cylinder seals (Brodie 2011a: 126–129, Figures 7.6 and 7.7). This association of size and price for antiquities of a single style or type is probably because larger objects are usually better quality examples of their type. So for cuneiform tablets a larger sized tablet will normally carry a longer inscription, which is likely to be of more scholarly interest than a shorter inscription. For cylinder seals and the Attic pottery discussed by Delaloye (and paintings), the increased surface area of a larger object allows more freedom of expression for the artist. Thus, within limits, size might be considered to be a proxy indicator of quality. As Delaloye put it, 'bigger is generally better'.

Delaloye's post was introducing the sale of a collection of Greek figure-decorated pottery from a 'Manhattan Private Collection', which included 15 Attic black-figure vessels. Lot 202 of that sale, a black-figure hydria, had an impeccable provenance that could be traced back to the collection of Reverend John Hamilton-Gray and Elizabeth Caroline Hamilton-Gray, which had been sold at auction at Sotheby's London in 1888. Lot 206, a trefoil oinochoe, also had a long provenance, first seen at the Paris-based auction house Hôtel Drouot in 1903 and featured in several publications since then. Alongside these two vessels with a published provenance that could be traced back to before 1910, lot 207 had been first published in 1962, six vessels had been first published later than 1970, and six had not been published at all. Figure 6.6 plots the price of each vessel sold against its maximum dimension. In graphic confirmation of Delaloye's prediction, there is a strong correlation between size and price. The three largest vessels achieved the three highest prices, and not one of those three vessels had a published provenance that could be traced back to before 1970.

In this data set, then, size, and therefore, arguably, quality, is without doubt the primary determinant of price. As regards provenance, there is a suggestion that when compared to vessels of similar size, the well-provenanced lots 202 and 206 performed better than their more poorly-provenanced counterparts, but not well enough to overturn Delaloye's accurate prediction, born out of experience, that at the end of the day it is size that matters. This correlation between size and price is more generally demonstrable. Figure 6.7 plots the price of each single ceramic

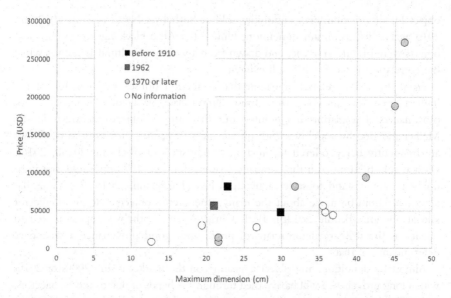

**FIGURE 6.6** Plot of price against vessel size for Attic figure-decorated pottery sold by auction at Christie's New York on 25 April 2017, showing the strong correlation between price and size. (All prices in US dollars, all sizes in centimetres).

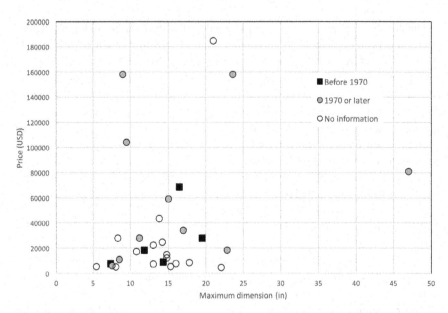

**FIGURE 6.7** Plot of price against vessel size for all lots comprising a single ceramic Precolumbian object sold at Sotheby's New York in 2012 and 2013, showing the correlation between price and size. (All prices in US dollars, all sizes in inches).

object lot of Precolumbian antiquities sold at Sotheby's New York in 2012 and 2013 against its maximum dimension. Unlike the Attic black-figure vessels, these objects were of different types and drawn from a variety of cultural styles, yet while the correlation is weaker it is still evident.

From this evidence, it is apparent that if auction houses are keen to sell the highest-price lots possible, they must discriminate in favour of quality, not provenance. Tsirogiannis has pointed out that suspect objects identified in the Medici and Becchina archives with provenances stretching back only to the 1980s are frequently being offered for auction at Christie's (Tsirogiannis 2015b, 2016). Most would be stopped if the company would adopt the 1970 threshold, but in so doing it would stand to suffer a financial loss (Tsirogiannis 2016: 70). A similar argument could be made about the many other stolen objects that are offered for sale at auction (Brodie 2014b). Both Christie's and Sotheby's appear to regard quality as the primary determinant of price, with good provenance a secondary determinant—if that.

Almost by definition, any object appearing on the market in the 2000s or 2010s with a long provenance will have passed through the hands of one or more collectors, and will therefore have been subject to the filtering effects of their tastes and budgets (Nørskov 2002: 301–311). Successive collectors will have chosen 'good' quality objects and rejected 'poor' quality ones. The longer an object has been in circulation, the more prolonged and cumulative this filtering will have been. Thus, it should be expected *a priori* that on average objects coming to market with a long provenance will be of higher artistic or art historical significance than objects with only a short provenance, and it should in consequence be no surprise when good quality, high-priced objects have a long provenance. It is not the length of provenance in itself that is setting price, but the perceived quality of the objects, as endorsed by their collecting histories and associated scholarship. The apparent correlation of provenance and price shown in Figure 6.4 does not establish a causal association. The correlation reflects the discriminating agency of successive collectors and their quest for quality, not the ethical or financial qualms of present-day purchasers.

To the extent that quality assessment is inter-subjective, it is possible that attributions of artistic or art historical importance might accrete, so that in effect the quality of an object is something that can be created, agreed, recognized or discovered and thus improve over time. It is also the case that the reputation of a previous owner might in itself add to the market value of a piece, either because of the owner's celebrity, which might add associative lustre, or because of high regard for the owner's taste, which would then act as a proxy judgement or imprimatur of quality. If this view of quality as a consensual product is correct, then the quality of objects only recently arrived on the market might be better considered as uncertain than as poor, and that it is customer uncertainty over quality that is depressing prices rather than concern over illicit trade. A previous high price in itself, might also render an object desirable for conspicuous acquisition by payment of a further high price, the so-called Veblen effect (Velthuis 2005: 104-107). Again, this would be a provenance-related effect based more upon a purchaser's desire for social positioning than avoiding a stolen or trafficked object.

## The internet market and the invisible market

In terms of material volume, auction sales comprise only a small part of the destination market for antiquities. Alongside auction houses, there is a thriving trade to be seen on the internet, there are physical sales galleries, and the intimate settings of the commercial circuits described in Chapter 4. As already described in Chapter 4, provenance provision for antiquities sold on the internet is minimal at best. Yet on the internet poorly-provenanced and unprovenanced objects consistently command higher prices than objects with a pre-1970 provenance. Table 6.A provides statistics for Precolumbian objects sold on the internet over the years 2012 and 2013, with statistics from Sotheby's New York included for comparative purposes. For internet dealers and auctioneers, lots with a post-1970 provenance consistently outperformed lots in other provenance classes. There is no evidence for autoregulation of internet sales.

It is well-documented that some high-profile, illicitly-traded objects have broken price records when first sold, albeit through private transactions and not at public auction (Nørskov 2002: 291-2). Thus, it must be remembered that recently trafficked, good quality objects might be sold away from the public gaze, and that the likely operation of autoregulation cannot be assessed from auction data alone. In Chapter 4, we characterised the destination market as a circuit of commerce,

**TABLE 6A** Earliest verifiable provenance, median maximum diameter and median price of single ceramic lots of Precolumbian material offered and sold during 2012 and 2013 (after Brodie 2014c: 258, table 13.6)

|  | Earliest provenance | No lots offered | No lots sold | Percen- tage lots sold | Median size (ins) | Median price (USD) |
|---|---|---|---|---|---|---|
| Internet dealers | Pre-1970 | 179 | 7 | 4 | 4.7 | 353 |
|  | 1970 or later | 16 | 8 | 50 | 10.5 | 2600 |
|  | None | 1,249 | 472 | 38 | 7.3 | 750 |
| Internet auctions | Pre-1970 | 45 | 36 | 80 | 8.2 | 368 |
|  | 1970 or later | 96 | 80 | 83 | 9.5 | 738 |
|  | None | 190 | 109 | 57 | 7.5 | 450 |
| Sotheby's | Pre-1970 | 9 | 5 | 56 | 14.3 | 18,750 |
|  | 1970 or later | 13 | 10 | 77 | 13.1 | 46,875 |
|  | None | 21 | 15 | 71 | 14.2 | 12,500 |

where deals might be arranged in intimate social gatherings far removed from the commercial premises of auction houses such as Sotheby's or Christie's, and noted the increasing importance of art fairs for contriving such occasions. Nørskov (2002: 291–292) characterised these private sales as comprising an 'invisible market', pointing out that the invisible market had been in the past the source of many important museum acquisitions, and that the prices agreed in many of these invisible transactions were higher than anything achieved at auction.

In October 2011, the Asian art dealer Subhash Kapoor was arrested in Germany and in July 2012 extradited to India on charges relating to the trafficking of antiquities (Brodie 2019). Kapoor was proprietor of the sales gallery Art of the Past, in New York City. The case against Kapoor in India hinged upon the theft between 2006 and 2008 of eleventh to twelfth century Chola period bronze idols from temples in the towns of Suthamalli and Sripuranthan, in the state of Tamil Nadu. Following Kapoor's arrest in Germany, starting in January 2012, US Immigration and Customs Enforcement (ICE), Homeland Security Investigation (HSI) agents launched a series of raids on Kapoor's gallery and associated storage facilities in New York City, seizing business records and material stock. Customs, journalists and individual investigators identified objects from the temple thefts in several private and museum collections, which were subsequently returned to India. From these investigations and seizures, something is known about the prices paid by museums and private collectors in private transactions for recently stolen and trafficked objects. Table 6B lists the prices paid to Kapoor between 2006 and 2008 for four of the stolen objects. Figure 6.8 plots in ascending order of magnitude the prices paid for these objects together with prices paid for comparable Indian objects at Sotheby's New York over the same period. The four

Kapoor objects, coloured black on the chart, were amongst the highest priced, with the Shiva Nataraja, bought by the National Gallery of Australia in 2008 for $5 million being the most expensive.

Interestingly, the two objects coloured white on the chart and interleaved with the Kapoor objects were deaccessioned from the Albright-Knox Art Gallery (at the same time as the Artemis and the Stag discussed previously) and sold at the Sotheby's Indian and Southeast Asian sale of March 2007. Lot 26 was a Chola copper alloy figure of Saint Sambandar, sold for $408,000, acquired by the Albright-Knox in 1937 from the Heeramaneck Galleries in New York. Lot 27 was a Chola granite figure of Shiva and Brahma, sold for $4,072,000, which had been with dealer C.T. Loo in New York in 1927 before being acquired by the museum. If Kapoor had not been arrested and information relating to his business practices had remained secret, no doubt the Albright-Knox objects would be proposed as examples of how a good provenance helps determine a high price, as has happened with the previously discussed case of the Albright-Knox Artemis and Stag. But with the inclusion of the Kapoor objects transacted on the invisible market, the argument is rendered specious.

## The effect of suspect provenance on saleability and price

There are several well-known private collections of largely unprovenanced high-quality objects that have been assembled over the past twenty or thirty years (Chippindale and Gill 2000), including some collections that are openly suspected of containing stolen and trafficked objects. If good provenance is a determinant of price, then it would be expected that the prices of such suspect objects would be depressed at auction. This seems not to be the case.

On 15 October 2008, for example, the London auction house Bonhams offered material from the collection of Graham Geddes. Geddes, described by Bonhams as 'Australia's foremost dealer and collector' (Rountree 2008: 43), had built up his collection from the 1970s onwards. The Bonhams sale was intended to comprise 193 lots, but the day before auction the Italian authorities informed Bonhams that 10 of the antiquities offered for sale probably derived from illegal digs conducted during the 1970s, and Bonhams subsequently withdrew 13 lots

**TABLE 6B** Prices paid to Kapoor for objects stolen from Suthamalli and Sripuranthan temples. (All prices in US dollars)

| Date | Object | Purchaser | Price ($) |
|------|--------|-----------|-----------|
| February 2008 | Shiva Nataraja | National Gallery of Australia | 5 million |
| March 2006 | Manickavasagar | Private collector | 650,000 |
| 2007 | Uma Parameshvari | Singapore Asian Civilisations Museum | 650,000 |
| May 2006 | Ganesha | Toledo Museum of Art | 245,000 |

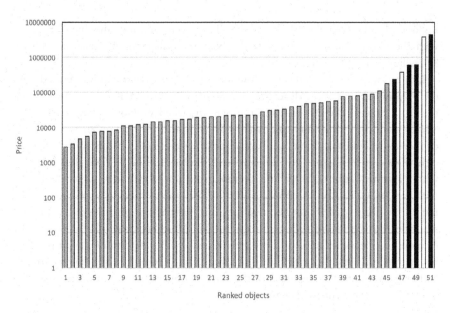

**FIGURE 6.8** Ranked order plot of prices achieved by Indian objects sold at Sotheby's New York Indian and Southeast Asian sales between 2006 and 2008, together with prices of four Kapoor objects listed in Table 6B. Sotheby's objects comprise all sold stone and metal figural objects dating to between 700 AD and 1300 AD. Sotheby's objects are coloured grey and white, Kapoor objects coloured black. (All prices in US dollars standardised to 2005).

from auction (Squires 2008). On the day of the sale, 120 of the remaining 180 lots sold. The auction catalogue included 52 lots of Classical Greek or South Italian figure-decorated pottery. Seven of the lots were among those withdrawn at the request of the Italians, and five failed to sell. None of the 40 lots that actually sold had a long provenance, they were all post-1970, but the vessels comprising the lots could be divided into two provenance groups according to their place of purchase.

Geddes had acquired the first group, 17 lots in total, at Sotheby's London in the 1980s. Large numbers of unprovenanced Classical Greek and South Italian vessels that were sold at Sotheby's London in the 1980s and early 1990s are now known to have been consigned by the convicted dealer Giacomo Medici (Watson 1997; Watson and Todeschini 2007). By 2008, it should have been common knowledge in the collecting and trade communities that any South Italian or Classical Greek vessel with a provenance dating back only to a Sotheby's auction during the 1980s or 1990s had quite possibly been excavated and traded illegally.

The second group of pottery comprised 23 lots Geddes had acquired from other sources. Thus, if good provenance is a primary concern of collectors, it would be expected that lots with an obviously suspect provenance (those bought at

Sotheby's), would perform less well than those with a seemingly better provenance (those not bought at Sotheby's). Table 6C shows that in terms of mean price the Sotheby's group performed better than the Not-Sotheby's group, and thus there is no evidence of customers discriminating against the Sotheby's vessels on account of suspect provenance.

**TABLE 6C** The mean price of Greek and South Italian figure-decorated pottery from the Graham Geddes collection offered for sale at Bonhams London on 15 October 2008. (All prices in GB pounds).

| Provenance group | Mean price |
| --- | --- |
| Sotheby's | 11,343 |
| Not Sotheby's | 7,341 |

On 20 November 2016, Christian McCann Auctions of Melbourne, Australia offered for sale the fine and decorative art collection of Stewart Macciolli. The collection included a range of Classical Greek and South Italian pottery, including five of the vessels that had been withdrawn by Bonhams in 2008. Presumably the Italian authorities had not reclaimed them and they had been returned to their consignor. None of the provenance entries for the Christian McCann auction made mention of the 2008 Bonhams catalogue or the Italian objection. Despite the questionable provenance of the originally-withdrawn vessels, prices held up well. Table 6D compares the prices achieved at Christian McCann with the 2008 Bonhams estimates. Direct comparison is potentially misleading because of the lapsed interval of time, but still, there is little evidence of questionable provenance having a serious negative impact on price, as is often claimed. Perhaps buyers in Melbourne in 2016 were unaware of events in London in 2008 because the actors involved were careful to keep them secret. Or perhaps the buyers just didn't care about the possibility that what they were buying had been trafficked. Either way, it is difficult to discern the hidden hand of autoregulation in such circumstances.

**TABLE 6D** Prices achieved by four vessels sold at the 2016 Christian McCann auction compared to Bonhams estimates for the same vessels in 2008. (All prices in US dollars, standardised to 2005).

| Christian McCann lot number | Christian McCann price | Bonhams estimate |
| --- | --- | --- |
| 331 | 21,287 | 29,120–40,040 |
| 335 | 9,579 | 11,830–17,290 |
| 336 | 3,784 | 2,275–3,458 |
| 337 | 5,440 | 2,275–3,458 |

## A discourse heavy with creative compliance

In this chapter we have used long-term and aggregate sales data to examine and reject claims that it is in the financial interest of the destination market to clean itself of trafficked objects. We have argued instead that trafficked objects continue to be sold for good prices while incriminating information about their sources is suppressed, thereby sanitising discourse about the market rather than the market itself. This might perhaps be seen as another form of creative compliance, as we discussed in Chapter 5. In the following chapter, we continue this line of thinking about types of regulation and their prospects for success in the antiquities trade.

# 7

# REGULATION, SELF-REGULATION AND ETHICAL CONSUMPTION MARKETS

In Chapter 3, we introduced and discussed four modalities of crime reduction: situational, social, legal, and economic. We considered the difficulties facing legal invocations of the criminal justice system, particularly the problem of proving dishonest intent. In this chapter, we look at another aspect of the legal approach, examining how object recovery actions are used as a restorative but also possibly deterrent response to the antiquities trade. We also consider the application of normative or ethical derivatives of legal controls through self-regulation. But we continue to recognise that within the wider regulatory context, law plays only one part in controlling the illicit antiquities trade. Thus we will combine our reflections on white-collar crime in Chapter 5 with the core imperatives of our discussion of the economic and social modes of crime prevention in Chapter 3 to present in the second half of this chapter a discussion of what an ethical consumption market might look like for the antiquities trade, and how it might be encouraged and enforced. In so doing, we move beyond a strict prescriptive view of what regulation might entail, and introduce ideas of how negotiation and compromise might encourage voluntary participation in a demonstrably licit antiquities market—one that might discourage and even actively work against illicit trade. Our proposition in this regard takes forward the discussion of information in the market which we introduced in Chapter 4, suggesting how market transparency might be improved without encroaching upon the personal and commercial confidentiality of legitimate market actors.

## Recovering stolen and trafficked antiquities

Alongside criminal prosecution, another commonly-used legal approach to the illicit trade is the recovery of looted and trafficked objects through civil (private) law actions or customs seizure and forfeiture. The advantage of such methods over criminal law is that the standard of proof is lower. Instead of a need to prove guilt 'beyond reasonable doubt', as is usual in criminal proceedings, lawful ownership is decided on a 'balance of probabilities'. There is no need to prove the dishonest intent of suspected offenders, though problems of evidence remain, and different countries have different rules for securing title through honest transaction or possession. Nevertheless, it is easier to recover stolen or trafficked material for return to a dispossessed owner than it is to convict criminal actors and disrupt criminal trading networks.

The recovery of a trafficked antiquity can be viewed as an exercise in asset confiscation—an attempt to deter criminal action through sequestering financial proceeds. There are also good cultural reasons for recovering trafficked antiquities that are not directly related to the deterrent effect of monetary loss. Sometimes the return of a trafficked antiquity can help restore the damage caused by its looting or theft. The repatriation of the Duryodhana to Cambodia, for example, discussed in Chapter 5, was associated with the return of related pieces from Christie's auction house, the Metropolitan Museum of Art, the Norton Simon Museum, and the Cleveland Museum of Art. They are believed to have been forcibly removed from the temple complex of Koh Ker in Preah Vihear Province sometime during the 1970s. Their original placements are known and so in theory the original architectural complex could be restored (Hauser-Schäublin 2016: 67, Figure 3.1). The recovery of stolen and trafficked antiquities can also be justified for political or historical reasons. The high-profile acquisition and display of what are commonly believed to be looted antiquities by foreign museums and collectors can be viewed by a source country or community as a flagrant violation of its sovereignty and a material and very visible expression of its lack of international influence or respect. The return of such an object can offer symbolic recognition of a source country or community's right to cultural self-determination and for formerly colonized states it might help foster a process of reconciliation for wrongs committed during colonial rule (Lee 2017: 172; O'Keefe 2017: 9–10).

There have been some successful civil recovery actions. In 1987, for example, as we have mentioned previously, Turkey initiated civil proceedings in New York to reclaim the so-called Lydian Hoard. The Lydian Hoard, also called the Karun Treasure and the Croesus Treasure, comprised more than 360 precious antiquities dating to the sixth century BC that had been illegally excavated in the Uşak Province of Turkey in the 1960s before being acquired by the Metropolitan Museum of Art between 1966 and 1970. In 1993, in an out-of-court settlement, the Metropolitan agreed to return the material to Turkey (Kaye 2014: 189–192). But civil recovery actions can be expensive because of the legal costs involved (Kaye 2014: 191; O'Keefe 2007: 242). Bipartite negotiation or voluntary return offer cheaper options. For another Turkish example, in 2012 the country recovered a second-century AD mosaic of Orpheus from the Dallas Museum of Art through negotiation. Turkish police had obtained photographic evidence showing it to have been illegally excavated in Şanlıurfa Province in 1998 before its sale at Christie's New York in December 1999 (Kuşseven and Yilmaz 2014).

Destination market countries can help shoulder the financial burden of recovery through seizure and forfeiture of demonstrably stolen material or of material traded in violation of customs laws, usually involving false declaration of material or origin, or breaking nationally or internationally agreed trade controls. In February 2009, for example, the United Kingdom returned to Afghanistan more than 1,500 antiquities weighing together 3.4 tons. These had been seized by Her Majesty's Revenue and Customs during random searches of the luggage of incoming passengers from Pakistan and the United Arab Emirates made from 2002 to 2004 at London's Heathrow airport (Peters 2009). Most of the antiquities had been illegally excavated and exported. However, notifications of success such as this one are sporadic, leading to suspicions that for antiquities, customs laws are unevenly enforced, probably because antiquities are considered low priority alongside more politically-sensitive goods such as drugs and arms.

Police and customs recovery actions can be aided by targeted trade controls imposed by national implementations of international instruments such as the 1970 UNESCO Convention. In the US, Articles 7(b) and 9 of the UNESCO Convention were implemented in 1983 as the Convention on Cultural Property Implementation Act (CCPIA). CCPIA allows the US to impose import controls unilaterally on material from countries suffering from antiquities theft or looting in the form of emergency import restrictions, or as part of a more wide-ranging bilateral agreement at the request of an antiquities source country. In 2016 Germany strengthened its implementation of the 1970 UNESCO Convention with the Kulturgutschutzgesetz (Cultural Property Protection Act) that places import controls on material from other States Parties to the Convention. United Nations Security Council Resolutions (UNSCRs) have also place trade controls on material from Iraq (UNSCR 661 and 1483) and Syria (UNSCR 2199).

Despite the apparent success of customs actions aimed at recovering material for customs violations or other trade-related offences, they have been criticized for encouraging a policy of 'recovery and return' (Brodie 2015c: 324–326) or 'seize and send' (St Hilaire 2016), whereby customs and other law enforcement agencies prioritise the recovery and return of antiquities to their country of origin over the investigation and prosecution of criminals engaged in trafficking. In the Heathrow seizures, for example, the fact that more than 1,500 objects were discovered in the luggage of incoming air passengers suggests a substantial number of individual interceptions of people passing through customs, but the police reported not securing a single conviction (Lamb 2006). Presumably any criminals involved were left free to continue offending.

The material recovered through customs seizures is often (though not always) of variable quality and of little intrinsic monetary value or scientific interest, so that the cultural arguments justifying recovery at the expense of criminal prosecution might not apply. An expert working with the National Museum of Afghanistan, for example, reported that something like 90 per cent of the objects recovered at Heathrow were of limited importance and would not be placed on display (Peters

2009). Unlike the Cambodian Koh Ker pieces, which were looted from above the ground, the recovery and return of objects obtained at source through clandestine excavation does not and cannot repair the damage caused by that excavation, no more than the return of a few shards of glass can repair a broken window. The argument that the financial loss caused by such recoveries deters future trafficking is also hard to sustain for such low-value material. The seizure of major pieces from market actors worried as much about reputational as financial harm might exert a deterrent effect—Sotheby's, for example, may have become more circumspect about offering poorly-provenanced Cambodian objects since it was caught offering the Cambodian Duryodhana. But for many traders, particularly less-public ones with only limited reputational capital who deal in large quantities of low-value objects, the occasional loss of material through customs seizure can be accepted as a cost of doing business to be factored into the pricing arrangement. Criminal traders are left at large to continue offending. Thus, the cultural benefit or deterrent effect of recovering material does not always outweigh the harmful consequences of failing to disrupt ongoing illicit trade. St Hilaire (2016: 3) points to the political overtones of customs recoveries when he quotes US Immigration and Customs Enforcement (ICE): 'Returning a nation's looted cultural heritage or stolen artworks, promotes goodwill with foreign governments and citizens, while significantly protecting the world's cultural heritage and knowledge of past civilisations'. In such circumstances, the imposition and enforcement of customs regulations and other trade controls can be viewed as another example of performative regulation as discussed in Chapter 5. The appearance of taking action is more important than the material outcome of the action.

## Self-regulation

Although the recovery of trafficked material through civil or customs actions has become a dominant regulatory response to the illicit trade in antiquities, it does not exhaust all regulatory options. Such actions can be characterized as examples of 'command and control' regulation—government-imposed rules governing commercial practice established by law and backed by penalties for non-compliance. Another option is to promote commercial self-regulation, whereby market actors pledge to adhere to certain self-imposed standards of practice. For the destination market, antiquities trade organisations and associations advertise self-regulation through their codes of practice or ethics, but the content of these codes can be criticised. Their wording is sometimes ambiguous and open to misinterpretation, and due diligence advice is poorly developed. Standards of compliance are also open to question.

The International Association of Dealers in Ancient Art (IADAA) provides a good example of such a code, and of the uncertainties surrounding content and compliance. The IADAA is regarded by itself and by other market actors as the premier trade association and publishes its Code of Ethics and Practice on its website. Article 2 of the Code states that:

> The Members of IADAA undertake not to purchase or sell objects until they have established to the best of their ability that such objects were not stolen from excavations, architectural monuments, public institutions or private property.

It is not clear from this text whether objects 'stolen from excavations' should be taken to mean objects 'obtained through clandestine and illegal excavation', or 'stolen from already-established, legitimate excavations'. The distinction is an important one, because many if not most unprovenanced antiquities in circulation on the destination market derive from clandestine excavations. If Article 2 of the Code is not regarded by members as applying to clandestine excavations, then the Code cannot be considered to comprise a regulatory instrument as conventionally understood by the international community as it would not prohibit trade in looted antiquities. It is not clear either whether or not the prohibition is time-limited. In other words, does the code consider stolen antiquities to be 'laundered' or legitimized for commerce after a period of time in open circulation? The text makes no such reservation, though in Chapter 6, for example, we described how Christie's auction house has adopted a series of what are, from a legal perspective, arbitrary date thresholds, designed to separate, what are for Christie's, acceptable consignments from unacceptable ones. Christie's does not seem overly concerned to establish that antiquities were not 'stolen from excavations', whatever that might mean.

The stipulation in Article 2 of the IAADA Code for dealers to exert themselves to the 'best of their ability' is also vague. There are attached Due Diligence Guidelines, but they contain no requirement to establish a full account of legitimate provenance from the time of an antiquity's modern discovery, thereby ensuring an object was not stolen, asking only that a member should obtain a signed and dated form from a vendor testifying to lawful ownership. Again, given the known legal mechanisms for acquiring title to stolen property, this requirement does more to protect the dealer from knowingly transacting in stolen property than it does to prevent the dealer from unknowingly transacting in stolen property. Looking closely at what dealers say about a licit antiquities trade, it seems that they base their understanding of 'licit' on knowability. The antiquities trade is licit because dealers are not knowingly transacting in trafficked objects, and therefore should not be considered offenders in any normal criminal sense. The limits of knowability of course are set close by the commercial practices of the trade itself, which restrict information flow and obstruct due diligence and provenance research.

We have mentioned the concept of 'due diligence' at several points in this book. In the context of the antiquities market due diligence describes the process of search and discovery undertaken by a prospective buyer before agreeing a purchase (Prott 1997: 46–51). It is, in effect, an information search. Throughout the 2000s and later, increasingly more rigorous standards of due diligence were developed for the antiquities market, such as the Due Diligence Guidelines introduced by the

IADAA. These guidelines were thought necessary because of hardening regulatory and criminal justice environments (Ulph in press). Due diligence has also been an issue for the larger art market, though for different reasons. By the 2010s, economic crimes such as insider trading, tax evasion and money laundering were beginning to undermine public confidence in the propriety of the art market, and questions were being asked about the need for regulation to improve market transparency (Reyburn 2015; Macquisten 2016). But although guidelines such as those produced by IADAA point towards the increasing salience of due diligence for destination market actors, whether out of self-interest or not, and aim to increase market transparency internally, there are no requirements to make antiquities provenance information available to external actors, except for meeting legal obligations to comply with law enforcement. This sharpens the distinction between published provenance and documented provenance noted in Chapter 4 (Levine 2009: 229–232), with more rigorous due diligence increasing the availability and quality of documented provenance, but not that of published provenance. The dealership Phoenix Ancient Art, for example, has stated that 'it is acceptable and common practice, for obvious competitive reasons, to omit all but the last decade of ownership in publishing a history, provided that the previous ownership has been satisfactorily established' (Aboutaam and Aboutaam 2004). As we show in the case study appendix to this book, published provenance may omit information about tainted transactions present in the documented provenance (Tsirogiannis 2015b), thereby sanitising ownership history and warding off unwelcome attention and investigation. But withholding provenance information also raises the suspicion and scepticism of critics and other outside observers that the antiquities trade has 'something to hide'.

Perhaps the most problematic aspect of self-regulation, however, is the fact that members of antiquities trade associations are frequently exposed either engaging in criminal acts or, more often, transacting in what is subsequently shown to be stolen material in apparent violation of their professed standards of practice. The IADAA claims 'Our members adhere to the highest professional standards as set out in our stringent code of ethics'. However, among its founding members in 1993 (IADAA 1993) were Frederick Schultz, who in 2003 was convicted in the US, after appeal, of federal offences relating to the theft and trafficking of antiquities from Egypt (Gerstenblith 2002, 2003); the Merrin Gallery, whose proprietor Edward Merrin was convicted in the US in 2007 of federal charges of defrauding clients (Kaufman 2007); and Michael Ward, who in 1993 was caught in possession of the trafficked Aidonia Treasure (subsequently returned to the ownership of Greece). Through the 2000s and 2010s, other members of the IADAA were discovered selling objects that could be sourced to the convicted dealers Giacomo Medici and Gianfranco Becchina (Tsirogiannis 2013a, 2015b). It is always possible that these publicly-recognised legal or ethical infractions were in fact exceptions to the general rule that IADAA members conduct their businesses in a lawful and ethical manner. It might equally be argued, however, that the known infractions are the tip of a much larger iceberg of malpractice that remains hidden from view.

There are good reasons for antiquities market actors to keep quiet about ethical violations. In the first place, such reticence would seem necessary to prevent reputational harm, to an individual dealer, an association, or the antiquities trade generally. But more broadly, trade associations view themselves and are viewed by governments and other policy-making organisations as legitimate stakeholders entitled to a seat at the table when any decisions are taken about market governance. If ethical non-compliance was demonstrably routine, this perceived legitimacy would evaporate. More insidiously, it allows trade associations to resist calls for the design and implementation of stronger 'command and control' regulation, insisting that the destination market is already self-regulated and reasonably free of trafficked antiquities, even though there is no mechanism for independent verification of those claims. This discussion of self-regulation has focused on the IADAA, which is, to repeat, generally regarded even by its critics as the most principled trade association. In the broader destination marketplace, it is commonplace to see traders banding together into dubious 'associations', no doubt aimed at reassuring potential customers about the probity of member dealers and the legitimacy and authenticity of their stock. The nature of self-regulation among some of these associations can only be guessed at.

Ultimately, the credibility of antiquities trade self-regulation is fatally undermined by its demonstrable failures and the absence of any means of external audit. The operation of self-regulation is not visible and not open to assessment by outside observers. In Chapter 4, we proposed that the destination market can be conceived as a mutually-engaged circulation of money, material and information, but argued that information is a closely guarded resource. Recovery actions and self-regulation are ostensibly aimed at diminishing the quantity of illicit antiquities in circulation, but not so much at increasing information availability and market transparency. Another regulatory option therefore would be to remove barriers obstructing the free circulation of information, both within and without the antiquities market. In other words, regulation could be designed and adopted that would improve market transparency both internally and externally. For example, it could be made mandatory for dealers to publish everything that is known about an object's ownership history, without suppressing any incriminating information, thereby allowing a good-faith customer to be more careful and discriminating about purchases. In Chapters 1 and 4 we described several legitimate reasons why information is a restricted commodity on the destination market. Dealers might want to keep the identity of a source secret to avoid attracting the attention of competing dealers, or to prevent questioning of their profit margins. Sellers might have good personal reasons for wanting to keep their identities secret, particularly with regard to their financial affairs. But there are also some less-than-legitimate reasons for withholding provenance-related information, such as when it helps suppress or disguise evidence of theft or illicit trade and provides plausible deniability about the provenance of trafficked antiquities to forestall criminal investigation. A credible and effective system of regulation would need to reconcile these apparently incompatible policy goals of increasing transparency while protecting confidentiality.

## Beyond self-regulation, autoregulation, and traditional legal regulation: meta-regulation and the possibility of an ethical consumption market

Recovery actions conceived and implemented within the legal mode of crime reduction draw largely upon a set of principles and procedures first developed by the 1970 UNESCO Convention. The Convention can be characterized as prescriptive, in that it sets out a series of conditions States Parties are expected to meet upon joining. These conditions are largely concerned with establishing and maintaining the necessary human and material capacity for protecting cultural heritage from theft or looting, and implementing the Convention's requirements for preventing illicit trade and effecting the recovery of illicitly-traded objects. The 1970 UNESCO Convention provides the foundation for a series of subsequently clarifying and strengthening laws and normative recommendations such as the 1995 Unidroit Convention on Stolen or Illegally Exported Cultural Objects and the 2001 UNESCO Convention on the Protection of Underwater Cultural Heritage, and thus for the legal approach more generally. The Convention is often described as 'standard setting', but might also less charitably be considered as an example of 'command and control' regulation—a regulatory instrument expressing the will of the international community through a prescriptive series of 'dos and don'ts'. There is only limited consideration in the Convention of actions that might be taken within what we have identified as the social and economic modalities of crime reduction, and they are largely concerned with awareness-raising. Perhaps the prescriptive nature of the UNESCO Convention is simply a sign of the time of its formulation and adoption. Since its adoption in 1970, a more nuanced body of regulatory theory and practice has developed, for white-collar crime in particular, which treats people as responsible citizens rather than criminal offenders and moves away from draconian expressions of 'command and control'. Persuasion and negotiation might have a greater deterrent effect than the elusive threat of punishment (Chappell and Polk 2011: 106–111). It is here that the social and economic modes of crime reduction come into to their own.

Critics of an overly legal and prescriptive approach to trade control have long objected that it merely acts to drive the trade underground and create a black market (Bator 1983: 41–43). The usual retort is that the antiquities trade is largely underground anyway, or least must be considered 'grey' because of the considerable information asymmetries that exist, as we explained in Chapter 2. Nevertheless, from a grey market perspective, an alternative strategy to suppressing a diffuse and intentionally disguised illicit trade would be to encourage the development of a demonstrably licit one by differentiating the grey trade into its black and white constituent parts. It is a move that might be welcomed by some antiquities traders, who have long sought to gain acceptance for the idea of separate licit and illicit trades, or have argued that the trade is largely licit though tainted by the presence of a few 'rotten apples' (Ede 2014; Eisenberg 1995a: 216). As leading London dealer James Ede once wrote, 'This attempt to unify the whole trade [as illicit] has as much validity as grouping back street abortionists with the consultants at Guys Hospital' (Ede 1995: 211). Yet if the antiquities trade is by its very nature grey, it does just that—it fails to distinguish between knowingly criminal actors and those struggling to do the right thing. As we saw with self-regulation, the problem is one of transparency.

We have argued in this chapter that neither command and control regulation nor self-regulation has succeeded in suppressing the flow of trafficked antiquities onto the destination market. We have further argued that self-regulation is not credible because of poor market transparency and the absence of any independent oversight. Between the two polarities of (strong) command and control regulation and (weak) self-regulation, however, there are intermediate control strategies that can be grouped together under the heading of meta-regulation (Baldwin et al. 2010: 8–9; Coglianese and Mendelson 2010) or enforced self-regulation (Ayres and Braithwaite 1992: 101–132), which have not been tested for their utility in reducing antiquities trafficking.

The essence of a meta-regulatory control strategy is to strengthen self-regulation through oversight and enforcement by a designated third party, thus reducing the opportunity for non-compliance. The third party would comprise what Ayres and Braithwaite (1992: 54–57) term a public interest group—a group or organization recognized as representing the constituency at risk of harm from the business in question. Following up Ede's medical analogy, for example, the activities of consultants at Guys are overseen and regulated by the General Medical Council (GMC), while those of back street abortionists are not. The GMC describes itself as 'an independent organisation that helps to protect patients and improve medical education and practice across the UK' (www.gmc-uk.org/about/role.asp). It has a senior management team drawn from outside the medical profession, working in conjunction with a council containing 50 per cent medical practitioners. Patients are reassured by GMC oversight to choose Guys over the back street. There is no comparable body to oversee the antiquities trade and to ensure and be seen to ensure that its harmful externalities are minimised. Thus, unintentionally perhaps, Ede's analogy highlights the need for independent oversight of professional practice and the lack of any such provision for the antiquities trade. For dealers who see themselves and want to be seen by others as the Guys' consultants of the antiquities trade, perhaps a comparable independent body should be necessary. Third-party oversight could also provide a mechanism for overcoming the apparent conflict between increasing market transparency and maintaining personal and commercial confidentiality.

Looking outside the antiquities trade, a commercial example of how a meta-regulatory solution might function is offered by the idea of an 'ethical consumption' or 'fair trade' market (Gourevitch 2011). An ethical consumption market (ECM) is an ameliorating or correcting commercial alternative to a commodity-producing business that is known to be socially or environmentally harmful (Nicholls and Opal 2005). Harmful businesses typically aim to increase profitability by exploiting primary producers financially or by utilising a production process known to be unnecessarily damaging to the natural environment. An ECM aims to diminish or eliminate these social or environmental harms, with the increased costs of a less harmful production process or trading model being absorbed into commodity pricing. Consumers are willing to pay a price premium for reassurance that consumption is not unnecessarily harmful. Typically, an independent NGO monitors and guarantees certain economic, environmental, and social standards of production and trade for consumers concerned about possible harms. To confirm compliance with stated standards and to enable consumers to make an informed choice, business participating in an ECM are entitled to badge products with a distinctive logo, something like the Fairtrade Mark of the Fairtrade Foundation, an easily recognizable and copyrighted sign. Participation in an ECM is voluntary on the part of producers, traders and consumers alike. There is no element of regulatory compulsion. The advantage for producers and traders is that higher prices allow them to cover the increased costs of ethical production and to protect their reputation, while at the same time minimising any moral concerns they themselves might harbour about engaging in harmful production processes. Thus, returning to our typology of crime reduction modalities developed in the previous chapter, an ECM presents as a combined socio-economic approach, with the social and economic agency of concerned actors structuring a market solution to a harmful practice.

A complete ECM solution is probably inappropriate for the antiquities trade. It would entail legalizing and commercializing archaeological excavation and trade at source so that profits derived from the destination market could be passed down to pay excavators or be used by appropriate agencies in heritage protection. Legalisation would most likely be used by dealers to increase market demand, and any money passed back would be soaked up by developing the human and physical capacity necessary for ensuring competent, well-documented standards of excavation along with matching standards of conservation and curation of found objects. We have already touched upon objections to this scenario in Chapter 6: it is at odds with both the ethical foundations of the archaeological profession and the regulatory systems and social outlooks of antiquities source countries.

Not all collectible antiquities could be made available for legal trade. Many antiquities in circulation have been obtained through theft from museums or other cultural institutions, including active religious establishments, and their trade would never be legalised. The Nataraja Shiva stolen from the temple of Sripuranthan, India, which has been mentioned several times already in this book, is one such example. Many antiquities available on the market have been forcibly and damagingly removed from standing architectural remains, and likewise such pieces would not be available for the market. The Cambodian Duryodhana and its companion pieces from the temple complex of Koh Ker are relevant examples here. Any source government introducing such a scheme would no doubt expect to keep any significant and thus monetarily valuable objects, reducing market supply and diminishing potential income even further, while incentivizing collectors to acquire comparable pieces obtained through illicit means.

It also seems inevitable that a fully legalized trade would be more concerned with conserving the tradeable commodity—the antiquity—than with preventing damaging practices of site excavation and conservation that a hypothetical ECM would be intended to prevent. The scholarly importance of an object with no recorded excavation context will not always if ever correlate with its monetary value. In any case, many archaeological sites do not contain saleable antiquities, and many antiquities, particularly those fabricated from perishable and organic materials require delicate excavation and expert (and therefore expensive) conservation.

More serious even than these practical objections, however, might be the fact that source governments would view the introduction of a legal antiquities market as an expensive and unnecessarily disruptive change to long-standing domestic practices of heritage management, one brought about to meet the demand of foreign collectors. The right of source country governments to determine their own domestic policies as regards the management of cultural heritage would be overturned to sate the desires of citizens from wealthier and more powerful demand countries. This outcome is not too far removed from the challenge to sovereignty and cultural self-determination posed by the illicit trade in the first place. So while it is possible to imagine how a legalized antiquities trade might operate, it is much harder to see how it would fulfil the necessary harm-reducing criteria in such a way as to be considered an ethical trade.

For the antiquities trade, a workable ECM would need to diminish the damaging externalities of the illicit trade by increasing the volume of demonstrably licit trade. Licitly-traded objects would comprise those objects that left their country of excavation legally, quite often decades or centuries ago before export was banned or controlled. An ECM would need to increase market transparency, while at the same time meeting legitimate concerns about maintaining confidentiality. The aim would be to assure customers that antiquities being sold through an ECM were offered in accord with stated standards of provenance and legality, and that participating dealers (badged accordingly) were in compliance with advertised codes of practice and ethics. Discriminating collectors could then choose to acquire antiquities from ECM dealers, and the demand for unprovenanced, likely trafficked, objects would diminish accordingly.

In such a system there would be financial benefits for participating dealers. As is the case for fair trade products, and as already claimed for the antiquities market (though disputed in the Chapter 6 discussion of autoregulation), some customers at least will pay a price premium for an object deemed licit according to a specified provenance standard. The hope would also be that good-faith and ethically-demanding customers would gravitate towards the ECM, taking business away from the increasingly recognisable 'rotten apples'. Antiquities dealers who regard themselves as law-abiding have argued in the past that they should be a part of any regulatory solution, and that the more punitive weapons in the regulatory armoury, particularly criminal sanctions, should be reserved for use only against unprincipled dealers and the illicit trade. This suggestion has often fallen upon deaf ears because of the difficulty in distinguishing between licit and illicit components of the grey antiquities trade, and the scepticism surrounding the effectiveness of self-regulation. Participation in an ECM, however, would overcome these problems, allowing other market control measures, particularly criminal justice responses, to focus more aggressively on dealers working outside the ECM, as the dealers themselves have suggested.

To overcome uncertainties of content and definition, a functioning ECM would require an association of dealers to formulate and agree a clear code of practice with one or more non-governmental or private sector organisations, building upon the one already existing for the IADAA or ideally the 1999 UNESCO International Code of Ethics for Dealers in Cultural Property, and agree a mechanism of third-party oversight to ensure compliance. The code might, within specified limits and with appropriate reservations, guarantee the legitimate provenance of material offered for sale. No doubt controversially, to ensure compliance, the sales and stock records of participating dealers would be open to inspection by the third party. As provenance determinations are rarely definitive, and fraudulent documentation is widespread, an indemnity scheme would be needed to back the ECM and protect dealers or customers against the loss of objects bought in good faith but subsequently shown to be stolen. The third-party should not be expected to provide a window onto to the inner workings of the trade, but rather to confirm to outsiders that the inner-workings are in full compliance with stated standards of provenance. This solution would go some way to reconciling the opposing demands for increased market transparency and continuing commercial confidentiality by extending the envelope of confidentiality to include the third party.

We suggested in Chapter 3 that the underlying philosophy of the social approach to crime reduction might be about 'changing people for the better', but equally, it might be about allowing them to act in ways that are less harmful. This might be achieved by changing their contexts of action rather than changing their predispositions to action. We have argued that the asymmetric availability of information, particularly of provenance-related information, frustrates even well-intentioned market actors. We have previewed here in bare-bones outline how an ECM might work advantageously in the destination market to provide a more open and rewarding context for market actors and other stakeholders alike. Clearly the devil is in the detail, and negotiation would be needed to overcome mutual suspicion and hostility before a workable ECM could be implemented to the satisfaction of all. But by introducing here the concept of an ECM, we are keen to show that there are as yet untested methods of market control drawing upon ideas developed outside the legal approach to crime reduction, and away from the hard prescription of command and control regulation, that might be productively applied to market governance.

# 8

# POLICY FAILURE, POLICY FUTURE

## Policy failure

The 1954 Hague Convention for the Protection of Cultural Property in the Event of Armed Conflict and the 1970 UNESCO Convention on the Means of Prohibiting and Preventing the Illicit Import, Export and Transfer of Ownership of Cultural Property have provided the backbone to the formation and implementation of international antiquities protection policy, with the 1995 Unidroit Convention on Stolen or Illegally Exported Cultural Objects also contributing, albeit muted in effect by the reluctance of antiquities market countries to accept it into their law. The policy approach developed by these international treaties and the institutions which promote and monitor them falls very much within what we have characterized as the legal mode of crime reduction and has been described as one of 'protection and recovery' (Brodie 2015c). This policy aims to protect cultural heritage sites at source, and to provide mechanisms for the return of trafficked antiquities to their dispossessed owners, often source states. Protection and recovery—and in particular the 'recovery' element—stems from the development from the mid twentieth century onwards of attempts by various decolonised countries to reclaim as part of their sovereign identity and cultural self-determination the great volumes of antiquities that had been removed to collections in the west. These national sentiments around repatriation were joined in the 1960s by converging concerns about the ongoing loss of antiquities through looting and illicit trade.

The continuing levels of looting documented around the world by our research and others' can lead to no other conclusion but that this policy focus on protection and recovery is failing to safeguard the world's cultural heritage. We propose four main reasons for this failure.

First, the emphasis of policy initiatives on cultural site protection at the source is unrealistic. This model cannot offer comprehensive, longer-term site protection due to the strain it puts on local resources. In the various source countries mentioned in this book, sites are often so numerous and remote that guarding even a selection of them would put untenable strain on policing and archaeological budgets. At the time of writing Syria is currently in the news, and by extension is the focus of a raft of source protection initiatives (Brodie 2015c). Yet there are estimated to be 10,000 archaeological sites in Syria and even in peacetime observers estimated that there were only enough resources to post a guard at around one site in every five (Ali 2013). In Iraq, under similar strain even pre-conflict, difficult decisions were made in weighing up the significance of the very many sites needing protection, with resources allocated accordingly, resulting in protection focused on the larger and more important sites (Russell 2008). In his review of the evidence Brodie concludes that such targeted measures may at best ameliorate rather than solve problems of looting, but he also observes that there is a distinct possibility that funds directed to site protection are in some cases diverted to fund militia groups or simply lost to corruption (Brodie 2015c). Site protection which may be difficult in peacetime will tend to be even more so during times of conflict, when it is needed the most.

Second, the reactive nature of policy initiatives means that they come too late to prevent either the establishment of regional looting and trafficking networks, or the massive damage such networks cause to cultural heritage sites. By definition, reactive policy apparatus is responsive to issues that appear on the international policy 'radar', and to achieve this level of recognition (a) significant and sustained destruction must be taking place to a country's cultural heritage and (b) the media must be raising it to global attention. There was widespread looting in Syria, for example, throughout the 1990s and 2000s and organized smuggling groups were therefore well placed to take advantage of the conflict after 2011 when it presented new opportunities for illicit business (Cunliffe 2012; Casana and Panahipour 2014). International policy was slow to react in the case of Syria, as it was for Iraq, even once the serious scale of conflict looting became apparent. ICOM's Emergency Red List of Syrian Cultural Objects at Risk was not produced until 2013, two years after the outbreak of conflict in 2011, and international capacity building funds did not begin to flow into Syria until 2014 when UNESCO implemented the Emergency Safeguarding of the Syrian Heritage Project, supported for three years by $2.46 million of European Union funding (Brodie 2015c).

Third, the targeting of policy initiatives at single countries follows developments in media coverage, as we have alluded to above. It has become increasingly obvious through the source-focussed policy initiatives and funding aimed at Iraq and Syria that in this field of antiquities trafficking, as no doubt in many others, policy follows media. Many countries have suffered extensive looting and trafficking in the past, and in some cases this destruction continues. But these countries are almost entirely overlooked by the officials and institutions in major aid-giving and support-giving countries like the US and UK, who decide where their funded interventions will be targeted. Looting in Iraq began to take a back seat in the policy field to the situation in Afghanistan in the 1990s, culminating in the destruction of the Bamiyan Buddhas by the Taliban in 2001 (Lawler 2001). After the 2003 coalition invasion, Iraq was in the spotlight and other countries, including Syria, received little or no attention in policy discussions despite experiencing high levels of looting. Subsequently the focus of international antiquities protection policy shifted to Syria, with Iraq increasingly overlooked, until reports of looting and destruction there by the Islamic State of Iraq and Syria (ISIS) gave rise to another 'emergency response action plan' by UNESCO in 2014. This meant that by 2014 there was one such plan for Iraq and another for Syria. There were none, however, for neighbouring countries haemorrhaging cultural property to looting and trafficking throughout this period, and continuing to do so, such as Libya, Jordan, Yemen, and perhaps Iran and Turkey (Bisheh 2001; ; Politis 2002; Contreras and Brodie 2010; Brodie and Contreras 2012; Kersel and Chesson 2013; Kersel and Chesson 2015; Brodie 2015c), and these are only examples from the immediate surrounding region which have been largely overlooked as policy has chased after media headlines of destruction elsewhere.

Further, concentrating emergency policy actions on single countries causes inevitable detection and enforcement problems because ancient borders do not follow modern borders: archaeological cultures are not confined within the boundaries of modern states. Thus, when the United Nations intervenes with a Security Council Resolution banning trade in antiquities originating in a particular country and that cannot be proven to have been exported before a given date, as it has done for both Iraq and Syria, identifying material surfacing on the international market in breach of such a ban is often fraught with uncertainty. There is clear evidence that Syrian and Iraqi material is sold on the market as originating in neighbouring countries where the UN controls do not apply (Brodie 2015c). Indeed, this is a fairly old antiquities laundering trick that has been well used in the market for many years, as we have already observed, so this is hardly a new development with which regulators could justifiably claim to have been blindsided.

Fourth, the emphasis of policy initiatives on securing the recovery and return of stolen and looted antiquities may be positive for dispossessed owners, including source states concerned with the cultural aspects of nationhood, but it does little to deter looting and trafficking, and return cannot repair the damage which looting does to an archaeological site. Seizure of antiquities at customs in destination market and transit countries may, as we have seen, lead to the confiscation of objects but rarely leads to criminal prosecution of traffickers. Occasional interceptions and civil forfeitures can be written off by traders in illicit material as a cost of doing business. Analysis of the usual mark-ups in the international antiquities market have suggested that if an importer is forced to bear the financial loss of a forfeiture, it can be written off by the subsequent sale of the next successfully received shipment (Brodie 2015c).

These four failings of the current 'protection and recovery' approach to international policy support the assertion, strongly made throughout this book, that we should look to controls that regulate the destination market for antiquities. After all, the sources of supply of illicit antiquities are manifold, with a significant number of source states worldwide being implicated in, and suffering the effects of, 'supply'. The global centres of trade, however, where collectors convene to buy, and to which dealers are drawn to sell, are relatively few in number by comparison. In Chapter 3 we noted that for the various other comparable transnational criminal markets which can be analysed alongside antiquities trafficking, supply-side controls have a considerably less impressive record of success than market-end regulation, and indeed criminologists who study the illicit antiquities trade have for some time made the case that it should be seen 'as a criminal market' (Polk 2000) which then points towards demand reduction for illicit artefacts as the appropriate strategy (Polk 2009), a call which has also been made by illicit antiquities researchers out-side the field of criminology, whose personal experiences and clear thinking about solutions have led them to the same conclusion (e.g. Russell 2008; O'Keefe 1997).

## Policy future

We have set out in this book several components of an overall market-oriented solution to the problem of looting and trafficking in antiquities. We have noted the creative compliance strategies employed by major market actors, who negotiate their relationship with the law so as to pay it lip service but to subvert its general sentiments. We have considered the exonerating discourse that has built up to enable and justify such participation in criminal activity—for let us make no mistake, this is at its root a straightforward case of large-scale crime we are dealing with. Those in the market may wish to present the issue as a difficult grey area in which the damage done by looting should be overlooked in a moral balancing act where the preservation and display by those who buy loot justifies the social and historical cost of the theft and trafficking that brings the objects to market (Mer-ryman 1988; Cuno 2008, 2014). These are, however, the kinds of normal 'techniques of neutralisation' that the study of the sociology of crime has found are quite usual in white-collar criminals. If anything, the identification of these ways of thinking, these cognitive distortions, makes it more, rather than less, clear that what is at stake here is the challenge of policing a criminal market.

Through the chapters in this book we have brought empirical study to bear on some of the justifying, neutralizing, and trivializing discourse in the market. This includes suggestions such as that autoregulation will lead to the market sanitizing itself, where we showed in Chapter 6 that it will not. It includes suggestions that the trend towards institutions publishing more provenance information will allow buyers to make informed ethical choices. As is illustrated in the case studies in the appendix, however, even the oldest and supposedly most venerable institutions in the market, those that exist and do business in public view in noteworthy premises in world cities, choose not to publish the 'inconvenient truths', which are scattered throughout the provenance histories of objects circulating on the market. We have shown in Chapter 2 that in source countries, networks of traffickers connect to local areas where looting happens, moving the objects overseas and on through well-connected intermediaries so there are often only a few steps in the chain between the original point of theft and a public international sale. That many of the market actors we have termed Janus figures—international brokers who can receive stolen goods and sell them on publicly—are known to established dealers, collectors and museums in the worldwide trade as having dubious reputations while still being able to sell into the global market is a serious indictment of the suggestion that any kind of self-regulation might clean the trade up. Our review of other transnational criminal markets in Chapter 3 showed that insofar as 'best practice' might be identifiable across this eclectic and disjointed field of international controls of illicit trades, the best prospects lie in regulation of the destination market and in ways that make more rather than less clear the links between that destination market and the sources of supply.

Through that process of moving our analytical lens across the three phases of the illicit antiquities market that we outlined in Chapter 1—source (supply), transit, and destination market (demand)—we have used case study examples and a framework of thinking primarily about economic and sociological approaches to regulation. We have considered the antiquities market as a connected economic and social network constituted as a field of communications, a circuit of commerce, and we have proposed that the regulation of those communications holds promise as a project to increase control over illicit trade in the market. Improving the information flow throughout the antiquities trade so that the true provenance histories of objects, and the implications of these, are known to buyers would be an important step. So too, alongside this, would be developing incentives for buyers to care about the legitimacy of those provenances (both in terms of how they have been produced and what they say about the transaction history of the object) and for sellers to care about trying to produce them in a way that has genuine integrity and that can be relied upon. Whether ethical consumption markets provide the best model for achieving those communication goals remains to be seen but the principles, at least, are clear.

# APPENDIX: CASE STUDIES

As a postscript to the main themes and arguments in this book, we can provide a snapshot of some aspects of the illicit antiquities market, to illustrate some elements of one particular narrative in the recent critical analysis of illicit dealing in the market. This narrative revolves around the dealer Giacomo Medici. There follow some short case-study style summaries of some of the known facts of Medici's illicit enterprise. Some of these are taken from our encyclopaedia of case studies, available on our website at traffickingculture.org, while others have been written especially for this book by our colleague Dr Christos Tsirogiannis.

## Giacomo Medici

Medici started dealing in antiquities in Rome during the 1960s (Silver 2009: 25). In July 1967, he was convicted in Italy of receiving looted artefacts, though in the same year he met and became an important supplier of antiquities to US dealer Robert Hecht (Silver 2009: 27–29). In 1968, Medici opened the gallery Antiquaria Romana in Rome and began to explore business opportunities in Switzerland (Silver 2009: 34). It is widely believed that in December 1971 he bought the illegally-excavated 'Euphronios (Sarpedon) krater' from tombaroli before transporting it to Switzerland and selling it to Hecht (Silver 2009: 50, and see below).

In 1978, he closed his Rome gallery, and entered into partnership with Geneva resident Christian Boursaud, who started consigning material supplied by Medici for sale at Sotheby's London (Silver 2009: 121–122, 139; Watson and Todeschini 2007: 27). Together, they opened Hydra Gallery in Geneva in 1983 (Silver 2009: 139). It has been estimated that throughout the 1980s Medici was the source of more antiquities consignments to Sotheby's London than any other vendor (Watson and Todeschini 2007: 27). At any one time, Boursaud might consign anything up to seventy objects, worth together as much as £500,000 (Watson 1997: 112). Material would be delivered to Sotheby's from Geneva by courier (Watson 1997: 112).

In October 1985, the Hydra Gallery sold fragments of the 'Onesimos kylix' to the J. Paul Getty Museum for $100,000, providing a false provenance by way of the fictitious Zbinden collection, a provenance that was sometimes used for material offered at Sotheby's (Silver 2009: 145; Watson and Todeschini 2007: 95). The Getty returned the kylix to Italy in 1999 (see below).

In 1986, bad publicity surrounding the sale of looted Apulian vases at Sotheby's London caused Medici and Boursaud to part company, and Medici bought the Geneva-based Editions Services to continue consigning material to Sotheby's (Watson 1997: 117, 183–186; Watson and Todeschini 2007: 27; Silver 2009: 147). From 1987 until 1994, he also consigned material to Sotheby's through other 'front companies', including Mat Securitas, Arts Franc and Tecafin Fiduciaire (Watson and Todeschini 2007: 73). He developed a triangulating system of consigning through one company and purchasing the same piece through another company. There were two potentially positive outcomes of this triangulation manoeuvre: first, it artificially created demand, suggesting to potential customers that the market was stronger than it actually was; and second, it was a way of providing illegally-excavated or -exported pieces with a 'Sotheby's' provenance, and, in effect, laundering them (Watson and Todeschini 2007: 135–141).

By the late 1980s, Medici had developed commercial relations with other major antiquities dealers including Robin Symes, Frieda Tchacos, Nikolas Koutoulakis, Robert Hecht, and the brothers Ali and Hischam Aboutaam (Watson and Todeschini 2007: 73–74). He was the ultimate source of artefacts that would subsequently be sold through dealers or auction houses to private collectors, including Lawrence and Barbara Fleischman, Maurice Tempelsman, Shelby White and Leon Levy, the Hunt brothers, George Ortiz, and José Luis Várez Fisa (Watson and Todeschini 2007: 112–134; Isman 2010a), and to museums including the J. Paul Getty, the Metropolitan Museum of Art, the Cleveland Museum of Art, and the Boston Museum of Fine Arts.

In 1995, a Sotheby's London auction catalogue advertised for sale a sarcophagus recognized by the Carabinieri to have been stolen from the church of San Saba, in Rome. Sotheby's informed the Carabinieri that it had been consigned by Editions Services (Watson and Todeschini 2007: 19). This was around the same time that the 'organigram' (see below), an organizational chart revealing Medici's central position in the organisation of the antiquities trade out of Italy, was discovered, (Watson and Todeschini 2007: 19). Putting the evidence together, the Carabinieri decided to act. On 13 September 1995, in concert with Swiss police, they raided Medici's storage space in the Geneva Freeport, which comprised five rooms with a combined area of about 200 square metres (Silver 2009: 174; Watson and Todeschini 2007: 20). One room was equipped as a laboratory for cleaning and restoring artefacts, another was fitted out as a showroom, presumably for receiving potential customers (Silver 2009: 180–181). In January 1997, Medici was arrested in Rome (Silver 2009: 175–176), and in July 1997, his Geneva storerooms, which had remained sealed since 1995, were opened again for the process of examination and inventory.

The official report of the contents of Medici's storerooms was submitted in July 1999. The storerooms had been found to contain 3,800 whole or fragmentary objects, more than 4,000 photographs of artefacts, and 35,000 sheets of paper containing information relating to Medici's business practices and connections. The seized artefacts were mainly from Italy, but there were also hundreds from Egypt, Syria, Greece and Asia. The Swiss authorities turned over Italian material to Italy, but returned the rest to Medici (Silver 2009: 192). The photographs were mainly Polaroids, showing what appeared to be illegally-excavated artefacts, sometimes with several views of the same object in various stages of restoration. Some artefacts were shown still covered with dirt after their excavation, some fragmentary, and others cleaned and reassembled prior to sale (Watson and Todeschini 2007: 54–68). In 2002, Carabinieri raided Medici's home in Santa Marinella (Watson and Todeschini 2007: 200).

Medici was charged with receiving stolen goods, illegal export of goods, and conspiracy to traffic, and his trial in Rome commenced on 4 December 2003. On 12 May 2005, he was found guilty of all charges. The judge declared that Medici had trafficked thousands of artefacts, including the sarcophagus fragment that had started the investigation, and the 'Euphronios (Sarpedon) krater' (Silver 2009: 212). He was sentenced to ten years in prison and received a €10 million fine, with the money going to the Italian state in compensation for damage caused to cultural heritage (Silver 2009: 214). In July 2009, an appeals court in Rome dismissed the trafficking conviction against him because of the expired limitation period, but reaffirmed the convictions for receiving and conspiracy. His jail sentence was reduced to eight years, but the €10 million fine remained in place (Scherer 2009). In December 2011, a further appeal failed (Felch 2012).

The evidence recovered during the investigation into Medici's business was instrumental in forcing several museums and private collectors to return artefacts to Italy, and triggered further investigations and ultimately the prosecutions of J. Paul Getty Museum curator Marion True and antiquities dealer Robert Hecht.

## Organigram

The 'organigram' (Figure 9.1) is a handwritten organizational chart that was recovered in September 1995 during a Carabinieri raid on the premises of Danilo Ziccho (Watson and Todeschini 2007: 16–18). Drawn by dealer Pasquale Camera, it presents a view of the antiquities trade within Italy as envisaged by Camera in the early 1990s. The US dealer Robert Hecht occupies a central place on the chart, with links to collectors and museums in the US, to major antiquities dealers Nikolas Koutoulakis, Eli Borowsky and Frieda Tchacos, and to the collector George Ortiz (who was in fact Bolivian, not Argentinian as suggested on the chart). Hecht is also shown to stand at the head of two chains of dealers and

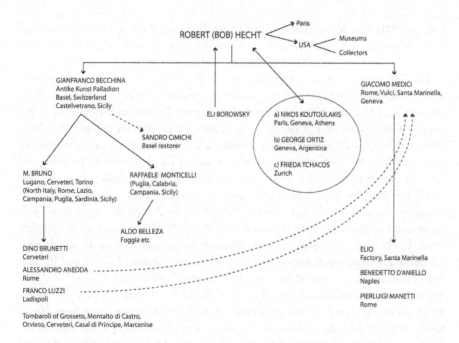

**FIGURE 9.1** The 'organigram' as interpreted by Watson and Todeschini (2007: 17–18) and Mazur (2006).

tombaroli within Italy, one orchestrated by Gianfranco Becchina, the other by Giacomo Medici. The assumption when the organigram was first discovered, which was later substantiated by investigations of Becchina and Medici, was that these chains were responsible for supplying Hecht with artefacts illegally excavated from within Italy that he would then sell on to museums and collectors in the US (Isman 2011; Silver 2009). A notable feature of the organization presented on the chart is that the Becchina and Medici chains are largely independent of one another. Members of each separate chain referred to themselves as being part of a cordata, the Italian term for a group of mountaineers roped together (Watson and Todeschini 2007: 79). It was later revealed that dealer Nino Savoca headed a third cordata not shown on the organigram (Watson and Todeschini 2007: 150, 153).

## The Euphronios (Sarpedon) Krater

The Euphronios (Sarpedon) krater is a red-figure calyx krater made in Athens *circa* 515 BC, 46 cm high and 55 cm in diameter, signed by Euxitheos as potter and Euphronios as painter. It is decorated on the front with a scene depicting the death of Sarpedon, who is attended by Hypnos and Thanatos with the god Hermes looking on. On the reverse are three Athenian youths arming themselves for battle. It was bought by the Metropolitan Museum of Art in 1972 for the then record-breaking price of $1 million, and is thought to have been excavated illegally in

Italy in 1971. The Metropolitan's director at the time, Thomas Hoving, described it as '... a work that would force the history of Greek art to be rewritten' (Hoving 1993: 318). In 2006, the Metropolitan restored ownership of the krater to Italy.

The find spot and early provenance of the Euphronios krater have never been firmly established. However, the krater is generally believed to have been discovered in December 1971 by tombaroli digging illegally on private land in the Greppe Sant'Angelo area of the Etruscan cemetery of Cerveteri (Silver 2009: 287–290). The tombaroli are said to have sold the krater to Medici for something in the region of $88,000, with Medici, in turn, arranging for the krater to be smuggled into Switzerland, where he sold it to Hecht for $350,000 (Silver 2009: 37–52, 287–290). By this time, the krater was in a fragmentary though completely restorable state, so Hecht left it with Fritz Bürki in Zurich for restoration. The provenance of the krater after its arrival in Zurich is well-documented. In February 1972, Hecht alerted the Metropolitan Museum to the existence of the krater with a letter to Dietrich von Bothmer, the Metropolitan's Curator of Greek and Roman Art. In June 1972, von Bothmer, along with Hoving and Hoving's deputy Theodore Rousseau, visited Zurich to view the krater (Hoving 2001e). In August 1972, after some haggling, the Metropolitan agreed to buy the krater from Hecht for $1 million (Hoving 2001a). The money was raised through the sale of the Durkee and Ward collections of 11,000 coins and medals, which had been donated to the Metropolitan in the early twentieth century. Sotheby's agreed to handle the coin sale and offered the Metropolitan a $1.5 million payment in advance, plus 84 per cent of all gross receipts in excess of $1 million (Hoving 2001a). The Metropolitan ultimately received nearly $2.3 million from the coin auctions (Hoving 1993: 316). The krater arrived in the US on 31 August 1972.

Hecht claimed to be acting on ten per cent commission as agent for the krater's owner, whom he identified as Lebanese collector and dealer Dikran Sarrafian (Hoving 2001a). Hecht supplied two documents of provenance for the acquisitions committee meeting that approved the purchase. First, was a letter dated 10 July 1971, written by Sarrafian to Hecht, in which Sarrafian declared that he would deliver the vase to Hecht in expectation of a final sale price of $1 million. Second, was another letter from Sarrafian to Hecht, dated 9 September 1972, stating that Sarrafian's father had obtained the krater in 1920 in London and that because it was in fragments it had been sent [to Switzerland] for restoration three years before the writing of the letter (Hoving 1993: 319; 2001b).

On 12 November 1972, the *New York Times* announced the krater's acquisition with a cover story for its Sunday magazine (Mellow 1972). The price and provenance of the krater were both withheld, with the Metropolitan claiming that it was maintaining secrecy in order to protect a potential source of future acquisitions (Gage 1973b). On 19 February 1973, however, a more critical account of the krater's provenance was published (Gage 1973c), heralding a series of articles that questioned the museum's account and suggesting instead that the krater had been excavated illegally at Cerveteri in late 1971. The names of Hecht and Sarrafian and the $1 million price tag were revealed to the public (Gage 1973b). It was during this time in a TV interview that Hoving referred to the krater as the 'hot pot'—a name that stuck (Hoving 2001b).

The new and potentially damaging allegations of illicit provenance caused the Metropolitan to send lawyers to visit Sarrafian in Beirut (Hoving 2001c). They obtained documents from Sarrafian confirming that he had received payment for the krater of $909,000 in Swiss francs on 25 October 1971. They also obtained testimony from a clerk who had seen the vessel in fragments with Sarrafian in Beirut in the early 1960s. The Metropolitan's legal team also collected affidavits from Bürki, confirming that he had received a fragmentary krater from Sarrafian in August 1971, and a photographer in Basel who had seen the fragments in September 1971 (Gage 1973a; Hoving 1993: 333; 2001c). This evidence was made public in June 1973, and seemed to confirm that the krater was in Switzerland before the suggested December 1971 date of illegal excavation, as well as refute allegations of illicit provenance (Gage 1973a).

In July 1973, Hoving received a copy of a letter that art collector Muriel Newman had sent Sarrafian stating that she had seen a fragmentary Euphronios vessel with him in Beirut in 1964. Newman subsequently signed an affidavit confirming this statement (Hoving 1993: 335–336; 2001c).

By the end of 1973, the question of provenance seemed settled in favour of the Hecht/Metropolitan account of Sarrafian's ownership, and thus legitimate provenance. Hoving subsequently wrote, however, that in private, he had still harboured doubts. This was largely because, in various statements, Sarrafian had referred to the krater as comprising a hatbox of fragments and implying that it was incomplete (e.g. Gage 1973b, 1973a; Van Gelder 1973; Hoving 2001c, 2001d). The krater bought by the Metropolitan was complete, and was considered by Hoving to be too large, even in fragments, to have fit into a hatbox. Hoving resigned from the Metropolitan in 1977, but by 1993 he had come to believe that there were in fact two Euphronios kraters: one that had been illegally excavated in 1971 and subsequently acquired by the Metropolitan, and a second less-well-preserved one that had been in the possession of Sarrafian as claimed and documented, but that had subsequently turned up in the collection of Bunker Hunt (Hoving 1993: 338–339, 2001d). Hecht had simply taken the provenance and documentation from the Sarrafian/Bunker Hunt krater and attached it to the illegally-excavated and better-preserved Sarpedon krater bought by the Metropolitan. Sarrafian had been killed in a car crash in 1977 (Hoving 2001c), and so was unavailable for further comment. When challenged by Hoving about this switch, Hecht himself was ambivalent (Hoving 2001d). This second (Bunker Hunt) krater, however, was bought by Leon Levy and Shelby White in 1990, and returned to Italy in 2010 when evidence emerged that it too had been illegally excavated (Povoledo 2008b). If Sarrafian did indeed possess a Euphronios krater, as the evidence collected by the Metropolitan suggests, then its identity and whereabouts remain unknown.

Matters rested there until the Italian investigations of Medici and Hecht gained momentum though the 1990s and early 2000s. Two photographs were discovered in Medici's Geneva storerooms, apparently taken in May 1987, one showing Medici standing next to the Euphronios krater on display in the Metropolitan, the second showing Hecht in a similar pose (Watson and Todeschini 2007: 107). On 16 February 2001, the Carabinieri raided Hecht's apartment in Paris. They recovered a handwritten 'memoir' of Hecht's, setting out an autobiographical account of his life in the antiquities trade. It contains two accounts of the Sarpedon Euphronios: the first admitting to the fact that Hecht had bought the krater from Medici and that it had been excavated illegally in 1971; the second reiterating the Sarrafian provenance as provided to the Metropolitan. Finally, in June 2001, Marion True informed Italian investigators in a sworn deposition that van Bothmer had pointed out to her on an aerial photograph the location of the looted tomb from which the krater was allegedly taken, though von Bothmer subsequently denied this allegation (Felch and Frammolino 2005; 2011: 209, 211; Watson and Todeschini 2007: 206–207).

On 3 February 2006, the Metropolitan reached an agreement with Italy about the return of twenty objects, including the Euphronios krater. Although the evidence for illegal excavation and trade was still largely circumstantial, the Metropolitan's then-director, Philippe de Montebello, clearly thought it was convincing when he was quoted as saying that it was 'highly probable' that the vessel had been stolen from an Etruscan tomb (Kennedy and Eakin 2006). The krater arrived back in Italy on 18 January 2008, where it was put on display with other returned objects at the exhibition *Nostoi: Capolavori Ritrovati*, before being curated permanently at the Villa Giulia in Rome (Povoledo 2008a).

## Fifth-century BC Attic red-figured kylix, signed by Euphronios as potter and painted by Onesimos with scenes of the Trojan War

The J. Paul Getty Museum started acquiring fragments of this kylix in the 1980s, paying $180,000 to Frieda Tchacos of Galerie Nefer in Zurich for pieces comprising approximately 40 per cent of the whole. Tchacos said that she had in turn bought them from Nino Savoca of Munich (Watson and Todeschini 2007: 92; Silver 2009: 142). Other pieces were obtained from the Schweitzer collection of Arlesheim, a collection which has been reported as having often been used as a false provenance (Watson and Todeschini 2007: 94–95), and from the Geneva Hydra Gallery, under the proprietorship of Medici and Christian Boursaud (Watson and Todeschini 2007: 94–95). Boursaud provided as provenance the name of the Zbinden Collection, which is believed to have been invented in an attempt to 'legitimise' the piece for acquisition (Watson and Todeschini 2007: 95). Another piece of the vessel was donated by the Metropolitan Museum's von Bothmer in the mid-1980s, which he had obtained from Hecht in 1968 (Watson and Todeschini 2007: 210; Silver 2009: 142–143). The kylix was still not complete when it was published in 1991 by Dyfri Williams of the British Museum, who reported that he had seen a photograph of a missing fragment comprising three joining pieces (Williams 1991: 61). The original of this photograph was found in the possession of Giacomo Medici when Carabinieri raided his Geneva storerooms in 1995 (Watson and Todeschini 2007: 94), and Medici handed over the pieces shown in the photograph in April 1999 once the rest of the kylix had been returned to Italy (Silver 2009: 187). The Medici storerooms also contained photographs of the fragments that the Getty owned, showing that they had passed through Medici's hands, even though he had not sold them directly to the Getty (Watson and Todeschini 2007: 92–95).

In the 1997 conference Antichità Senza Provenienza, held at Viterbo University in Italy, archaeologist Maria Rizzo presented evidence that the kylix had in fact been excavated illegally from the Etruscan cemetery of Cerveteri, and directly addressing Marion True, who was attending the conference, asked for its return (Rizzo 1997: 156–157; Felch and Frammolino 2011). After receiving corroborating information from Italy, the Getty complied with Rizzo's request (Felch and Frammolino 2011: 176–177).

## A Greek bronze figure of a sow

As previously discussed, when on 13 September 1995 the Swiss and Italian authorities raided the warehouses of Medici at the Freeport of Geneva, thousands of antiquities and a photographic and document archive of Medici's activities were found and seized. Among the seized antiquities were objects not depicted in the archive, indicating that the photographs do not comprise a complete record of the antiquities that Medici traded in his career as an intermediary and a dealer. One such item is a Greek bronze figure of a sow.

The raid on Medici's warehouses and his arrest was reported by the journalist Peter Watson in Sotheby's: Inside Story (Watson 1997: 290–293). The hardback edition of this book includes a black-and-white image depicting twelve antiquities on two shelves; four of the antiquities bear paper tags of the distinctive shape used by Sotheby's auction house. Among the four antiquities is the bronze figure of a sow on the far right of the upper shelf. The caption to the image reads: 'A few of the tens of thousands of treasures found in one of four warehouses in Geneva used by Medici; the building was sealed after the revelations in this book' (Watson 1997: bottom image of the tenth unnumbered page of images in the middle of the book). This caption implies that the antiquities depicted were seized after their discovery in the 1995 raid.

Before it was photographed in connection to the Medici raid, this bronze figure of a sow had appeared in 1987 at an exhibition in the Geneva Museum of Art and History (1 October 1987–31 January 1988) as part of the collection of the 'Thetis Foundation'. There was no mention of any previous collecting history of the sow in the exhibition catalogue; the figure was presented as 'corinthien ou sicyonien' (Zimmerman 1987: 37). The bronze sow then appeared with 123 other antiquities belonging to the 'Thetis Foundation' at auction in Sotheby's London branch on 23 May 1991, and for 121 of these objects, the only collecting history given by Sotheby's was their previous appearance in the 1987 exhibition of the Geneva Museum of Art and History, as part of the 'Thetis Foundation' collection. The sow appeared as lot 54 (Sotheby's 1991: 32–33), was valued at £6,000–8,000 and sold for £14,300.

In late January 2006, 11 years after the raid and with the Medici case not yet finished in the Italian courts, the Greek journalist Nikolas Zirganos interviewed Medici in Rome. The interview was published on 19 February 2006 in the Greek magazine *Epsilon* accompanying the newspaper *Eleutherotypia* (Zirganos 2006: 22–34) and on page 32 the same image that Watson had published in his 1997 book appeared, depicting the sow among other figurines. The image had been provided to Zirganos by Medici himself and the caption read (translated from the Greek text): 'One of the images that Medici used to send to potential buyers. The ruler helped them to estimate the scale of the antiquities'.

The Sotheby's tags attached to the figure raise the question of whether Medici, himself, was the buyer of the bronze sow in the 1991 Sotheby's auction. If that were the case, its discovery in the 1995 raid suggests that the figure remained in Medici's warehouse in the Geneva Free Port until then, and in fact until at least 1997 when it was officially seized by the Swiss and Italian authorities.

Although after seizure the figure of the sow was believed to have been confiscated, it reappeared on the market at auction in Christie's New York branch in 8 June 2012, as lot 65 (Christie's 2012: 56). The collecting history that Christie's offered for the sow was:

> The Thetis Foundation; Sotheby's, London, 23 May 1991, lot 54.
> Private Collection, Switzerland, 2004.
> Published:
> J.-L. Zimmermann, Collection de la Foundation Thetis, Geneva, 1987, pp. 37–38, no. 72.

Tsirogiannis identified the figure from the images in Watson 1997 and Zirganos 2006 and together with three more identifications from the Medici archive he notified the Italian public prosecutor Paolo Giorgio Ferri on 5 June 2012 (Tsirogiannis 2013b).

The figure was estimated to be worth $60,000–80,000 but remained unsold and it was returned to its anonymous consigner. The identification of the sow at the Christie's auction highlighted two issues requiring clarification. First, how was it possible for an antiquity found in 1995 and seized from an illicit antiquities dealer to appear on sale in a public auction house in 2012? Second, who, according to Christie's, was the private collector who owned the object in Switzerland in 2004 and the consigner of the sow in the 2012 auction?

Seeking answers to these two questions, Tsirogiannis contacted two Italian researchers, Daniela Rizzo and Maurizio Pellegrini of the National Etruscan Museum of Villa Giulia in Rome, who had accompanied the authorities investigating the Medici warehouse in Geneva (Watson and Todeschini 2006: 49–65). He also emailed Max Bernheimer, International Head of Christie's antiquities department. Rizzo and Pellegrini noted that the figure was indeed seized after the 1995 raid. Thereafter, based on their archaeological expertise and experience the two archaeologists had been instructed by the Swiss and Italian authorities to compile a list of the illicit antiquities of Italian origin discovered in the hands of Medici and a separate list of antiquities that could have been looted outside Italy. This second list included around 100 antiquities of Greek origin (among which was the figure of the sow, recorded as no. 1141), which remained in Switzerland awaiting a claim for repatriation by the Greek State. While the Italian state confiscated and repatriated thousands of antiquities, the Greek state did not claim the antiquities that the Italians excluded from their list, which were eventually returned to Medici after the expiration of the appropriate limitation period.

It is possible that Medici or a person acting on his behalf may have been either the seller of the figure to the 'Private Collection, Switzerland' or the 'private collector' himself, or even the consigner of the figure in the 2012 Christie's auction in New York. While Rizzo and Pellegrini were willing to answer questions about how this confiscated item could later appear at auction, the auction house representative was less forthcoming. Regarding the sow, Bernheimer's email reply to Tsirogiannis on 2 January 2013 read:

> In terms of the name of the consignor, again, that information is confidential; it is my understanding that our consignor acquired the piece from the Private Collection, Switzerland, in 2004, and that the Private Collector acquired it from Sotheby's London in 1991. The bronze has been returned to the seller.

The answers collected from the archaeologists and the auction house were important in that they show that police confiscation is not always the end of the journey of antiquities through the market. Repatriation does not always follow, a claim by an interested state authority is not always forthcoming, and the object may be returned to the dealer from whom it was seized. The object is then able to continue its journey through the marketplace. The case is particularly interesting in terms of the information provided in the subsequent auction sale: none of the documented history of the seizure of the object is imparted in the sale information provided by Christie's. Based on the reply of their representative one can only speculate as to whether this omission would have been due to a failure on the auction house's part to detect the previous involvement of Medici, or a deliberate decision to 'airbrush' him out of the provenance chain based perhaps on a perception that an object coming out of the hands of a dealer convicted of handling illicit antiquities may not be an attractive prospect for sale.

## A Greek bronze warrior

The same Medici image of several antiquities published by Watson in 1997 and by Zirganos in 2006 and discussed above, allowed the identification of a second antiquity within the market: a bronze figure of an archaic Greek warrior (upper shelf, third from the left). This bronze figure is depicted on the same shelf as the bronze sow and it has had a similar path through the market (Tsirogiannis 2015b).

The two bronze figures have a very similar collecting history: by 1987 the warrior, too, had become part of the 'Thetis Foundation' and was exhibited at the Geneva Museum of Art and History (Zimmerman 1987: 39, 148). The warrior was offered at the same Sotheby's London sale as the sow (23 May 1991) as lot 77 (Sotheby's 1991), where it was described as 'An East Greek Bronze Figure of a Running Hero, circa 540–530 B.C., probably Perseus'. The only collecting history accompanying this figure was its appearance in the 1987 Geneva exhibition ('Zimmermann, Thétis, p. 39, no. 74'). The figure was valued at £8,000–12,000 but was sold for only £7,700. The warrior and sow were both discovered and seized at the Geneva Freeport warehouse of Medici and they remained in Swiss custody (the warrior recorded as no. 1138 in the list compiled by Rizzo and Pellegrini) at least until 1997, but possibly for a few years more, until the expiration of the period in which the Greek state had the right to claim them.

The similarities in the collecting history of the two bronze figures continue, since the warrior, too, appeared on sale at Christie's New York in 2013, a year after the previously-discussed failed attempt to sell the sow. The warrior was offered as lot 543, estimated at $30,000–50,000 (Christie's 2013: 24–25) and Medici's involvement as well as the previous confiscation of the object was not mentioned in the collecting history that Christie's provided:

PROVENANCE:
Thétis Foundation, Geneva, acquired prior to 1987.
Thétis Foundation; Sotheby's, London, 23 May 1991, lot 77.
PUBLISHED:
J.-L. Zimmermann, Collection de la Fondation Thétis, Développements de l'art grec de la préhistoire à Rome, Geneva, 1987, pp. 39 and 148, no. 74.

Like the sow, the warrior failed to sell and was returned to its anonymous consigner. Like the sow, the warrior's whereabouts after the auction remain unknown at the time of writing (2018).

While the bronze figure of the warrior was moving between Medici and state authorities, antiquities dealer Kevin R. Cheek published a book entitled *Into the Antiquities Trade* (Cheek 2003). Cheek (2003: 122) includes the image of the warrior figurine from Sotheby's 1991 catalogue, repeating Sotheby's description of the object as 'Running Hero', with a caption referring to the seizure of the figurine in Geneva:

Greek bronze figure of a Running Hero, circa 540–530 B.C., as seen in Sotheby's London, Antiquities, auction May 23, 1991, number 77. This is the identical piece subsequently seized during the Geneva Seizure and later published by Peter Watson in *Sotheby's: Inside Story*.

Watson does not appear to have researched the collecting history of any of the antiquities depicted in the image he published in 1997, and Cheek 2003, three years before Zirganos' publication of the same image, seems to have been the first to identify the warrior in the 1991 Sotheby's auction as the one in the image in Watson's book. Cheek makes this connection (see also Cheek 2003: 176, 179) apparently with the aim of showing that Medici bought the object legitimately at auction. He says, for example, that 'what is perhaps the most shocking element of the *Geneva Seizure* is that the Italian government confiscated Medici's entire collection as property of the Italian state' (Cheek 2003: 178), suggesting that he did not consider this proper. Cheek and Watson constitute two publications of the bronze warrior in the period from 1997 to 2003, which connect the Sotheby's sale with Medici and the subsequent seizure of material in Geneva, information which the collecting history published in the Christie's 2013 auction catalogue omits. As with the case of the sow, the case of the bronze warrior shows how seized antiquities may continue their journey through the international antiquities market even after being taken from dealers accused of illicit activities.

Again, as in the case of the bronze sow, Christie's did not refer to the complete collecting history when at the time of the auction Watson's publication had been available for more than 16 years and Cheek's for 10 years. This calls into question the depth of meaning in the market's much advertised turn towards 'due diligence' standards. Due diligence may be a phrase that is used by the members of the antiquities market to attract and reassure potential buyers. Rigorous due diligence should include an assessment of the 'character of the parties' appearing in a provenance (Prott 1997: 48). Clearly, omitting mention of Medici in these catalogue descriptions of provenance prevents a good faith collector from conducting rigorous due diligence. In this respect, publishing only the unproblematic parts of a known collecting history could be fairly taken to be a form of creative compliance, similar to the strategies used by Sotheby's in Chapter 5. Or, on the other hand, not being diligent enough about your due diligence leads to a pervasive situation we may see as 'undue diligence', in which the proper inquiries are not made energetically enough, and information about suspicious or inopportune provenance histories is overlooked. As we described in Chapter 6, Christie's has adopted a 2000 provenance threshold, whereby if an object can be shown to have been out of its country of origin since before 2000, it will be deemed acceptable for auction. The legal or ethical underpinning of this threshold is obscure—if indeed it exists. It looks to be more of a commercial convenience for the auction house, sparing the expenditure of time and money on rigorous due diligence. As these case studies show, it is also convenient in another sense as it allows Christie's to exclude unsavoury aspects of provenance that date back to before 2000. Whether the issue is one of deliberately dropping inconveniently problematic parts of a provenance history, or not knowing about those parts in the first place due to a reluctance to put enough effort into investigating the case, the market effect is the same: customers are not given the opportunity to assess all of the facts surrounding the history of an object before they buy.

## An Attic red-figure lekythos attributed to the Nikon Painter

The auction house Münzen und Medaillen AG in Basel was opened in 1942 by the brothers Herbert Adolph Cahn (1915–2002) and Erich B. Cahn (1913–1993), gradually becoming one of the most famous auction houses worldwide; it deals mainly in coins and medals, but also in classical antiquities. In 1976, Herbert Cahn was convicted in Italy for acquiring illicit antiquities originating from Italy; he was given a brief suspended sentence (Watson and Todeschini 2007: 164–165). Herbert's son, Jean-David Cahn, is also active in the antiquities business and has been found in possession of illicit antiquities (Patris 2007; Godart et al. 2008: 204–205; Gill 2008), some of which are depicted in the confiscated Medici archive (Tsirogiannis 2013a: 12–13).

In 1986 the anonymous owner of a lekythos decorated with the images of Eos and Kephalos (or Tithonos), consigned the vase to Münzen und Medaillen AG to be auctioned on 14 November 1986, as lot 213 (Münzen und Medaillen AG 1986: 73–73, pl.51; Tsirogiannis 2015a). The lekythos was presented as part of the Ferruccio Bolla collection (Münzen und Medaillen AG 1986: 4, 59); it was attributed to the Nikon Painter and was valued at 10,000–12,000 Swiss francs.

Ferruccio Bolla died in April 1984 and there is no record of when or from whom he originally acquired the lekythos, who consigned the vase in the Münzen und Medaillen AG 1986 auction, or who bought it at this auction. However, a portion of an interview of Marion True, conducted by the Italian public prosecutor Paolo-Giorgio Ferri on 20 and 21 June 2001, may be relevant to this case (Ferri 2001: 12):

FERRI: The first question is this:
>     Do you know Mr. Giacomo Medici, and if you do, when—how many times did you meet with him?

TRUE: Yes, I do know Giacomo Medici. I believe the first time I met Giacomo was in 19 — around 1984 on the occasion of the sale of the Bolla collection. A collection of Greek vases that took place in Basel, Switzerland. Mr. Medici was buying actively at the sale. And following the sale he was introduced to me. I was with other people who knew him. And one of them, I do not know who it was, actually introduced us.

It is therefore possible that Medici acquired the vase during the 1986 auction, since he 'was buying actively at the sale' (True did not accurately recount the date). The same Nikon lekythos was offered for sale at Christie's London branch on 1 October 2015, as lot 93. The lekythos was offered among other antiquities under the title 'Various Properties' and their consigners were not named. The collecting history accompanying the lekythos in the Christie's catalogue was:

> Anonymous sale; Münzen und Medaillen AG, Basel, 14 November 1986, lot 213. Formerly private collection, Japan, acquired privately in 1997.

*(Christie's 2015: 65)*

This collecting history raises (at least) two queries. First, why did Christie's not state that the 1986 sale of the lekythos by Münzen und Medaillen was from the Bolla collection? It can be assumed that it would be to their advantage to point out that the object came from a known private collection. Second, what is meant by the ambiguous phrasing of the second sentence?

In 2015, Tsirogiannis had recorded the same vase on the website of Phoenix Ancient Art, a gallery with branches in New York and Geneva, owned by the brothers Hischam and Ali Aboutaam. The only collecting history accompanying the vase was 'Ex-Japanese private collection, acquired in 1997'; the vase appeared as 'SOLD', without any price given.

The omission of the Aboutaams from the 'provenance' section of the Christie's catalogue is probably not insignificant as the dealership has a troubled history. Each of the Aboutaam brothers has been arrested and convicted, one for his involvement in trading illicit antiquities (which he has denied) and the other for falsifying import documents (Amineddoleh 2009). Their Geneva warehouses, like those of Medici, have been raided by the Swiss and Italian authorities (Watson and Todeschini 2007: 183). It has also been alleged that they were involved in selling fakes to museums (see Ferri 2001: 78) and private collectors (Marton 2003; Muscarella 2008: 14–15). In 2009 the Aboutaam brothers returned 251 antiquities worth $2.7 million to the Italian state (Freeman 2009). Thus, individuals known to be in the collecting history of this lekythos were linked to illicit antiquities, yet this was not presented in the Christie's catalogue.

The inclusion of 'private collection, Japan' in the Christie's catalogue's 'provenance' section for the piece provided a clue for further research into the object's provenance. Having previously identified another antiquity in the Aboutaams' gallery as being connected to the Japanese antiquities dealer Noriyoshi Horiuchi, which was presented as 'Ex Japanese private collection' just as this lekythos was, Tsirogiannis again contacted Rizzo and Pellegrini, since they also recorded the antiquities found and confiscated in Horiuchi's warehouses following the raid by the Swiss and Italian authorities in the Geneva Freeport in 2008. They confirmed that the same Nikon lekythos was found and confiscated in Horiuchi's warehouses. As a result of this raid, 337 antiquities were repatriated to Italy (Isman 2010b), some of which Tsirogiannis identified in the confiscated photographic and documentary archives of the antiquities dealers Medici, Becchina and Symes-Michaelides. Rizzo and Pellegrini advised, however, that the Nikon lekythos among many other antiquities was returned to Horiuchi because the Italian authorities could not prove the illicit origin of the vase. It seems that subsequently Horiuchi sold the lekythos to the Aboutaam brothers, who advertised it as 'Ex Japanese private collection, acquired in 1997'. When compiling the vase's provenance for their catalogue Christie's appear to have adopted nearly the same wording as that used by the Aboutaams on their website ('Formerly private collection, Japan, acquired privately in 1997').

Before the Christie's auction on 1 October 2015, Tsirogiannis notified Interpol, Scotland Yard's Art and Antiques Unit and the Carabinieri Art Squad, supplying them with all the relevant evidence regarding the lekythos, as well as three more antiquities that he identified in the same auction from the confiscated Becchina archive. The cases were presented on the Looting Matters (Gill 2015b, 2015a) and ARCA blogs (Albertson 2015b, 2015a). Christie's withdrew all four antiquities before the auction. While the whereabouts of the other three identified and withdrawn antiquities remained unknown in 2018, a few days after its withdrawal from the Christie's auction, the lekythos reappeared on the Phoenix Ancient Art website on offer for 71,000 Swiss Francs, where it remained into 2018.

The lekythos represents a case in which an artefact was withdrawn from sale at an auction house due to questions it raised, to be returned to the consignor and thence making its way back into the market. Christie's withdrew the lekythos from the auction when presented with Tsirogiannis's research, but without incontrovertible proof of the illicit origin of the lekythos. The case is another in the line of studies that uncover dubious provenance practices in the marketing of antiquities, which can easily mislead researchers, authorities and customers while, at the same time, market actors advertise commitment to the highest ethical standards. These omissions in the provision of provenance details are 'whiter than white-collar' issues (McBarnet 1991), only becoming visible through careful documentary research revealing a somewhat ambiguous type of unethical behaviour that some may interpret simply as sharp and savvy marketing.

## Conclusion: From black and white to shades of grey

In Chapter 2 we described the antiquities market as a grey market. The case studies presented in this chapter offer more detailed insights into the process or processes of 'greying'. Medici himself, while buying antiquities illegally-sourced from Italy, some of which he subsequently tried to launder by passage through Sotheby's, was also buying antiquities openly and legally at Sotheby's. This is not to say, without further information, that the antiquities themselves were definitely 'clean': for example in the cases reviewed above there is an absence of any kind of provenance before entry into the Thetis Foundation. It does, however, go some way towards illustrating the grey nature of the market, trading in a mix of licit, illicit, and uncertain, inscrutable or questionable objects. In such a context, knowing only that an antiquity passed through the hands of a dealer convicted of offences involving illicit antiquities may well not be enough to deter a buyer professing adherence to a belief in 'innocent until proven guilty' when judging its legitimacy and suitability for purchase. A more risk-averse good-faith buyer or collector might decide otherwise, preferring a more cautious assessment of 'guilty until proven innocent'. But the greyness grows darker when the auction house, either deliberately or through limited due diligence, fails to name dealers convicted of offences involving illicit antiquities in its published provenance. It frustrates the intention of even the most cautious good-faith actors to purchase only legitimate material. Furthermore, the absence of information offers bad-faith dealers or collectors a defence of ignorance against any potentially damaging civil or criminal court case.

# REFERENCES

AAMD (2008) *Report of the AAMD Task Force on the Acquisition of Archaeological Materials and Ancient Art (revised 2008)*. New York: Association of Art Museum Directors.

Aboutaam, A. and Aboutaam, H. (2004) 'Unfair to the Aboutaams', *The Art Newspaper*, 21 November.

*Aboutaam v Dow Jones* (2017) Complaint. *Hicham Aboutaam v Dow Jones & Company*, 17 July. [Online]. Available at: www.courthousenews.com/wp-content/uploads/2017/07/Aboutaam-WSJ-COMPLAINT.pdf [accessed 9 May 2019].

Adam, G. (2013). 'The Art Market: Apples – Only $41.6m a Bowl', *Financial Times*, 10 May. [Online]. Available at: www.ft.com/content/10292934-b6f1-11e2-a249-00144feabdc0 [accessed 9 May 2019].

Al Quntar, S. (2017) 'Repatriation and the Legacy of Colonialism in the Middle East', *Journal of Mediterranean Archaeology and Heritage Studies*, 5(1): 19–26.

Albertson, L. (2015a) 'Christie's Withdraws Suspect Antiquities from Auction', *ARCA*. [Online]. Available at: http://art-crime.blogspot.co.uk/2015/10/christies-withdraws-suspect-antiquities.html [accessed 10 November 2016].

Albertson, L. (2015b) 'While the West Seeks Tighter Curbs on the Trade in Antiquities Looted by ISIS, Italian Suspect Antiquities Continue to Appear at Major Auction Houses', *ARCA*. [Online]. Available at: http://art-crime.blogspot.co.uk/2015/09/while-west-seeks-tighter-curbs-on-trade.html [accessed 10 November 2016].

Alder, C., Chappell, D., and Polk, K. (2009) 'Perspectives on the Organisation and Control of the Illicit Traffic in Antiquities in South East Asia', in S. Manacorda (ed) *Organised Crime in Art and Antiquities*. Milan, Italy: International Scientific and Professional Advisory Council of the UN Crime Prevention and Criminal Justice Programme, pp. 119–144.

Alder, C. and Polk, K. (2002) 'Stopping this Awful Business: The Illicit Traffic in Antiquities Examined as a Criminal Market', *Art Antiquity and Law*, 7: 35.

Ali, C. (2013) 'Syrian Heritage Under Threat', *Journal of Eastern Mediterranean Archaeology and Heritage Studies*, 1(4): 351–366.

Alsop, J. (1982) *The Rare Art Traditions: The History of Art Collecting and its Linked Phenomena*. New York: Harper and Row.

Amineddoleh, L. (2009) 'Phoenix Ancient Art and the Aboutaams in Hot Water Again', *Art & Cultural Heritage Law Newsletter*, 1(5): 13–15.

Anderson, M. (2017) *Antiquities: What Everyone Needs to Know*. Oxford: Oxford University Press.

Appadurai, A. (ed) (1986) *The Social Life of Things: Commodities in Cultural Perspective*. Cambridge: Cambridge University Press.

Appiah, K.A. (2006) *Cosmopolitanism: Ethics in a World of Strangers*. London: Allen Lane.

Asia Society (2012) 'The Future of the Past – Collecting Ancient Art in the 21st Century', *Asia Society, New York*, 18 March. [Online]. Available at: https://asiasociety.org/new-york/future-past-%E2%80%93-collecting-ancient-art-21st-century [accessed 9 May 2019].

Atwood, R. (2004) *Stealing History: Tomb Raiders, Smugglers, and the Looting of the Ancient World*. New York: St Martin's Press.

Ayling, J. (2013) 'Harnessing Third Parties for Transnational Environmental Crime Prevention', *Transnational Environmental Law*, 2(2): 339–362.

Ayres, I. and Braithwaite, J. (1992) *Responsive Regulation: Transcending the Deregulation Debate*. New York: Oxford University Press.

Bailey, M. and Gerlis, M. (2013) 'Guilty Plea Over Antiquities', *The Art Newspaper*, No 249, 10 September. [Online]. Available at: http://ec2-79-125-124-178.eu-west-1.compute.amazonaws.com/articles/Guilty-plea-over-antiquities/30312 [accessed 9 May 2019].

Balcells, M. (2015) 'Art Crime as White-Collar Crime', in J. Kila and M. Balcells (eds) *Cultural Property Crime: An Overview and Analysis of Contemporary Perspectives and Trends*. Leiden, Netherlands: Brill, pp. 96–110.

Baldwin, R., Cave, M., and Lodge, M. (2010) 'Introduction: Regulation – The Field and the Developing Agenda', in R. Baldwin, M. Cave, and M. Lodge (eds) *The Oxford Handbook of Regulation*. Oxford: Oxford University Press, pp. 3–17.

Bator, P.M. (1983) *The International Trade in Art*. Chicago, IL: University of Chicago Press.

Bauman, Z. (1989) *Modernity and the Holocaust*. Cambridge: Polity.

Beare, M.E. (ed) (2003) *Critical Reflections on Transnational Organised Crime, Money Laundering and Corruption*. Toronto, Canada: Toronto University Press.

Becker, H.S. (1982) *Art Worlds*. Berkeley, CA: University of California Press.

Beckert, J. and Wehinger, F. (2013) 'In the Shadow: Illegal Markets and Economic Sociology', *Socio-Economic Review*, 11(1): 5–30.

Beltrametti, S. and Marrone, J. (2016) 'Market Responses to Court Rulings: Evidence from Antiquities Auctions', *Journal of Law and Economics*, 59(4): 913–944.

Benson, M. (1985) 'Denying the Guilty Mind: Accounting for Involvement in a White-Collar Crime', *Criminology*, 23(4): 583–607.

Besson, S. and Campiotti, A. (2004) 'New York va juger un marchand d'art genevois', *Le Temps*, 16 July. [Online]. Available at: www.letemps.ch/culture/new-york-va-juger-un-marchand-dart-genevois[accessed 9 May 2019].

Bisheh, G. (2001) 'One Damn Illicit Excavation after Another: The Destruction of the Archaeological Heritage of Jordan', in N. Brodie, J. Doole, and C. Renfrew (eds) *Trade in Illicit Antiquities: The Destruction of the World's Archaeological Heritage*. Cambridge: McDonald Institute for Archaeological Research, pp. 115–118.

Blake, J. (1998) 'Illicit Antiquities and International Litigation: The Turkish Experience', *Antiquity*, 72: 824–830.

Blumenthal, R. and Mashberg, T. (2012) 'The Curse of the Outcast Object', *New York Times*, 12 July. [Online]. Available at: https://cn.nytimes.com/culture/20120726/26collectors/en-us [accessed 9 May 2019].

Blumenthal, R. and Mashberg, T. (2017) 'Expert Opinion or Elaborate Ruse? Scrutiny for Scholars' Role in Art Sales', *The New York Times*, 30 March. [Online]. Available at: www.

nytimes.com/2017/03/30/arts/design/expert-opinion-or-elaborate-ruse-scrutiny-for-scholars-role-in-art-sales.html [accessed 9 May 2019].

Bogdanos, M. (2005) *Thieves of Baghdad*. New York: Bloomsbury.

Borodkin, L.J. (1995) 'The Economics of Antiquities Looting and a Proposed Legal Alternative', *Columbia Law Review*, 95(2): 377–417.

Bottoms, A. and Wiles, P. (2002) 'Environmental Criminology', in M. Maguire, R. Morgan, and R. Reiner (eds) *The Oxford Handbook of Criminology*, 3rd edn. Oxford: Oxford University Press, pp. 620–656.

Bourdieu, P. (1984) 'The Market of Symbolic Goods', in P. Bourdieu (ed) *The Field of Cultural Production: Essays on Art and Literature*. New York: Columbia University Press, pp. 112–141.

Bourdieu, P. (1986) 'The Forms of Capital', in J. Richardson (ed) *Handbook of Theory and Research for the Sociology of Education*. New York: Greenwood, pp. 241–258.

Braithwaite, J. (2011) 'The Essence of Responsive Regulation', *UBC Law Review*, 44(3): 475–520.

Brantingham, P.J. and Brantingham, P.L. (eds) (1981) *Environmental Criminology*. Beverly Hills, CA: Sage.

Brodie, N. (1998) 'Pity the Poor Middlemen', *Culture Without Context*, 3(Autumn): 7–9.

Brodie, N. (2009) 'Consensual Relations? Academic Involvement in the Illegal Trade in Ancient Manuscripts', in S. Mackenzie and P. Green (eds) *Criminology and Archaeology: Studies in Looted Antiquities*. Oxford: Hart, pp. 41–58.

Brodie, N. (2011a) 'Academic Involvement in the Market in Iraqi Antiquities', in S. Manacorda and D. Chappell (eds) *Crime in the Art and Antiquities World: Illegal Trafficking in Cultural Property*. New York: Springer, pp. 117–133.

Brodie, N. (2011b) 'Congenial Bedfellows? The Academy and the Antiquities Trade', *Journal of Contemporary Criminal Justice*, 27(4): 408–437.

Brodie, N. (2014a) 'The Antiquities Market: It's All in a Price', *Heritage and Society*, 7(1): 32–46.

Brodie, N. (2014b) 'Auction Houses and the Antiquities Trade', in S. Choulia-Kapeloni (ed) *3rd International Conference of Experts on the Return of Cultural Property*. Athens, Greece: Archaeological Receipts Fund, pp. 71–82.

Brodie, N. (2014c) 'The Internet Market in Precolumbian Antiquities', in J. Kila and M. Balcells (eds) *Cultural Property Crime: An Overview and Analysis on Contemporary Perspectives and Trends*. Leiden, Netherlands: Brill, pp. 237–262.

Brodie, N. (2014d) 'Provenance and Price: Autoregulation of the Antiquities Market', *European Journal on Criminal Policy and Research*, 20(40): 427–444.

Brodie, N. (2015a) 'Archaeological and Criminological Approaches to Studying the Antiquities Trade: A Comparison of the Illicit Antiquities Research Centre and the Trafficking Culture Project', *Cuadernos de Prehistoria y Arqueología*, 25: 99–215.

Brodie, N. (2015b) 'The Internet Market in Antiquities', in F. Desmarais (ed) *Countering Illicit Traffic in Cultural Goods*. Paris, France: ICOM, pp. 11–20.

Brodie, N. (2015c) 'Syria and its Regional Neighbors: A Case of Cultural Property Protection Policy Failure?', *International Journal of Cultural Property*, 22: 317–335.

Brodie, N. (2015d) 'Why is No One Talking About Libya's Cultural Destruction?, *Near Eastern Archaeology*, 78: 212–217.

Brodie, N. (2018) 'Problematizing the Encyclopedic Museum: The Benin Bronzes and Ivories in Historical Context', in B. Effros and G. Lai (eds) *Unmasking Ideologies: The Vocabulary and Symbols of Colonial Archaeology*. Los Angeles, CA: Cotson Institute, pp. 61–82.

Brodie, N. (2019) 'The Criminal Organisation of the Transnational Trade in Cultural Objects: Two Case Studies', in S. Hufnagel and D. Chappell (eds) *Handbook on Art Crime*. New York: Palgrave, pp. 439–461.

Brodie, N. and Bowman Proulx, B. (2013) 'Museum Malpractice as Corporate Crime? The Case of the J. Paul Getty Museum', *Journal of Crime and Justice*, 37(3): 399–421.

Brodie, N. and Contreras, D. (2012) 'The Economics of the Looted Archaeological Site of Bab edh-Dhra: A View from Google Earth', in P.K. Lazrus and A.W. Barker (eds) *All the Kings Horses: Looting, Antiquities Trafficking and the Integrity of the Archaeological Record*. Washington, DC: Society for American Archaeology, pp. 9–25.

Brodie, N., Dietzler, J., and Mackenzie, S. (2013) 'Trafficking in Cultural Objects: An Empirical Overview', in S. Manacorda (ed) *Prevenzione e Contrasto dei Reati Contro il Patrimonio Culturale: la Dimensione Nazionale ed Internazionale*. Naples, Italy: Vita e Pensiero, pp. 19–30.

Brodie, N., Doole, J., and Renfrew, C. (eds) (2001) *Trade in Illicit Antiquities: The Destruction of the World's Archaeological Heritage*. Cambridge: McDonald Institute for Archaeological Research.

Brodie, N. and Kersel, M.M. (2014) 'WikiLeaks, Text, and Archaeology: The Case of the Schøyen Incantation Bowls', in M.T. Rutz and M.M. Kersel (eds) *Archaeologies of Text*. Oxford: Oxbow Books, pp. 198–213.

Brodie, N. and Renfrew, C. (2005) 'Looting and the World's Archaeological Heritage: The Inadequate Response', *Annual Review of Anthropology*, 34: 343–361.

Bunker, E.C. and Latchford, D. (2003) *Adoration and Glory: The Golden Age of Khmer Art*. Chicago, IL: Art Media Resources.

Byrne, D. (2016) 'The Problem with Looting: An Alternative Perspective on Antiquities Trafficking in Southeast Asia', *Journal of Field Archaeology*, 41(3): 344–354.

Campbell, P.B. (2013) 'The Illicit Antiquities Trade as a Transnational Criminal Network: Characterizing and Anticipating Trafficking of Cultural Heritage', *International Journal of Cultural Property*, 20: 113–153.

Casana, J. and Panahipour, M. (2014) 'Notes on a Disappearing Past: Satellite-Based Monitoring of Looting and Damage to Archaeological Sites in Syria', *Journal of Eastern Mediterranean Archaeology and Heritage Studies*, 2(2): 128–151.

Chappell, D. and Polk, K. (2011) 'Unravelling the "Cordata": Just How Organised is the International Traffic in Cultural Objects', in S. Manacorda and D. Chappell (eds) *Crime in the Art and Antiquities World*. New York: Springer, pp. 99–116.

Cheek, K. (2003) *Into the Antiquities Trade*. Bloomington, IN: Xlibris Corporartion.

Chippindale, C. and Gill, D.J.W. (2000) 'Material Consequences of Contemporary Classical Collecting', *American Journal of Archaeology*, 104: 463–511.

Christie's (2012) *Antiquities (8 June)*. Sale 2565. New York: Christie's.

Christie's (2013) *Antiquities (6 June)*. Sale 2709. New York: Christie's.

Christie's (2015) *Antiquities (1 October)*. Sale 10373 New York: Christie's.

CITES (1975) *Convention on International Trade in Endangered Species of Wild Fauna and Flora*. Washington, DC. [Online]. Available at: www.cites.org.

Ciudadanía and LAPOP (2012) *Cultura política de la democracia en Bolivia, 2012: Hacia la igualdad de oportunidades*, Vanderbilt. [Online]. Available at: www.vanderbilt.edu/lapop/bolivia/Bolivia-2012-Report.pdf [accessed 4 June 2018].

Clarke, R.V. (1997) *Situational Crime Prevention: Successful Case Studies*, 2nd edn. New York: Harrow and Heston.

Clarke, R.V. and Brown, R. (2003) 'International Trafficking in Stolen Vehicles', in M. Tonry (ed) *Crime and Justice: A Review of Research*, Vol. 30. Chicago, IL: University of Chicago Press, pp. 197–227.

Coglianese, C. and Mendelson, E. (2010) 'Meta-Regulation and Self-Regulation', in R. Baldwin, M. Cave and M. Lodge (eds) *The Oxford Handbook of Regulation*. Oxford: Oxford University Press, pp. 146–168.

Cohen, L.E. and Felson, M. (1979) 'Social Change and Crime Rate Trends: A Routine Activity Approach', *American Sociological Review*, 44: 588–608.

Cohen, S. (2001) *States of Denial: Knowing about Atrocities and Suffering*. Cambridge: Polity.

Conklin, J.E. (1994) *Art Crime*. Westport, CT: Praeger.

Contreras, D. and Brodie, N. (2010) 'Quantifying Destruction: An Evaluation of the Utility of Publicly Available Satellite Imagery for Investigating Looting of Archaeological Sites in Jordan', *Journal of Field Archaeology*, 35: 101–114.

Cunliffe, E. (2012) *Damage to the Soul: Syria's Cultural Heritage in Conflict*. Palo Alto, CA: Global Heritage Fund. [Online]. Available at: http://ghn.globalheritagefund.com/uploa ds/documents/document_2107.pdf.

Cuno, J. (2008) *Who Owns Antiquity? Museums and the Battle Over Our Ancient Heritage*. Princeton, NJ: Princeton University Press.

Cuno, J. (2014) 'The Case Against Repatriating Museum Artifacts', *Foreign Affairs*, 93(6): 119–124.

Davis, T. (2011) 'Supply and Demand: Exposing the Illicit Trade in Cambodian Antiquities Through a Study of Sotheby's Auction House', *Crime, Law and Social Change*, 56: 155–174.

Davis, T. (2015) 'The Lasting Impact of United States vs Cambodian Sculpture', in F. Desmarais (ed) *Countering Illicit Traffic in Cultural Goods*. Paris, France: ICOM, pp. 95–106.

Davis, T. and Mackenzie, S. (2015) 'Crime and Conflict: Temple Looting in Cambodia', in J. Kila and M. Balcells (eds) *Cultural Property Crime*. Leiden, Netherlands: Brill.

De Montebello, P. (2007) 'Whose Culture Is It? Museums and the Collection of Antiquities', *Berlin Journal*, 15: 33–37.

Delaloye, L. (2017) 'Collecting Guide: 7 Things to Know About Greek Vases', *Christie's*, 7 April.

Duster, T. (1971) 'Conditions for Guilt-Free Massacre', in N. Sanford and C. Comstock (eds) *Sanctions for Evil*. San Francisco FL: Jossey-Bass.

Eakin, H. (2007) 'Treasure Hunt. The Downfall of the Getty Curator Marion True', *New Yorker*, 17 December. [Online]. Available at: www.newyorker.com/magazine/2007/12/17/treasure-hunt-3 [accessed 9 May 2019].

Ede, J. (1995) 'The Antiquities Trade: Towards a More Balanced View', in K.W. Tubb (ed) *Antiquities: Trade or Betrayed*. London: Archetype, pp. 211–214.

Ede, J. (2014) 'In Defence of the Antiquities Trade', *Apollo Magazine*, 11 April. [Online]. Available at: www.apollo-magazine.com/defence-antiquities-trade [accessed 9 May 2019].

Efrat, A. (2013) 'The Rise and Decline of Israel's Participation in the Global Organ Trade: Causes and Lessons', *Crime, Law and Social Change*, 60: 81–105.

Eisenberg, J. (1993) 'The Embiricos Greek Vase Sale at Christie's', *Minerva*, 4(4): 23–25.

Eisenberg, J. (1995a) 'Ethics and the Antiquity Trade', in K.W. Tubb (ed) *Antiquities: Trade or Betrayed*. London: Archetype, pp. 215–221.

Eisenberg, J. (1995b) 'The Summer 1995 Antiquities Sales', *Minerva*, 6(5): 24–33.

Eisenberg, J. (2004) 'The Autumn 2003 Antiquities Sales', *Minerva*, 15(2): 25–32.

Eisenberg, J. (2006) 'The Spring 2006 Antiquities Sales', *Minerva*, 17(5): 36–45.

Eisenberg, J. (2008) 'The Proto-Elamite Guennol Lioness', *Minerva*, 19(2): 31.

Farrell, S. and Alberge, D. (1997) 'Sotheby's Cuts Antiquity Sales Over "Smuggling"', *The Times*, 19 July.

Faucon, B. and Kantchev, G. (2017) 'Prominent Art Family Entangled in ISIS Antiquities-Looting Investigations', *Wall Street Journal*, 31 May. [Online]. Available at: www.wsj.com/articles/prominent-art-family-entangled-in-investigations-of-looted-anti quities-1496246740 [accessed 9 May 2019].

Felch, J. (2012) 'Quick Takes', *Los Angeles Times*, 20 January.

Felch, J. and Frammolino, R. (2005) 'Italy Says it's Proven Vase at Met was Looted', *Los Angeles Times*, 28 October. [Online]. Available at: www.latimes.com/archives/la-xpm -2005-oct-28-me-met28-story.html [accessed 9 May 2019].

Felch, J. and Frammolino, R. (2011) *Chasing Aphrodite: The Hunt for Looted Antiquities at the World's Richest Museum*. Boston, MA/New York: Houghton Mifflin Harcourt.

Felson, M. (1995) 'Those Who Discourage Crime', in J.E. Eck and D. Weisburd (eds) *Crime and Place*, Vol. 4, Crime Prevention Studies. Monsey, NY: Criminal Justice Press, pp. 53–66.

Ferri, P.-G. (2001) *Examination of Marion True by the Italian public prosecutor Dr Paolo–Giorgio Ferri* (copy on file with Tsirogiannis). Los Angeles, CA: Getty Center.

Freeman, A.L. (2009) 'Swiss Gallery Surrenders EU2 Million in Antiquities to Italy', *Bloomberg*. [Online]. Available at: www.bloomberg.com/apps/news?pid=newsarchive& sid=a1km7Oa1Z2SU&refer=home [accessed 10 November 2016].

Gage, N. (1973a) 'Dillon Stands by Vase', *New York Times*, 27 June.

Gage, N. (1973b) 'Farmhand Tells of Finding Met's Vase in Italian Tomb', *New York Times*, 25 February.

Gage, N. (1973c) 'How the Metropolitan Acquired "The Finest Greek Vase There Is"', *New York Times*, 19 February. [Online]. Available at: www.nytimes.com/1973/02/19/a rchives/how-the-metropolitan-acquired-the-finest-greek-vase-there-is-how.html [accessed 9 May 2019].

Geertz, C. (1978) 'The Bazaar Economy: Information and Search in Peasant Marketing', *American Economic Review*, 68(2): 28–32.

Geismar, H. (2001) 'What's in a Price? An Ethnography of Tribal Art at Auction', *Journal of Material Culture*, 6(1): 25–47.

George, A.R. (2013) Babylonian Divinatory Texts Chiefly in the Schøyen Collection, Cornell University Studies in Assyriology and Sumerology, Vol. 18. Bethesda, MD: CDL Press.

Gerlis, M. (2016) 'Christie's and Sotheby's Battle for the Middle Market', *The Art Newspaper*, 1 February. [Online]. Available at: http://en.artintern.net/index.php/news/main/html/1/ 4256 [accessed 9 May 2019].

Gerstenblith, P. (2002) 'United States v. Schultz', *Culture Without Context: The Newsletter of the Illicit Antiquities Research Centre, University of Cambridge*, 10(Spring): 27–31.

Gerstenblith, P. (2003) 'The McClain/Schultz Doctrine: Another Step Against Trade in Stolen Antiquities', *Culture Without Context: The Newsletter of the Illicit Antiquities Research Centre, University of Cambridge*, 13(Autumn): 5–8.

Gerstenblith, P. (2007) 'Controlling the International Market in Antiquities: Reducing the Harm, Preserving the Past', *Chicago Journal of International Law*, 8(1): 167–195.

Gerstenblith, P. (2012) 'Has the Market in Antiquities Changed in Light of Recent Legal Developments?', in M.A. Adler and S.B. Bruning (eds) *The Futures of Our Pasts: Ethical Implications of Collecting Antiquities in the Twenty-first Century*. Santa Fe, NM: School for Advanced Research, pp. 67–84.

Gill, D.J.W. (2008) 'Marble Lekythos Returns to Greece', *Looting Matters*, 21 April. [Online]. Available at: http://lootingmatters.blogspot.co.uk/2008/04/marble-lekythos-re turns-to-greece.html [accessed 10 November 2016].

Gill, D.J.W. (2015a) 'Christie's withdraw lots from antiquities sale', *Looting Matters*, 1 October. [Online]. Available at: http://lootingmatters.blogspot.co.uk/2015/10/chris ties-withdraw-lots-from.html [accessed 9 November 2015].

Gill, D.J.W. (2015b) 'Further sightings on the London market', *Looting Matters*, 29 September. [Online]. Available at: http://lootingmatters.blogspot.co.uk/2015/09/further-sight ings-on-london-market.html [accessed 8 November 2015].

Global Witness (2000) 'Forests, Famine and War: The Key to Cambodia's Future', *Global Witness*. [Online]. Available at: www.globalwitness.org/en/archive/forests-famine-and-war-key-cambodias-future [accessed 9 May 2019].

Global Witness (2015) 'The Cost of Luxury: Cambodia's Illegal Trade in Precious Wood with China', London: Global Witness. [Online]. Available at: www.globalwitness.org/documents/17788/the_cost_of_luxury_1.pdf.

Godart, L., De Caro, S., and Gavrili, M. (eds) (2008) *Nostoi: Repatriated Masterpieces*. Athens, Greece: Greek Ministry of Culture.

Goddard, J. (2011) 'Anticipated Impact of the 2009 Four Corners Raid and Arrests', *Crime, Law and Social Change*, 56(2): 175–188.

Gourevitch, P. (2011) 'The Value of Ethics: Monitoring Normative Compliance in Ethical Consumption Markets', in J. Beckert and P. Aspers (eds) *The Worth of Goods*. Oxford: Oxford University Press, pp. 86–105.

Haines, F. (1997) *Corporate Regulation: Beyond Punish or Persuade*. Oxford: Clarendon Press.

Hanson, R., Warchol, G.L., and Zupan, L.L. (2007) 'Policing Paradise: Law and Disorder in Belize', *Police Practice & Research*, 5(3): 241–257.

Hauser-Schäublin, B. (2016) 'Looted, Trafficked, Donated and Returned: The Twisted Tracks of Cambodian Antiquities', in B. Hauser-Schäublin and L.V. Prott (eds) *Cultural Property and Contested Ownership*. London: Routledge, pp. 64–81.

Heath, C. (2012) *The Dynamics of Auction*. Cambridge: Cambridge University Press.

Heilmeyer, W.-D. (1997) 'The Protection of Archaeological Cultural Property from an Archaeological Perspective', *Law and State*, 56: 96–105.

Henkelman, W. (2003) 'Persians, Medes and Elamites: Acculturation in the Neo-Elamite Period', in G. Lanfranchi, M. Roaf, and R. Rollinger (eds) *Continuity of Empire: Assyria, Media, Persia (History of the Ancient Near East Monographs 5)*. Padova, Italy: S.a.r.g.o.n. Editrice e Libreria, pp. 73–123.

Hollowell, J. (2006) 'Moral Arguments on Subsistence Digging', in C. Scarre and G. Scarre (eds) *The Ethics of Archaeology: Philosophical Perspectives on the Practice of Archaeology*. Cambridge: Cambridge University Press, pp. 69–93.

Hope, T. and Karstedt, S. (2003) 'Towards a New Social Crime Prevention', in H. Kury and J. Obergfell-Fuchs (eds) *Crime Prevention: New Approaches*. Mainz, Germany: Weisse Ring Verlag.

Hoving, T. (1993) *Making the Mummies Dance: Inside the Metropolitan Museum of Art*. New York: Simon and Schuster.

Hoving, T. (2001a) 'Super Art Gems of New York City: "Hot Pot" Part II – Unexpectedly, the Money Source Opens Up', *artnet*. [Online]. Available at: www.artnet.com/magazine/features/hoving/hoving7-2-01.asp [accessed 7 August 2018].

Hoving, T. (2001b) 'Super Art Gems of New York City: The "Hot Pot" III – The Shit Hits the Fan', *artnet*. [Online]. Available at: www.artnet.com/magazine/features/hoving/hoving7-5-01.asp [accessed 7 August 2018].

Hoving, T. (2001c) 'Super Art Gems of New York City: The "Hot Pot" V – Utterly Unexpected Good News', *artnet* [Online]. Available at: www.artnet.com/magazine/features/hoving/hoving7-13-01.asp [accessed 7 August 2018].

Hoving, T. (2001d) 'Super Art Gems of New York City: The "Hot Pot" VI – The Old Switcheroo', *artnet*. [Online]. Available at: www.artnet.com/magazine/features/hoving/hoving7-16-01.asp [accessed 7 August 2018].

Hoving, T. (2001e) 'Super Art Gems of New York City: The Grand and Glorious "Hot Pot" – Will Italy Snag it?', *artnet*. [Online]. Available at: www.artnet.com/magazine/features/hoving/hoving6-29-01.asp [accessed 7 August 2018].

Hübschle, A.M. (2016) *A Game of Horns: Transnational Flows of Rhino Horn*. Cologne, Germany: International Max Planck Research School on the Social and Political Constitution of the Economy.

IADAA (1993) 'International Association of Dealers in Ancient Art', *Minerva*, 4(5): 36–38.

ICOM (2004) *Code of Ethics for Museums*. Paris, France: International Council of Museums.

Isman, F. (2010a) 'Looted from Italy and Now in a Major Spanish Museum?', *The Art Newspaper*, 13 July.

Isman, F. (2010b) 'Operazione Andromeda', *Il Messaggero*, 17 July, 151–162.

Isman, F. (2011) 'The Masterpiece Sold for $1000 and a Suckling Pig', *The Art Newspaper*, 225: 50–52.

Johnstone, R. and Sarre, R. (2004) 'Regulation: Enforcement and Compliance', *Research and Public Policy Series, No. 57*. Canberra, Australia: Australian Institute of Criminology.

Karpic, L. (2010) *Valuing the Unique: The Economics of Singularities*. Princeton, NJ: Princeton University Press.

Kaufman, J.E. (1997) 'Heavenly Showcase for Cult's Collection', *The Art Newspaper*, Dec.: 8–9.

Kaufman, J.E. (2007) 'Slap on the Wrist for Fraudulent Antiquities Dealer', *The Art Newspaper*, Oct., 63.

Kaye, L. (2014) 'The Fight against the Illicit Trafficking of Cultural Property: Best Practices in the United States of America', in J. Sánchez-Cordero (ed) *La Convención de la UNESCO de 1970*. Mexico City: Universidad Nacional Autónoma de México, pp. 175–210.

Kaye, L.M. and Main, C.T. (1995) 'The Saga of the Lydian Hoard: From Ushak to New York and Back Again', in K.W. Tubb (ed) *Antiquities Trade or Betrayed: Legal, Ethical and Conservation Issues*. London: Archetype, pp. 150–161.

Keefe, P.R. (2007) 'The Idol Thief: Inside One of the Biggest Antiquities Smuggling Rings in History', *The New Yorker*, 7 May. [Online]. Available at: www.newyorker.com/maga zine/2007/05/07/the-idol-thief.

Kelman, H.C. and Hamilton, V.L. (1989) *Crimes of Obedience*. New Haven, CT: Yale University Press.

Kennedy, R. and Eakin, H. (2006) 'Met Agrees Tentatively to Return Vase in '08', *New York Times*, 4 February. [Online]. Available at: www.nytimes.com/2006/02/04/arts/m et-agrees-tentatively-to-return-vase-in-08.html.

Kersel, M.M. (2006) 'From the Ground to the Buyer: A Market Analysis of the Trade in Illegal Antiquities', in N. Brodie, M.M. Kersel, C. Luke, and K. Walker Tubb (eds) *Archaeology, Cultural Heritage and the Antiquities Trade*. Gainesville, FL: University Press of Florida, pp. 188–205.

Kersel, M.M. and Chesson, M.S. (2013) 'Looting Matters: Early Bronze Age Cemeteries of Jordan's Southeast Dead Sea Plain in the Past and Present', in L. Nilsson Stutz and S. Tarlow (eds) *Oxford Handbook of the Archaeology of Death and Burial*. Oxford: Oxford University Press, pp. 677–694.

Kiel, K. and Tedesco, K. (2011) *Stealing History: How Does Provenance Affect the Price of Antiquities*, College of the Holy Cross, Department of Economics Faculty Research Series, Paper no. 11–05, Worcester, MA: Department of Economics College of the Holy Cross.

Kirkpatrick, S.D. (2002) *Lords of Sipan: A True Story of Pre-Inca Tombs, Archaeology, and Crime*. New York: William Morrow & Company.

Kleemans, E.R., Soudijn, M.R.J., and Weenink, A.W. (2012) 'Organized Crime, Situational Crime Prevention and Routine Activity Theory', *Trends in Organized Crime*, 15(2): 87–92.

Knowles, B. (2010) 'Looted Antiquities Worth Millions Recovered From Black Market by Italian Police', *The Independent*, 19 July. [Online]. Available at: www.independent.co.uk/life-style/history/looted-antiquities-worth-millions-recovered-from-black-market-by-italian-police-2030071.html [accessed 9 May 2019].

KPCS (2003) *The Kimberley Process Certification Scheme*. World Diamond Council. [Online]. Available at: www.kimberleyprocess.com.

Kuşseven, P. and Yilmaz, Z. (2014) 'Repatriating Antiquities: The Experience of Turkey', in S. Choulia-Kapeloni (ed) *3rd International Conference of Experts on the Return of Cultural Property*. Athens, Greece: Archaeological Receipts Fund, pp. 135–144.

Lamb, C. (2006) 'Looted Afghan Art Smuggled into UK', *The Times*, 12 March. [Online]. Available at: www.thetimes.co.uk/article/looted-afghan-art-smuggled-into-uk-zpp qt5b6cp9 [accessed 9 May 2019].

Lawler, A. (2001) 'Destruction in Mesopotamia', *Science*, 293: 32–35.

Lee, K.-G. (2017) 'International Conference on Return of Cultural Property: Progress and Prospects', *Proceedings of the 6th International Conference of Experts on the Return of Cultural Property*, 170–175. Seoul, South Korea: Overseas Korean Cultural Heritage Foundation.

Lee, M. (2009) *Against Environmental Criminology: Designing Out Crime and the Death of Utopian Vision*. Sydney, Australia: The Australian Sociological Association.

Lee, M. (2011) *Trafficking and Global Crime Control*. London: Sage.

Lemieux, A.M. and Clarke, R.V. (2009) 'The International Ban on Ivory Sales and its Effects on Elephant Poaching in Africa', *British Journal of Criminology*, 49: 451–471.

Levine, J. (2009) 'The Importance of Provenance Documentation in the Market for Ancient Art and Artifacts: The Future of the Market May Depend Upon Documenting the Past', *DePaul Journal of Art, Technology and Intellectual Property Law*, 19(2): 219–233.

Levine, M. and de Luna, L. (2013) 'Museum Salvage: A Case Study of Mesoamerican Artifacts in Museum Collections and on the Antiquities Market', *Journal of Field Archaeology*, 38: 264–276.

Loader, I. and Sparks, R. (2010) *Public Criminology?*London: Routledge.

Lobay, G. (2009) 'Border Controls in Market Countries as Disincentives to Antiquities Looting at Source? The USA–Italy Bilateral Agreement 2001', in S. Mackenzie and P. Green (eds) *Criminology and Archaeology: Studies in Looted Antiquities*. London: Hart, pp. 59–82.

Lufkin, M. (2004) 'Antiquities Dealer Arrested for Smuggling Iranian Object', *The Art Newspaper*, March: 8–9.

Lundin, S. (2015) *Organs for Sale: An Ethnographic Examination of the International Organ Trade*. Basingstoke, UK: Palgrave Macmillan.

Mackenzie, S. (2002) 'Illicit Antiquities, Criminological Theory and the Deterrent Power of Criminal Sanctions for Targeted Populations', *Art Antiquity and Law*, 7(2): 125–162.

Mackenzie, S. (2005a) 'Dig a Bit Deeper: Law, Regulation and the Illicit Antiquities Market', *British Journal of Criminology*, 45: 249–268.

Mackenzie, S. (2005b) *Going, Going, Gone: Regulating the Market in Illicit Antiquities*. Leicester, UK: Institute of Art and Law.

Mackenzie, S. (2006) 'Psychosocial Balance Sheets: Illicit Purchase Decisions in the Antiquities Market', *Current Issues in Criminal Justice*, 18(2): 221–240.

Mackenzie, S. (2007) 'Transnational Crime, Local Denial', *Social Justice*, 34(2): 111–124.

Mackenzie, S. (2009) 'Identifying and Preventing Opportunities for Organized Crime in the International Antiquities Market', in S. Manacorda (ed) *Organized Crime in Art and Antiquities*. Milan, Italy: International Scientific and Professional Advisory Council of the United Nations Crime Prevention and Criminal Justice Programme, pp. 41–62.

Mackenzie, S. (2010) 'Fakes', in F. Brookman, M. Maguire, H. Pierpoint, and T. Bennett (eds) *Handbook on Crime*. Cullompton, UK: Willan, pp. 120–136.

Mackenzie, S. (2011a) 'Illicit Deals in Cultural Objects as Crimes of the Powerful', *Crime, Law and Social Change*, 56: 133–153.

Mackenzie, S. (2011b) 'The Market as Criminal and Criminals in the Market: Reducing Opportunities for Organised Crime in the International Antiquities Market', in S. Manacorda and D. Chappell (eds) *Crime in the Art and Antiquities World: Illegal Trafficking in Cultural Property*. New York: Springer, pp. 69–86.

Mackenzie, S. (2013) 'Conditions for Guilt-Free Consumption in a Transnational Criminal Market', *European Journal on Criminal Policy and Research*, 20(4): 503–515.

Mackenzie, S. (2015) 'Do We Need a Kimberley Process for the Illicit Antiquities Trade? Some Lessons to Learn from a Comparative Review of Transnational Criminal Markets and their Regulation', in F. Desmarais (ed) *Countering Illicit Traffic in Cultural Goods: The Global Challenge of Protecting the World's Heritage*. Paris, France: International Council of Museums, pp. 151–162.

Mackenzie, S. and Davis, T. (2014) 'Temple Looting in Cambodia: Anatomy of a Statue Trafficking Network', *British Journal of Criminology*, 54(5): 722–740.

Mackenzie, S. and Green, P. (2008) 'Performative Regulation: A Case Study in How Powerful People Avoid Criminal Labels', *British Journal of Criminology*, 48(2): 138–153.

Mackenzie, S. and Green, P. (2009) 'Criminalising the Market in Illicit Antiquities: An Evaluation of the Dealing in Cultural Objects (Offences) Act 2003 in England and Wales', in S. Mackenzie and P. Green (eds) *Criminology and Archaeology: Studies in Looted Antiquities*. Oxford: Hart, pp. 145–170.

Mackenzie, S. and Yates, D. (2016) 'Collectors on Illicit Collecting: Higher Loyalties and Other Techniques of Neutralization in the Unlawful Collecting of Rare and Precious Orchids and Antiquities', *Theoretical Criminology*. Online first, 20(3) 340–357.

Mackenzie, S. and Yates, D. (2017) 'What is Grey About the "Grey Market" in Antiquities?', in J. Beckert and M. Dewey (eds) *The Architecture of Illegal Markets*. Oxford: Oxford University Press, pp. 70–86.

Macquisten, I. (2016) 'Should the Art Market be More Transparent?', *Apollo*, 16 September. [Online]. Available at: www.apollo-magazine.com/should-the-art-market-be-more-transparent [accessed 9 May 2019].

Mallonnee, L. (2015) *Why Is No One Talking about Libya's Cultural Destruction?* [Online]. Available at: https://hyperallergic.com/179246/why-is-no-one-talking-about-libyas-cultural-destruction [accessed 8 December 2017].

Manacorda, S. and Chappell, D. (eds) (2011) *Crime in the Art and Antiquities World: Illegal Trafficking in Cultural Property*. New York: Springer.

Marshall, C.E. (2002) 'Deterrence Theory', in D. Levinson (ed) *Encyclopaedia of Crime and Punishment*, Vol. 2. Thousand Oaks, CA: Sage Publications, pp. 512–514.

Marton, A. (2003) 'Problems of Sumerian Art, Looted and Fake Antiquities from Iraq', *Free Republic*, 16 April. [Online]. Available at: www.freerepublic.com/focus/f-news/894193/posts?page=2 [accessed 10 November 2016].

Matsuda, D. (1998) 'The Ethics of Archaeology, Subsistence Digging, and Artifact Looting in Latin America: Point, Muted Counterpoint', *International Journal of Cultural Property*, 7: 87–97.

Matsuda, D. (2005) 'Subsistence Diggers', in K. Fitz Gibbon (ed) *Who Owns the Past? Cultural Policy, Cultural Property, and the Law*. New Brunswick, NJ: Rutgers University Press, pp. 225–265.

Mazur, S. (2006) 'Add NYT to Bob Hecht Antiquities Ring Organigram?', *Scoop*. [Online]. Available at: www.scoop.co.nz/stories/HL0608/S00171.htm [accessed 7 August 2018].

Mazur, S. (2013a) 'A Fake? – "America's Souvenir to the Iranian People"', *Scoop*. [Online]. Available at: www.scoop.co.nz/stories/HL1310/S00063/a-fake-americas-souvenir-to-the-iranian-people.htm [accessed 7 August 2018].

Mazur, S. (2013b) 'ICE "incompetence" in Iranian Griffin Debacle', *Scoop*. [Online]. Available at: www.scoop.co.nz/stories/HL1310/S00114/ice-incompetence-in-iranian-griffin-debacle.htm [accessed 7 August 2018].

McBarnet, D. (1991) 'Whiter than White-Collar Crime: Tax, Fraud Insurance and the Management of Stigma', *British Journal of Sociology*, 42(3): 323–344.

McBarnet, D. (2003) 'When Compliance is Not the Solution but the Problem: From Changes in Law to Changes in Attitude', in V. Braithwaite (ed) *Taxing Democracy: Understanding Tax Avoidance and Evasion*. Aldershot, UK: Ashgate, pp. 229–244.

McBarnet, D. (2006) 'After Enron will "Whiter than White Collar Crime" Still Wash?', *British Journal of Criminology*, 46(6): 1091–1109.

Meier, B. (2004) 'Art Dealer Pleads Guilty in Import Case', *New York Times*, 24 June. [Online]. Available at: www.nytimes.com/2004/06/24/arts/art-dealer-pleads-guilty-in-import-case.html.

Melikian, S. (2008) 'A Wake-up Call for the Antiquities Market', *New York Times*, 12 June. [Online]. Available at: www.nytimes.com/2008/06/14/arts/14iht-melik14.1.13666041.html.

Melikian, S. (2010) 'Wanted: Antiquities Beyond Reproach', *New York Times*, 17 December. [Online]. Available at: www.nytimes.com/2010/12/18/arts/18iht-melik18.html.

Melikian, S. (2012) 'How UNESCO's 1970 Convention Is Weeding Looted Artifacts Out of the Antiquities Market', *Art+Auction*, September.

Melikian, S. (2013) 'Antiquities, With a Proven Record, Drive Auction Market', *New York Times*, 14 June.

Mellow, J. (1972) 'A New (6th Century B.C.) Greek Vase for New York', *New York Times Magazine*, 12 November. [Online]. Available at: www.nytimes.com/1972/11/12/archives/a-new-6th-century-b-c-greek-vase-for-new-york-greek-vase-the-other.html [accessed 9 May 2019].

Merryman, J.H. (1986) 'Two Ways of Thinking about Cultural Property', *American Journal of International Law*, 80: 831.

Merryman, J.H. (1988) 'The Retention of Cultural Property', *University of California Davis Law Review*, 21: 477.

Merryman, J.H. (2005) 'Cultural Property Internationalism', *International Journal of Cultural Property*, 12: 11–39.

Merton, R.K. (1938) 'Social Structure and Anomie', *American Sociological Review*, 3: 672–682.

Merton, R.K. (1968) *Social Theory and Social Structure*. Glencoe, IL: Free Press.

Messner, S.F. and Rosenfeld, R. (1994) *Crime and the American Dream*. Belmont, CA: Wadsworth.

Michalowski, R.J. and Kramer, R.C. (1987) 'The Space Between the Laws: The Problem of Corporate Crime in a Transnational Context', *Social Problems*, 34: 34–53.

Münzen und Medaillen AG (1986) *Auktion 70. Kunstwerke der Antike. Antike Gläser, griechische, etruskische und römische Bronzen, Schmuck der Antike, griechische Vasen*. Basel, Switzerland: Münzen und Medaillen.

Murphy, J.D. (1995) *Plunder and Preservation: Cultural Property Law and Practice in the People's Republic of China*. Hong Kong, China: Oxford University Press.

Muscarella, O.W. (2000) 'Excavated in the Bazaar: Ashurbanipal's Beaker', *Source: Notes in the History of Art*, 20(1): 29–37.

Muscarella, O.W. (2008) 'The veracity of 'scientific' testing by conservators', in E. Pernicka and S. von Berswordt-Wallrabe (eds) *Original—Copy—Fake?: Examining the Authenticity of*

*Ancient Works of Art*. Havertown, PA: David Brown Book, , pp. 9–18. [Online]. Available at: http://savingantiquities.org/wp-content/uploads/2015/03/Muscarella-Veracity-Scientific-Testing.pdf [accessed 10 December 2017].

Muscarella, O.W. (2012) 'An Unholy Quartet: Museum Trustees, Antiquity Dealers, Scientific Experts, and Government Agents', in H. Fahimi and K. Alizadeh (eds) *Namvarnameh: Papers in Honour of Massoud Azarnoush*. Tehran, Iran: IranNegar, pp. 185–190.

Nagin, D.S. (1998) 'Criminal Deterrence Research at the Outset of the Twenty-first Century', in M. Tonry (ed) *Crime and Justice: A Review of Research*, Vol. 23. Chicago, IL: University of Chicago Press, pp. 1–42.

Naylor, R.T. (2004) *Wages of Crime: Black Markets, Illegal Finance and the Underworld Economy*. Ithaca, NY: Cornell University Press and McGill-Queen's University Press.

Naylor, R.T. (2011) *Crass Struggle: Glitz, Greed and Gluttony in a Wanna-have World*. Montreal, Canada: McGill-Queen's University Press.

Nicholls, A. and Opal, C. (2005) *Fair Trade: Market-Driven Ethical Consumption*. London: Sage.

Nørskov, V. (2002) *Greek Vases in New Contexts: The Collecting and Trading of Greek Vases - an Aspect of the Modern Reception of Antiquity*. Aarhus, Norway: Aarhus University Press.

O'Keefe, P.J. (1997) *Trade in Antiquities: Reducing Destruction and Theft*. London: Archetype.

O'Keefe, P.J. (2007) *Commentary on the UNESCO 1970 Convention on Illicit Traffic*, 2nd edn. Builth Wells, UK: Institute of Art and Law.

O'Keefe, P.J. (2017) *Protecting Cultural Objects: Before and After 1970*. Leicester, UK: Institute of Art and Law.

Oded, S. (2013) *Corporate Compliance: New Approaches to Regulatory Enforcement*. Cheltenham, UK: Edward Elgar.

Page, A. (2009) 'Ancient Art, New Rules', *Art and Antiques*, June. [Online]. Available at: www.artandantiquesmag.com/2009/06/ancient-art-new-rules [accessed 9 May 2019].

Palmer, N., Addyman, P., Anderson, R., Browne, A., Somers Cocks, A., Davies, M., Ede, J., Van der Lande, J., and Renfrew, C. (2000) *Ministerial Advisory Panel on Illicit Trade*, London: Department for Culture, Media and Sport.

Parcak, S., Gathings, D., Childs, C., Mumford, G., and Cline, C. (2016) 'Satellite Evidence of Archaeological Site Looting in Egypt: 2002–2013', *Antiquity*, 90: 188–205.

Paredes Maury, S. (1999) *Surviving in the Rainforest: The Realities of Looting in the Rural Villages of El Petén, Guatemala*, Report submitted to the Foundation for the Advancement of Mesoamerican Studies (FAMSI). [Online]. Available at: www.famsi.org/reports/95096/95096ParedesMaury01.pdf [accessed 11 January 2018].

Passas, N. (1999) 'Globalization, Criminogenic Asymmetries and Economic Crime', *European Journal of Law Reform*, 1(4): 399–423.

Passas, N. and Bowman Proulx, B. (2011) 'Overview of Crimes and Antiquities', in S. Manacorda and D. Chappell (eds) *Crime in the Art and Antiquities World: Illegal Trafficking in Cultural Property*. New York: Springer, pp. 51–68.

Patris (2007) 'Βρέθηκε το άγαλμα που έκλεψαν από τη Γόρτυνα', *Patris*, 15 June. [Online]. Available at: www.patris.gr/articles/111985/58368?PHPSESSID= -.UQEGJqOjaM8 [accessed 10 November 2016].

Peachey, P. (2014) 'Ex-BBC Man Attempted to Sell Artefact Plundered in Arab Spring', *The Independent*, 7 March. [Online]. Available at: www.independent.co.uk/news/uk/crime/ex-bbc-man-attempted-to-sell-artefact-plundered-in-arab-spring-9177690.html [accessed 9 May 2019].

Peters, G. (2009) 'More than 1,500 Stolen Afghan Artifacts Return to Kabul', *National Geographic*, 6 March.

Pires, S.F. and Clarke, R.V. (2011) 'Sequential Foraging, Itinerant Fences and Parrot Poaching in Bolivia', *British Journal of Criminology*, 51: 314–335.

Pires, S.F. and Moreto, W.D. (2011) 'Preventing Wildlife Crimes: Solutions that can Overcome the "Tragedy of the Commons"', *European Journal on Criminal Policy and Research*, 17: 101–123.

Pires, S.F., Schneider, J.L., and Herrera, M. (2016) 'Organized Crime or Crime that is Organized? The Parrot Trade in the Neotropics', *Trends in Organized Crime*, 19: 4–20.

Pogge, T.W. (2002) *World Poverty and Human Rights: Cosmopolitan Responsibilities and Reforms*. Cambridge: Polity Press.

Politis, K. (2002) 'Dealing with the Dealers and the Tomb Robbers: The Realities of the Archaeology of the Ghor es-Safi in Jordan', in N. Brodie and K.W. Tubb (eds) *Illicit Antiquities: The Theft of Culture and the Extinction of Archaeology*. London: Routledge, pp. 257–267.

Polk, K. (2000) 'The Antiquities Trade Viewed as a Criminal Market', *Hong Kong Lawyer*, Sept.: 82–92.

Polk, K. (2009) 'Whither Criminology in the Study of the Traffic in Illicit Antiquities?', in S. Mackenzie and P. Green (eds) *Criminology and Archaeology: Studies in Looted Antiquities*. Oxford: Hart, pp. 13–26.

Povoledo, E. (2008a) 'Ancient Vase Comes Home to a Hero's Welcome', *New York Times*, 19 January. [Online]. Available at: www.nytimes.com/2008/01/19/arts/design/19bowl.html [accessed 9 May 2019].

Povoledo, E. (2008b) 'Repatriated Art in Rome', *New York Times*, 29 March. [Online]. Available at: www.nytimes.com/2008/03/29/arts/29arts-REPATRIATEDA_BRF.html [accessed 9 May 2019].

Pratt, J. (2007) *Penal Populism*. London: Routledge.

Prott, L.V. (1997) *Commentary on the UNIDROIT Convention on Stolen and Illegally Exported Cultural Objects 1995*. Leicester, UK: Institute of Art and Law.

Prott, L.V. (2000) 'UNESCO Celebrates Thirtieth Anniversary of its Convention on Illicit Traffic', *International Journal of Cultural Property*, 9: 347–349.

Prott, L.V. (2005) 'The International Movement of Cultural Objects', *International Journal of Cultural Property*, 12: 225–248.

Prott, L.V. and O'Keefe, P.J. (1989) *Law and the Cultural Heritage, Vol. 3: Movement*. London: Butterworths.

Redmond-Cooper, R. (1997) 'Good Faith Acquisition of Stolen Art', *Art, Antiquity and Law*, 2(2): 55–61.

Reyburn, S. (2014) 'The Lure of Antiquities', *New York Times*, 15 August. [Online]. Available at: www.nytimes.com/2014/08/18/arts/international/the-lure-of-antiquities.html [accessed 9 May 2019].

Reyburn, S. (2015) 'A Tug of War Over Art-Sales Transparency', *New York Times*, 25 September. [Online]. Available at: www.nytimes.com/2015/09/28/arts/international/a-tug-of-war-over-art-sales-transparency.html [accessed 9 May 2019].

Rizzo, M.A. (1997) 'La coppa con Ilioupersis al J.P. Getty Museum di Malibu con dedica ad Hercle ed il santuario di Hercle a Cerveteri: Storia di una ricontestualizzazione', in *Antichità Senza Provenienza II*. Atti del Colloquio Internazionale, Viterbo – Palazzo del Rettorato, 17–18 ottobre 1997. Rome, Italy: Ministero per i Beni e le Attività Culturali.

Rountree, C. (2008) 'The Geddes Collection', *Bonhams Magazine*, Autumn, 43.

Russell, H. (2004) 'Western Antiques: The Past Year Has Seen a Concerted Effort by Auction Houses and Dealers to Put Past Troubles in the Market Behind Them, and Concentrate on Well-Provenanced Objects of High Quality', *Apollo*, 1 December. [Online]. Available at: www.thefreelibrary.com/Western+antiques%3A+the+past+year+has+seen+a+concerted+effort+by%E2%80%A6-a0126194880 [accessed 9 May 2019].

Russell, J. (2008) 'Efforts to Protect Archaeological Sites and Monuments in Iraq, 2003–2004', in G. Emberling and K. Hanson (eds) *Catastrophe! The Looting and Destruction of Iraq's Past*. Chicago, IL: Oriental Institute of the University of Chicago, pp. 29–44.

SAFE (2016) 'Exclusive Interview: Sandra L. Cobden', *SAFE. Saving Antiquities For Everyone*. [Online]. Available at: http://savingantiquities.org/executive-interview-sandra-l-cobden/ [accessed 10 December 2017].

Scherer, S. (2009) 'Rome Court Upholds Conviction of Antiquities Dealer', *Bloomberg*. [Online]. Available at: www.bloomberg.com/apps/news?pid=newsarchive&sid=asneBHwVx9wU [accessed 17 July 2012].

Schneider, J.L. (2008) 'Reducing the Illicit Trade in Endangered Wildlife: The Market Reduction Approach', *Journal of Contemporary Criminal Justice*, 24(3): 274–295.

Scott, M. and Lyman, S. (1968) 'Accounts', *American Sociological Review*, 33: 46–62.

Sherman, L.W., Gottfredson, D.C., MacKenzie, D.L., Eck, J., Reuter, P., and Bushway, S. (1998) 'Preventing Crime: What Works, What Doesn't, What's Promising', in *National Institute of Justice: Research in Brief*. Washington, DC: US Department of Justice.

Siegel, D. (2009) *The Mazzel Ritual: Culture, Customs and Crime in the Diamond Trade*. Dordrecht, Netherlands: Springer.

Silver, V. (2009) *The Lost Chalice: The Epic Hunt for a Priceless Masterpiece*. New York: HarperCollins.

Sotheby's (1991) *Antiquities. The property of Thetis Foundation and other owners (23 May)*. London: Sotheby's.

Sparkes, B.A. (1996) *The Red and the Black*. London: Routledge.

Squires, N. (2008) 'Suspicions that Roman Artefacts were Illegally Traded', *Daily Telegraph*, 16 October.

St Hilaire, R. (2016) *How to End Impunity for Antiquities Traffickers: Assemble a Cultural Heritage Crimes Prosecution Team*, Antiquities Coalition Policy Brief Series, No. 1. Washington, DC: Antiquities Coalition. [Online]. Available at: http://thinktank.theantiquitiescoalition.org/wp-content/uploads/2015/10/Policy-Brief-1Nov.17-2016.pdf [accessed 9 May 2019].

Staley, D.P. (1993) 'St Lawrence Island's Subsistence Diggers: A New Perspective on Human Effects on Archaeological Sites', *Journal of Field Archaeology*, 20: 347–355.

Sutherland, E., Cressey, D.R., and Luckenbill, D. (1995) 'The Theory of Differential Association', in N.J. Herman (ed) *Deviance: A Symbolic Interactionist Approach*. Lanham, MD: General Hall, pp. 64–68.

Sutherland, E.H. and Cressey, D.R. (1974) *Criminology*, 9th edn. Philadelphia, PA: Lippincott.

Sutton, M. (1998) *Handling Stolen Goods & Theft: A Market Reduction Approach*, Home Office Research Study 178. London: Home Office.

Sutton, M., Schneider, J., and Hetherington, S. (2001) *Tackling Theft with the Market Reduction Approach*, Crime Reduction Research Series Paper 8. London: Home Office.

Sykes, G.M. and Matza, D. (1957) 'Techniques of Neutralisation: A Theory of Delinquency', *American Sociological Review*, 22: 664–670.

Thomas, S. (2012) 'Searching for Answers: A Survey of Metal-detector Users in the UK', *International Journal of Heritage Studies*, 18(1): 49–64.

Thompson, D. (2008) *The $12 Million Stuffed Shark*. New York: Palgrave.

Thompson, E. (2010) 'The Relationship Between Tax Deductions and the Market for Unprovenanced Antiquities', *Columbia Journal of Law and the Arts*, 33: 241–265.

Tijhuis, E.A.J.G. (2006) *Transnational Crime and the Interface between Legal and Illegal Actors: The Case of the Illicit Art and Antiquities Trade*. Nijmegen, Netherlands: Wolf Legal Publishers.

Tremain, C. (2017) 'Fifty Years of Collecting: The Sale of Ancient Maya Antiquities at Sotheby's', *International Journal of Cultural Property*, 24: 187–219.

True, M. (1997) 'Refining Policy to Promote Partnership', in *Antichita Senza Provenienza II, Bolletino d'Arte*. Rome, Italy: Ministero per i Beni e le Attivita Culturali.

Tsirogiannis, C. (2013a) 'Something is Confidential in the State of Christie's', *Journal of Art Crime Research*, 9: 3–20.

Tsirogiannis, C. (2013b) *Unravelling the Hidden Market of Illicit Antiquities: The Robin Symes–Christos Michaelides Network and its International Implications*. University of Cambridge: Unpublished PhD Thesis.

Tsirogiannis, C. (2015a) '"Due Diligence"? Christie's Antiquities Auction, London, October 2015', *Journal of Art Crime*, 14: 27–36.

Tsirogiannis, C. (2015b) 'Mapping the Supply: Usual Suspects and Identified Antiquities in "Reputable" Auction Houses in 2013', *Cuadernos de Prehistoria y Arqueología*, 25: 107–144.

Tsirogiannis, C. (2016) 'Nekyia. Reasons to Doubt: Misleading Assertions in the London Antiquities Market', *Journal of Art Crime, Spring*: 67–72.

Tubb, K.W. (2002) 'Point, Counterpoint', in N. Brodie and K.W. Tubb (eds) *Illicit Antiquities: The Theft of Culture and the Extinction of Archaeology*. London: Routledge.

Tubb, K.W. (2013) 'Shifting Approaches to Unprovenanced Antiquities among Conservators', in L.V. Prott, R. Redmond-Cooper, and S. Urice (eds) *Realising Cultural Heritage Law: Festschrift for Patrick O'Keefe*. Builth Wells, UK: Institute of Art and Law, pp. 145–162.

Tucker, R.L. (2011) 'Stolen Art, Looted Antiquities, and the Insurable Interest Requirement', *Quinnipiac Law Review*, 29: 611–663.

Ulph, J. (in press) 'Re-conceptualising Due Diligence Measures in the Art Market', in V. Mitsilegas and S. Hufnagel (eds) Research Handbook on Transnational Crime.

UNESCO (1970) *Convention on the Means of Prohibiting and Preventing the Illicit Import, Export and Transfer of Ownership of Cultural Property*. Paris, France: UNESCO.

UNIDROIT (1995) *Convention on Stolen or Illegally Exported Cultural Objects*. Rome, Italy: UNIDROIT.

United Nations (2000) *Convention Against Transnational Organized Crime*. Palermo, Italy: UN.

United States Attorney - Southern District of New York (2004) 'Art Dealer Pleads Guilty in US Court to Customs Violation in Iranian Antiquity Case', Press Release, 23 June.

Van Gelder, L. (1973) 'Odyssey of the Vase: Contradictions and Conflicts', *New York Times*, 25 February. [Online]. Available at: www.nytimes.com/1973/02/25/archives/farmhand-tells-of-finding-mets-vase-in-italian-tomb-farmhand-tells.html [accessed 9 May 2019].

van Uhm, D. and Moreto, W.D. (2018) 'Corruption within the Illegal Wildlife Trade: A Symbiotic and Antithetical Enterprise', *British Journal of Criminology*, 58: 864–885.

Vander Beken, T. and Van Daele, S. (2008) 'Legitimate Businesses and Crime Vulnerabilities', *International Journal of Social Economics*, 35(10): 739–750.

Vaughan, D. (1996) *The Challenger Launch Decision: Risky Technology, Culture, and Deviance at NASA*. Chicago IL: The University of Chicago Press.

Vaughan, D. (1998) 'Rational Choice, Situated Action, and the Social Control of Organizations', *Law and Society Review*, 32(1): 23–61.

Vaughan, D. (1999) 'The Dark Side of Organizations: Mistake, Misconduct, and Disaster', *Annual Review of Sociology*, 25: 271–305.

Vaughan, D. (2004) 'Organizational Rituals of Risk and Error', in B. Hutter and M. Power (eds) *Organizational Encounters with Risk*. New York: Cambridge University Press, pp. 33–66.

Velthuis, O. (2005) *Talking Prices*. Princeton, NJ: Princeton University Press.

Vlasic, M.V. and DeSousa, J.P. (2012) 'Stolen Assets and Stolen Culture: The Illicit Antiquities Trade, the Perpetuation of Violence, and Lessons from the Global Regulation of Blood Diamonds', *Durham Law Review*, 2: 159–180.

Vold, G.B., Bernard, T.J., and Snipes, J.B. (2002) *Theoretical Criminology*, 5th edn. New York: Oxford University Press.

von Hirsch, A., Bottoms, A., Burney, E., and Wikström, P.-O.H. (1999) *Criminal Deterrence and Sentence Severity: An Analysis of Recent Research*. Cambridge: University of Cambridge Institute of Criminology.

Watson, P. (1997) *Sotheby's: The Inside Story*, Hardback edn. London: Bloomsbury.

Watson, P. (1998) *Sotheby's: The Inside Story*, Paperback edn. London: Bloomsbury.

Watson, P. and Todeschini, C. (2006) *The Medici Conspiracy*, 1st edn. New York: Public Affairs.

Watson, P. and Todeschini, C. (2007) *The Medici Conspiracy: The Illicit Journey of Looted Antiquities. From Italy's Tomb Raiders to the World's Greatest Museums*, Revised edn. New York: Public Affairs.

Wellsmith, M. (2010) 'The Applicability of Crime Prevention to Problems of Environmental Harm: A Consideration of Illicit Trade in Endangered Species', in R. White (ed) *Global Environmental Harm: Criminological Perspectives*. Cullompton, UK: Willan, pp. 132–149.

Westenholz, A. (2014) 'A Third-Millennium Miscellany', *Cornell University Studies in Assyriology and Sumerology*, 27. Bethesda, MD: CDL.

Williams, D. (1991) 'Onesimos and the Getty Iliupersis', in M. True (ed) *Greek Vases in the J. Paul Getty Museum, Vol. 5*. Occasional Papers in Antiquities (OPA), No. 7. Malibu, CA: J. Paul Getty Museum, pp. 41–64.

Windsor, J. (1998) 'Ancient Tablets with a Price Tag', *The Independent*, 19 September.

Yates, D. (2006) *South America on the Block: The Changing Face of Pre-Columbian Antiquities Auctions in Response to International Law*. MPhil dissertation, University of Cambridge.

Yates, D. (2014) 'Church Theft, Insecurity and Community Justice: The Reality of Source-End Regulation of the Market for Illicit Bolivian Cultural Objects', *European Journal of Crime Policy and Research*, 20: 445–457.

Yates, D. (2015) 'Value and Doubt: The Persuasive Power of Authenticity in the Antiquities Market', *Parse Journal*, 2: 71–84.

Yates, D. (2016) 'Museums, Collectors and Value Manipulation: Tax Fraud through Donation of Antiquities', *Journal of Financial Crime*, 23(1): 173–186.

Yates, D. (2017) 'Community Justice, Ancestral Rights, and Lynching in Rural Bolivia', *Race and Justice*, Online First. [Online]. Available at: https://doi.org/10.1177/2153368717713824 [accessed 9 May 2019].

Yates, D., Mackenzie, S. and Smith, E. (2017) 'The Cultural Capitalists: Notes on the Ongoing Reconfiguration of Trafficking Culture in Asia', *Crime, Media, Culture*, 13(2): 245–254.

Zelizer, V.A. (2004) 'Circuits of Commerce', in J.C. Alexander, G.T. Marx, and C.L. Williams (eds) *Self, Social Structure and Beliefs*. Berkeley, CA: University of California Press, pp. 122–144.

Zerubavel, E. (2006) *The Elephant in the Room: Silence and Denial in Everyday Life*. Oxford: Oxford University Press.

Zimmerman, J.-L. (1987) *Collection de la Fondation Thétis*. Geneva, Switzerland: Editions du Tricorne.

Zirganos, N. (2006) 'Υπόθεση Γκετί, μέρος Β', *Epsilon*, 19 February.

Zirganos, N. (2007) 'Operation Eclipse', in P. Watson and C. Todeschini (eds) *The Medici Conspiracy*. New York: Public Affairs, pp. 306–324.

# INDEX

Figures are indicated by italic type and tables by bold type. Authors are listed where their names appear in the text outside brackets. For a full list of authors, see the References section.